The Complete
BREAD BOOK

● *Dresdner Stollen*

The Complete
BREAD BOOK

150 Traditional Recipes from around the World

GAIL DUFF

PAVILION

For Mick and Lucy, who seemed to eat
nothing but bread for six months

First published in Great Britain in 1993 by
Pavilion Books Limited
26 Upper Ground
London SE1 9PD

Conceived and produced by Breslich & Foss
Golden House
28-31 Great Pulteney Street
London W1R 3DD

Project editor: Catriona Woodburn
Art director: Nigel Osborne
Design: Sally Stockwell
Original photography: Nigel Bradley for Visuel 7
Styling for original photography: Sue Skeen
Illustrator: Carol Wilhide

Printed in Italy

Typesetting by BMD Graphics, Hertfordshire, England
Film origination by Dot Gradations, Essex, England

A CIP record for this book is available from the British Library.
ISBN 1 85145 944 8

2 4 6 8 10 9 7 5 3 1

CONTENTS

FOREWORD

Anyone can make bread. There is no magic to it at all.
You don't need expensive equipment, and for some recipes you don't even
need an oven. If you have never baked bread before, it is best to
learn the basic recipe first (see page 12).
From this humble beginning, you can widen your horizons,
and take yourself on a culinary adventure of tastes, smells and
textures from around the world.

In the most up-to-date of baking plants today, the whole process
of bread-making is completely mechanical.
Ingredients are mixed at high speed into a dough, and the bread is

*actually baked 'on the move', whilst passing slowly on
a conveyor belt through a huge oven.
When the loaves are done, they are turned out of the tins,
sliced and bagged – all by machines.*

*By contrast, I visited a rural bakery at a watermill.
There was one baker who made a hundred loaves, almost totally
by hand, before 9.30 every morning, and his process was so simple that
it could have been taking place in my own kitchen.
He weighed out fresh yeast, flour, salt and fat.
He didn't even activate the yeast. He switched on the mixer and
added water by eye, before giving the dough a kneading
of about five minutes. He then turned it out
on to a wonderful old wooden baker's table and
gave it a final kneading by hand. An array of wreaths,
four strand plaits, Cottage Loaves and Bloomers, were formed
in a matter of minutes.*

*These extremes of craftsmanship and commercialization
exist all over the world. We need them both.
Sadly, there are too many people wanting bread for everyone
to enjoy the luxury of a local baker, but
if you are lucky enough to be able to buy handmade bread regularly,
you'll know the difference.
Best of all, of course, is the satisfaction of taking a home-baked
loaf out of the oven in your own kitchen.*

MAKING BREAD

The ingredients that you really need for making a good loaf are remarkably simple: flour, yeast, salt and water. However, to produce different textures and flavours, other ingredients can be added in varying amounts. Sugar, eggs, and fats such as butter, lard, oil or shortening, can give an altogether richer dough; and using alternative liquids such as milk, beer, white wine, or even brandy, will subtly influence the flavour.

To make a specific kind of loaf, you need the right kind of flour. Flour is milled from grains. The most commonly used is wheat, but bread can also be made from rye, barley, oats, buckwheat or cornmeal, though almost always in combination with wheat flour.

Every cereal grain is made up of the outer layer called the bran, the main starchy part called the endosperm, and the germ. The bran contains B vitamins and minerals, the endosperm is rich in carbohydrates, and the germ, although the smallest part, is the richest in B vitamins, vitamin E and protein. It is obvious that to obtain the most complete goodness you have to eat all of it, and that is why many people over the past few years have chosen whole-wheat bread. However, when you eat a balanced diet, there is no reason why you should not include a whole range of breads – whole-wheat, white and in between. There are particular breads, the richer ones especially, for which only white flour will do. Others can be made successfully with a mixture. Once you have tried a few of the recipes in this book you will be able to adapt them to your own tastes.

That is all I will say about the health aspects of the various flours. The rest of the information is about choosing the right kind for the right recipe.

FLOUR MADE FROM WHEAT

There are really three types of wheat: durum wheat, soft wheat and hard wheat. Durum wheat is grown in many places, including the United States and Canada and is used in making dry pasta. Soft wheat has a lower protein content than the hard wheats, and when it is ground it makes a fine, powdery flour that is best suited to cakes and biscuits and to some breads which are raised with baking powder or bicarbonate of soda. In the recipes throughout the book I have referred to it as 'ordinary plain flour'.

The wheat that is needed for bread making is known as hard wheat. At one time it was produced mainly in the United States and Canada, but now new types are being grown in Britain and Europe. Hard wheat has a high content of two proteins. When water is mixed with the flour, these combine to form gluten. Yeast mixed into this dough causes the release of carbon dioxide, and as this happens the gluten forms a stretchable network that expands and sets when the bread is baked. The flour has to be able to withstand this expansion and is therefore known as strong flour. When you feel strong flour in your hands it has a grainier texture than soft flour.

Strong flour is also called, simply, bread-making flour or bread flour. It has no raising agents added and in the recipes throughout the book I have referred to it as 'strong plain flour'.

Where a bread recipe requires wholemeal or whole-wheat flour, use a designated wholemeal bread flour if possible.

White Flour: white flour is produced mainly from the endosperm of the wheat. The bran and most of the germ are removed in the milling process. Depending on the country of origin, white flour is made up of between 70% and 78% of the wheat grain. White flour was once uniformly chemically bleached but in many countries this is no longer the case. Naturally, it is a pale creamy colour.

Wholemeal or Whole-wheat Flour: wholemeal or whole-wheat flour (the names are synonymous) is made up of 98% to 100% extraction of the wheat grain, and contains the bran, endosperm and germ of the wheat. There are two different methods of producing wholemeal flour. Most flour in the world today is ground on roller-mills. The grains are split open and by the end of the process the white flour, bran and germ are separated. Some flour is left white, while some is made into wholemeal flour by mixing the bran and germ back in. Roller-milling has been accused of creating high temperatures that damage some of the nutrients in the wheat, but water-cooled rollers now counteract this.

Stone-ground wholemeal flour is produced from wheat that is ground between mill stones. The whole of the grain is crushed, thus the bran, germ and endosperm are never separated. To produce stone-ground

● *Grains of Wheat*

white flour, the wholemeal flour is passed through a highly efficient sieve.

The vast majority of bread-making flour available is roller-milled unless otherwise stated on the package, but stone-ground flour is also widely available in health food stores and in many supermarkets.

All-Purpose Flour: widely available in the United States, this is a mixture of strong and soft wheat flours and can be used for any of the recipes in this book that call for non self-raising white flour. However, where available, use of the designated bread-making flour is recommended.

Graham Flour: Graham flour is a whole-wheat flour that has been more finely milled. It is called after Dr. Sylvester Graham a nineteenth-century clergyman from Massachusetts who, at a time when everyone was after white bread, persistently extolled the virtues of brown.

Wheatmeal or Brown Flour: wheatmeal or brown flour can have an extraction of 79% to 90%, and it is usually about 85%. It contains all the endosperm and germ and a little of the bran and makes lighter-textured loaves than wholemeal flour. This type of flour was popular in Britain in the 1970s and early 1980s but is now quite hard to come by. You can get similar results in baking if you mix about one half white flour and one half wholemeal flour.

Cracked Wheat: cracked wheat consists of coarsely broken up wheat grains. They are scattered on top of wholemeal loaves for decoration and can be soaked and added to wholemeal flour to make a moist, nutty-flavoured loaf.

Organic Flour: organic flour is produced from wheat that has been grown without chemical fertilisers or pesticides. Both white and wholemeal organic flours are available in limited quantities.

Self-raising Flour: self-raising flour is a soft flour into which have been mixed raising agents, usually bicarbonate of soda and an acid (such as cream of tartar) which neutralizes its flavour.

Semolina: semolina consists of the larger parts of the endosperm which are sifted out during the milling process. Semolina is the flour of choice in making fresh pasta, but is rarely used in bread making. I've included one recipe in the Middle Eastern section.

FLOUR MADE FROM OTHER GRAINS

Mixed Grain Flour: mixed grain flours are generally based on a wheat flour of about 85% extraction and contain malted grains of wheat and rye. One brand name for this type of flour is Granary flour. Bread made with mixed grain flour rises well and the pieces of whole grain produce an interesting texture. Any of the plainer breads in this book that are made with white flour can be made with mixed grain flour.

Rye Flour: after wheat, rye is the most popular grain for bread making. However, it contains gum-like substances that inhibit the development of gluten and so, used alone, makes a very close-textured loaf. It is often mixed with wheat flour. Rye flour comes in various grades of coarseness. Light rye flour is produced mainly from the endosperm and is a pale fawn colour. Rye meal, or dark rye flour, is made from the whole grain. It is a grey-brown colour and similar in texture to whole-wheat flour.

Barley Flour: barley flour is usually available from health food stores and specialist shops, but is rarely used by commercial bakers. It is a pale, grey-brown colour and makes a rather grey loaf. Because it does not contain enough gluten-producing proteins, barley flour is usually mixed with wheat flour when making yeasted breads. However, it can be used successfully for unleavened breads or thin soda breads.

Oatmeal: oatmeal comes in a variety of textures, ranging from fine, cream-coloured flour to more coarsely-ground grains known as pin-head oatmeal. Oatmeal lacks gluten but it can be mixed successfully with wheat flour to make bread with a soft, moist texture. Rolled oats can be used in the same way.

Buckwheat Flour: buckwheat flour is a dark grey flour, sometimes speckled with black pieces of bran, which is silky smooth to the touch. Bread made from it will not rise greatly due to the lack of gluten-forming proteins, but buckwheat flour does make delicious yeasted pancakes. For bread, it is best mixed with a wheat flour.

Cornmeal: cornmeal is produced by grinding the whole kernels of sweet corn. It is a coarse, pale yellow flour which is entirely lacking in gluten-producing proteins. For yeasted breads it is often mixed with wheat flour. Cornmeal is popular for breads raised with bicarbonate of soda or baking powder.

RAISING AGENTS

Yeast: in order for dough to rise, gas has to be produced within it to swell and stretch the gluten network. Today, yeast is the most common raising agent.

Yeast is a growing organism which occurs naturally in the air and on the skins of certain fruits. It will begin to grow when it comes into contact with moist, starchy substances and, as it grows, it produces carbon dioxide. A warm, moist, flour-based dough is a perfect environment.

Over the years, bakers have used homemade yeasts and the by-products of brewing in order to raise their breads successfully. Nowadays, yeast is made commercially and bread making is no longer a hit and miss affair. Yeast is available fresh or dried.

Fresh Yeast: fresh yeast comes in the form of a light brown, moist, compressed lump which can be crumbled easily. You can buy it by the ounce or gram, from bakeries, health food stores and specialist shops. Wrap it in grease-proof paper and store it in a plastic bag in the refrigerator and it will keep for up to two weeks. If you cannot obtain fresh yeast, use half the amount of dried yeast.

Dried Yeast: dried yeast comes in the form of small brown granules. Check for the expiry date on the packet. Dried yeast needs to be left far longer than fresh yeast for it to activate. Once in the specified amount of liquid, leave it to stand for about 15 minutes (see page 12).

Easy-Bake Yeast: easy-bake yeast is made from a strong yeast strain that rises in about half the usual time and can be added dry to the flour. Follow the instructions given on the packet as to amounts needed.

OTHER RAISING AGENTS

Bicarbonate of Soda: bicarbonate of soda is an alkaline raising agent which, like yeast, gives off carbon dioxide when moistened and heated.

Baking Powder: when bicarbonate of soda is used on its own, it produces an alkaline 'soapy' flavour. In many soda breads, sour milk or buttermilk is used – their acids neutralizing the soda's flavour. Cream of tartar will produce the same effect. Commercial baking powder is made from bicarbonate of soda and cream of tartar mixed with a small amount of starch, such as cornflour, to keep the mixture dry and flowing.

Most baking powders sold today are "double acting". The first action occurs when the powder comes into contact with liquid, the second during the heat of baking.

Sourdough Starters: sourdough starters are an easy-to-make alternative to buying fresh yeast. You will have to wait a little time before they get going, but once you have begun you can have bowls of starter at various stages of development. There are several unique starter recipes throughout this book, but the two that follow here are the most popular and universal methods.

Sourdough is "alive" and needs to be replenished with more flour and water or it will eventually "die".

Potato Sourdough Starter

1 medium potato, scrubbed, not peeled

warm water

1 lb (450 g) strong plain flour, whole-wheat flour or rye meal

8 oz (225 g) sugar

Halve the potato. Place in a saucepan, cover with water and boil until it is tender. Drain it, reserving the water. Peel the potato, put it into a medium-sized bowl and mash it. Make up the potato water to 30 fl oz (850 ml) with more warm water. Stir it into the mashed potato and then stir in the flour and sugar. Cover the bowl with clingfilm and put it into a warm place for about three days or until it is bubbling and smells slightly sour.

You can use your starter immediately or stir in another handful of flour and a little more warm water to keep it going (use approximately equal amounts of flour and water). If you don't use it all at once, you can keep the starter going for months, or even years, by stirring in more flour and water.

Rye and Yeast Sourdough Starter

25 fl oz (700 ml) warm water
1 oz (25 g) fresh yeast or 1 tablespoon dried
1 lb (450 g) rye flour or meal
1 small onion, peeled and halved

Pour 16 fl oz (450 ml) of the water into a large bowl and sprinkle in the yeast. Leave this to stand — five minutes for fresh yeast and 15 for dried. Beat in half the flour and add the onion halves. Cover the bowl with clingfilm and leave it in a warm place for 24 hours. Remove the onion and stir in the remaining flour and water. Cover the starter again and leave it in a warm place for two to three days or until it is bubbling, has a slightly sour smell and has tripled in volume.

Although this Sourdough Starter requires yeast initially, like the potato starter, you can keep it going by replenishing it as you use it, with equal amounts of flour and warm water.

OTHER INGREDIENTS

Liquids: the main liquid used for bread-making is water. However, some or all of this can be replaced with milk or the equivalent volume of beaten egg. Generally, one large egg has a liquid capacity of 2 fl oz (55 ml). Breads that contain milk or egg are softer than those made with water, but may not have such good keeping qualities. Milk does not inhibit the rising properties of dough, but large quantities of egg may. With egg breads you will find the dough slow to rise at the kneading and proving stage, but it will nevertheless rise considerably in the oven. It is worth bearing this in mind when you are shaping rich breads or choosing a baking container.

In some more unusual recipes, beer or white wine are used as the liquids but these are rare.

Fats: butter, vegetable shortening, lard and olive oil are all put into breads to enrich them. The hard fats are either melted and added or they are kneaded-in at room temperature. Olive oil can be added with the liquids or kneaded-in after the dough is mixed. All fats may inhibit the initial rising of the dough.

Salt: unless salt is added to the flour, your bread will have a bland, sweetish flavour. More salt is generally added to plainer breads than to sweet breads, but all breads should contain some. Fine salt can be mixed with the flour or dissolved in a little of the warm liquid before mixing. If you use a coarse salt, always dissolve it in the liquid first.

Sugar: if you use fresh yeast, there is no need to add any sugar at all to plain breads. The yeast will work quite happily on the warm water and moist dough. Dried yeast, depending on the brand that you use, may or may not need a teaspoon of sugar to get it going. Read the instructions on the packet, but it is also worth experimenting. If you do add sugar, use white for white bread so that you do not spoil the colour. For whole-wheat or mixed grain breads, you can use white or brown, or honey or molasses.

For sweetened breads, the sugar is usually added to the flour at some point during the mixing of the dough. Where a recipe just says 'sugar', ordinary granulated sugar is called for. Where special sugars are required it will be stated. Like eggs and butter, sugar may well inhibit the initial rising of the dough, but will not affect its ability to rise on baking.

Equipment

For a basic bread recipe you will need:

scales
a measuring jug
a small mixing bowl
a large mixing bowl
a tablespoon or a round-bladed knife
a large, clean, smooth surface on which to knead the bread
a clean dry cloth
an oven

If you find kneading bread difficult you can use a food mixer or large food processor fitted with a dough hook.

Professional bakers use a dough scraper. This is made of either metal or a very durable but flexible plastic material. It is about 5 inches (13 cm) long, thin, and about 3 inches (7.5 cm) wide. It is used for scraping the dough out of the mixing bowl and pulling it together on the work surface. Some dough scrapers can be used to cut thinly-rolled dough. A dough scraper is not essential but, if you make a lot of bread, treat yourself to one.

There is no need for any kind of mechanical equipment. To my mind, bread making is an enjoyable craft which demands a little skill but which gives much pleasure. At the time of writing, bread-making machines are becoming very popular in the United States. For the person who enjoys freshly-baked homemade bread, but has limited time, these may well be the answer. However, the proportions of flour to other ingredients differ from those needed for oven-baked bread, which is the subject of this book. Should you wish to use one of these machines for making your bread, consult the manufacturer's instructions for recipes and methods.

For yourself, make sure your hands are clean and take off any rings that might get in the way. Wear short sleeves or sleeves that stay up when pushed or rolled up and take off any bracelets. To stop yourself from getting floury, wear an apron or overall.

MAKING BASIC BREAD DOUGH

Let us look at a basic recipe and take it step by step. The importance of yeast activity, kneading, and leaving dough to rise in a warm place, are fundamental to bread making and the following method can be applied to all the recipes in this book.

Ingredients

1 oz (25 g) fresh yeast or 1 tablespoon dried yeast

10 fl oz (275 ml) warm water

sugar, optional

1 tablespoon salt

1 lb (450 g) flour (strong plain, wholemeal, or a mixture) plus extra for kneading – most recipes never state this but you will always need more

1. Weigh out the yeast.

2. Pour half the water into a small bowl. Crumble the fresh yeast into it or simply sprinkle over the dried yeast. If you need the sugar, sprinkle it into the water with the dried yeast. It is not necessary if you are using fresh yeast. Leave this mixture for the yeast to begin to work. The standard times for this are about 5 minutes for fresh yeast and 15 minutes for dried. However, I rarely leave fresh yeast for longer than 2 minutes and dried for longer than 10 minutes. If you feel safer leaving them longer, go ahead.

3. Dissolve the salt in the remaining water.

4. Place the flour in a mixing bowl. If it is a cold day and your room temperature is low, it will help to warm the flour slightly, by a radiator or open fire, or on top of a boiler or wood-burning stove.

5. Make a well in the centre of the flour. Pour in the yeast mixture and mix in a little of the flour from the sides of the well. Pour in the remaining water with the salt dissolved in it and, using a long, round-bladed knife or a tablespoon, begin to mix everything together to make a dough. Bring it all together into a rough ball with your fingers. It will be a lumpy, uneven mixture of dry pieces and wet pieces.

6. Sprinkle some flour on your work surface. Turn the dough on to it, scraping it from the sides of the bowl. Push it together into a rough round.

7. Knead the bread. When you knead the dough you are producing a smooth mixture, assisting the development of gluten, and pushing out any pockets of air that might eventually make a hole in the loaf. Begin by pushing the dough away from you with the palms of your hands and pulling it back with your fingers and, in the very short space between the two processes, giving it a quick squeeze. Do this about six times. Fold the ends of the dough over the top, give the dough a quarter turn and start pushing, squeezing and pulling again. After five minutes you should notice that the flour and water have become evenly mixed and that the texture of the dough is changing.

You can actually see the gluten developing in strong, flexible strands. The more you knead, the more the bread will be able to rise. Most people knead for 5 to 7 minutes, but do not go over 10 minutes.

If you have judged your liquid content correctly and the dough is a plain one you will not have to use much extra flour as you knead. Use just enough to keep your hands and the work surface dry. See the notes below for richer doughs: Kneading in the Bowl.

8. When your dough is ready, return it to the bowl to rise or 'prove'. Some people like to put it into a greased plastic bag, and some like to rinse out the bowl and grease it. Neither of these are necessary. Unless otherwise specifically stated in the recipe, just return the dough to the original bowl.

9. Cut a cross shape in the top of the dough. Ancient folklore tells us that this is to keep the devil out. Actually, it helps the dough to rise.

10. Cover the bowl. I have always used a clean, dry cloth for this. If the bread rises above the bowl, the cloth simply gets pushed up. If you have used clingfilm, the rising dough will stick to it. You can also place the bowl in a plastic bag which works quite well.

11. Place the bowl of dough somewhere where it will keep warm. If you have turned the oven on but not the rings, stand the bowl on top. It can also go by a radiator, on a covered wood-burning or solid-fuel stove, on the central heating boiler, or on a sunny windowsill, as long as the position is draught-free. Leave the dough until it has doubled in size. The average time is about an hour, but plain doughs very often rise in half the time.

12. Knead the dough again. It is now ready for shaping (see pages 16 to 21).

Before you go on, here are some notes and variations:

Adding Salt: when you are making up the basic recipe, as above, fine salt can be mixed into the flour and the liquid added separately.

Amount of Liquid: 10 fl oz (275 ml) per 1 lb (450 g) of flour is about right, but some flours, especially some brands of whole-wheat, soak up liquid fast and need a little bit more. If, after all the liquid has been added and you have begun to bring the dough together in the bowl, it still feels a bit dry, add another 4 tablespoons gradually. After a while, you will come to know your favourite flour and get used to the feel of your dough. I would rather err on the wet side than the dry. When the dough is on the work surface it is easy to knead in more flour, but adding water to mixed dough is exceptionally difficult and very messy.

Alternative Way of Mixing: once you are absolutely certain how much liquid your flour is going to require, you can, if you like, mix your bread in the Scandinavian way, which saves on time and washing up, but is slightly more messy on your hands in the initial mixing. For this, the yeast and water are mixed in a large mixing bowl. After the yeast has risen, the extra water is added and the flour and salt are stirred into it. You then carry on as usual, mixing everything together to make a dough.

Adding Fats: If your butter, vegetable shortening and lard are sufficiently soft, you will be able to add them to the flour without melting them first. Melting is time consuming, messy, wasteful and not necessary. If you are only adding a small amount of fat, cut it into small pieces, and put it into the well together with the liquid. As the bread is kneaded, it will mix in easily. Where a large amount of butter is added it is often kneaded in after the dough has become smooth. Punch the dough down on the work surface and dot one third of the butter on it. Fold it up and knead it until the butter is completely incorporated. Knead in the rest of the butter in the same way. Oil is added in a similar way: punch the dough on its surface and make a little dip in the centre. Add as much oil as the dip will take, knead it in and carry on in the same way.

Adding Sugar and Dried Fruits: these can be added to the flour before the liquids. Other recipes call for them to be kneaded in. Do it in the same way as kneading in butter.

Kneading in the Bowl: when you have a very liquid dough you can knead it in the bowl. You will often have to use this method where you have an enriched dough containing a lot of butter, eggs and sugar. Hold the bowl in your left hand and rotate it towards the right hand. With your right hand bring a portion of the dough from the sides into the middle. Work in the pattern of rotate-knead-rotate-knead. It is quite hard work but eventually you will find that the structure of the dough begins to change and, even if it is still moist, it will lose its stickiness. Cover the dough and let it rise. It will probably take longer than a dough that is less rich. Once it has risen, you will be able to knead it successfully on the work surface, but even so, treat it gently and do not squeeze it too hard.

EATING AND STORING BREAD

Most breads are not suitable for eating as soon as they come from the oven. I can think of notable exceptions such as Croissants, Danish Pastries and some of the flat, Middle Eastern and Indian breads, but most of the more everyday breads should be given a cooling-off period first. Very fresh, warm bread tends to be doughy in texture and, if you cut a warm loaf, the next slice will be unusable as it will harden as it cools. So, for loaves, resist the temptation for at least an hour and for rolls, 20 minutes.

Bread is at its peak as soon as it has cooled and ideally it should be eaten within two days. You can store it in a special earthenware bread crock, or in a wooden bread keeper, whatever is best for you. It will keep equally well in a sealed plastic bag in a cool larder.

Most bread freezes well. Wait until it is completely cool and then seal it in a plastic bag. Frozen bread can be thawed in the bag at room temperature or unwrapped in a low oven. If you are desperate, use the microwave. There is no need to use the defrost setting. One of my plain whole-wheat loaves takes 4 minutes on the high setting. Follow your manufacturer's instructions or carry out some experiments, beginning at a short time and working up.

Bread will keep for up to three months in the freezer.

SHAPING AND MOULDING BREAD DOUGH

After the long rising and the second kneading (see page 12), it is time for you to stamp your own character on the bread, by shaping it. Certainly, some special breads, such as the French Brioche or the Austrian Gugelhupf, do have their own particular moulds and tins, rarely used for other recipes, but the basic bread dough that is the staple of so many households can be as

● *Kneading the dough*

creatively used as potter's clay. Use a baking sheet, a tin, a mould, or even a flowerpot, slash the top of the dough or sprinkle it with grains and seeds to make a loaf that suits your mood or occasion.

Baking Sheets, Tins and Moulds

Using a baking sheet: loaves baked on a flat baking sheet, not confined in a mould or tin, will rise both upwards and sideways. Commercial bakers call them 'crusty', meaning that there is a good, crisp crust all over the surface. The texture of the crumb (the inside of the loaf) is slightly more airy than that of loaves baked in a container.

A good-quality baking sheet should last you for years. Choose one that is made from fairly thick metal so that it will neither wobble out of shape as you are lifting a heavy loaf nor warp in a hot oven. The best surfaces are either textured and dull or coated with a non-stick silicon-type material. You will also find it practical to buy as big a one as will fit inside your oven.

You will find many recipes that tell you to grease and flour or simply grease your baking sheet, but this really isn't necessary. Over many years of baking, I have found that a fairly thick sprinkling of flour is all you need. Apart from being time-consuming and messy, greasing may well shorten the life of your baking sheet because of the extra scrubbing needed to get it clean afterwards. If you are using white flour which is very fine, you can add a little coarse semolina or yellow cornmeal to add to its non-stick properties. Any type of whole-wheat flour, wheat or rye for example, will work well on its own.

Plain yeasted loaves and buns and also soda breads baked on floured baking sheets will never normally stick. If your dough is rich and moist, you may simply need to ease off the bread using a wide palette knife.

After baking, wipe off browned flour with a soft, damp cloth.

If, however, you are over-zealous with an egg-based glaze, it may well form a cooked brown ring on the baking sheet. The bread will come off easily enough, after which the sheet should be soaked in warm soapy water for about half an hour. You should then be able to rub the egg off with a soft cloth assisted occasionally by a scouring pad. Do not scour the sheets with metal pads or you will spoil the surface.

Making a Dome Oven: early 'hearth breads' were baked underneath an iron pot or kettle which was piled high with hot ashes. You can achieve a similar effect by inverting a large earthenware or pyrex bowl or a clean earthenware flowerpot over the loaf on your baking sheet. This will surround the baking loaf with steam, causing it to rise beautifully and producing a thin, crisp crust and moist crumb.

Have a trial run first, simply by putting the bowl or pot on to the empty tray. Make sure you can lift it properly and that it will fit into your oven. Rearrange the oven shelves if necessary.

To remove the hot bowl from an equally hot tray, slip a sturdy palette knife between the two and gently lift up one side of the bowl.

Using Tins, Moulds and other Containers: bread tins make even-shaped loaves that rise upwards only and have thinner crusts on the base and sides that are enclosed in the tin. The most popular shape is the rectangular, so-called two-pound or one kilo bread tin, which actually takes a loaf made with 1 lb (450 g) flour. One-pound (450 g) tins are available, but this smaller loaf size is not very practical for everyday bread. You can also buy sets of six or eight miniature tins and the resulting loaves can be used as bread rolls or sliced to make garnishes and canapés.

Choose sturdy tins, preferably with no seams and with a non-shiny, textured surface. Silicon-coated tins also work well and both types should last a long time. Before using, the tins should be greased. Some recipes specify using butter to fit with the ingredients and character of that particular loaf. For making plain loaves, however, simply brush the insides of the tins with a thin coating of good-quality cooking oil, such as sunflower oil. The cooked loaves should be quite loose in the tins and will turn out easily. After use, the tins will not need to be washed and regular use will build up their non-stick qualities. If, however, some dough (perhaps from a rich, sticky mixture) does stick, soak and wash the tins as for the baking sheets and make sure that you oil them well the next time that you use them.

Bread can also be baked in round cake tins and French Charlotte tins, prepared in a similar way. Also good are shallow round tins, such as the German spring-form tin, which give an even shape to the base of the loaf, but allow the top to rise both up and sideways. The French expanding cake hoop gives a similar effect. It consists of a wide steel band coiled round into an adjustable circle and should be used in conjunction with a baking sheet.

If you like to make a bread with a soft, thin crust and a close crumb, you can use a hinged mould. Hinged moulds are usually cylindrical in shape and completely enclose the dough, thus producing a perfectly even-shaped loaf that cuts crossways into round slices.

Two special types of bread tin which are used in this book are the slightly conical-shaped and fluted French Brioche and the Austrian Gugelhupf mould, again slightly conical, with a central column and spiral fluted patterns around the sides. Ordinary ring moulds can be used as a substitute.

Many of these bread moulds are now available in materials which are suitable for use in microwave ovens, usually some sort of durable and heat-proof plastic. Some of these can also be used in conventional ovens up to a certain temperature. If you frequently use both a microwave and a conventional oven, these dual purpose moulds, particularly for the speciality breads, are a good buy. However, always check the manufacturer's instructions before use.

A popular way of cooking whole-wheat loaves during the wholefood boom of the 1980s was to bake them in flowerpots. Use earthenware pots that are unglazed on both outside and inside. If you are bringing them in from the garden, make sure they are clean, dry them well after washing and leave them in a warm place for 24 hours to dry out completely.

Flowerpots, like bread moulds, need to be seasoned before you use them. Grease or oil them well and put them into a preheated 400°F/200°C/gas 6 oven for 45 minutes. Once they are cool they can be used in the same way as the bread tins. However, only use them for plain breads and do not wash them after use – just wipe them round with paper towels.

Specially-made earthenware bread pots are obtainable from some cookery stores and potters. They are unglazed, round, with a flat base and sides that slope slightly outwards towards the top, and come in several different sizes. Use them in the same way as flowerpots.

● *Adding eggs or milk to dough will produce a softer, richer bread*

SHAPES, SLASHES AND FINISHES

Elaborate bread shapes come from all over the world. The examples on the following pages are the most universal and some of the simplest to make in your own kitchen. Most bread shapes are baked on a baking sheet, but decorative tops will enhance bread baked in tins and moulds as well. Slashing the top of the risen dough, glazing it and scattering it with grains and other ingredients will add considerably to the final appearance.

Bread is nearly always shaped after the second kneading (see page 12) by which time it will be non-sticky and pliable. Work on a dry, floured surface with clean, floured hands.

Whether you are dividing the dough into portions, rolling it flat or making long, sausage shapes, it should never be stretched. Dough that is stretched into its final shape may well shrink back during baking and its surface often looks pulled and broken. Bread should be eased naturally into shape and, where it needs dividing, it should always be cut using a sharp knife.

After the second kneading, dough can be handled easily, so make the shape you want on the work surface first and transfer it to the baking sheet when it is done. If you do not like a shape, you can quickly knead it into a ball and begin again, but do not over-knead it and do not add any extra flour at this point or it will become too dry.

Once a shape has been formed and is on the baking sheet, do not touch it again, unless you are going to slash the surface. Too much poking and prodding of proven dough will cause it to deflate or become lop-sided.

Slashed Patterns

A slashed pattern not only gives a better visual effect, but also gives more crust. For effective scoring, you will need a razor blade or wide craft knife – the sharper the better.

Depending on the final shape required of the loaf, the surface can be cut either before or after proving. If it is *after* proving, take care not to press on the surface of the loaf.

Shallow slashes simply give a pattern to the finished loaf. Deep slashes – up to ½ inch (1 cm) – can affect the overall shape.

Ideas of patterns are given with the basic bread shapes that follow.

Round loaves

To make a basic round shape, after finishing kneading, tuck the uneven sides of the dough underneath, turning the loaf round as you do so, so that you end up with a smooth dome of dough. Turn it round several times, gently easing it into shape with your hands.

The patterning on round loaves is generally carried out after proving. The following are the most popular patterns.

The Crown

Score a circle about 1 inch (2.5 cm) in from the sides of the loaf so that the centre part will rise slightly above the outside.

The Coburg

This is one of the standard English bread shapes. It is made by scoring a cross on the top of the loaf. Begin by scoring a straight line straight across the top. Then score the second line in two separate parts, working from the outside of the loaf to the centre. A deep score will cause the four quarters of the loaf to pull slightly apart when baked, and give the loaf a square shape.

A shallow-cut loaf will stay rounder. The cross need not go from side to side but can be confined more to the centre of the loaf, in which case, cut it quite deep.

The Miche

The Miche or Pain de Campagne, is a French loaf which has its top scored into six sections. After proving, slash one long line across the top, but not quite to the edges. Make two slashes on each side of this line, from just inside the edge of the loaf to the centre – so equally dividing the top of the loaf into six.

The Ring

If you do not have a ring mould, you can form a ring by hand. Shape the dough into a round. Push the handle of a wooden spoon down through the centre. Insert two fingers, then three and eventually your whole fist. Having said that dough should never be stretched, this is the one occasion where stretching is permissible,

16

but you will have to be careful. With your fingers inside the hole and your palms on the edge of the ring, gently enlarge it until it is about 6 inches (15 cm) across. Do this slowly, letting the dough rest between pulls. The dough can be left plain or, after proving, marked with shallow diagonal slashes round the edge.

The Chequerboard
The Chequerboard or College Loaf is slashed with four parallel lines across the loaf and then another four at right-angles to these, making a squared pattern. If this pattern is cut deep the result will be a knobbly, crusty top.

The Cottage Loaf
This is a peculiarly English loaf. Divide the dough into two pieces of one third, and two thirds. Form each into a round and place the smaller on top of the larger. Push the handle of a wooden spoon down through both pieces to the bottom and then slightly enlarge the hole with your fingers. (According to Eliza Acton in *The English Bread Book*, 1857, the hole was sometimes made even bigger by the baker pushing his elbow through it!) Cottage loaves are slashed before proving. Score in straight lines from the top to the bottom, taking in both sections of the loaf and making the scores about ¼ inch (5 mm) deep and 1 inch (2.5 cm) apart all the way round. Leave the loaf to prove and, just before baking, press down gently, but firmly, in the centre. This helps to maintain an even shape while the bread is baking.

Elongated Bread Shapes
The instructions for making a cylinder of dough sound complicated at first, but with only a little practice you will be able to do it quickly.

Basic Cylinder Shape
First make a round of dough and let it rest for about 5 minutes. Then, on a floured board, flatten the dough with your hands to a thickness of about 1 inch (2.5 cm). Roll it up and then roll it backwards and forwards under your hands working all the time from the centre outwards to make a long, even shape. Flatten it out again to make a long rectangle. Fold in both ends to the centre and press down hard again. This folding ensures all sides and corners are even. Roll up the dough tightly from one long side to make an even cylinder.

The Bloomer
How the Bloomer obtained its name is a mystery and Elizabeth David in her book *English Bread and Yeast Cookery* looks at its fascinating etymology without reaching any firm conclusions. My favourite origin is that it was named after the bicycling attire of Mrs. Amelia Bloomer – having the appearance of one half of what became known as 'a pair of bloomers'. This is probably not the correct one, but it makes a good story. The Bloomer is a large, cylindrical loaf, tapering at both ends, and has parallel diagonal slashes which are made after proving. To make a tapered cylinder, follow the instructions above, and at the final rolling bring the ends of the dough towards you with your palms and push the centre away with your thumbs so that you have a thick crescent. Straighten the loaf, making the side that pointed towards you the underside. Then roll the loaf backwards and forwards under your hands until you get the right shape, keeping your hands

mainly on the ends. Put the loaf on a floured baking sheet, leave it to prove and make a few short diagonal slashes all along its length, about 1½ inches (4 cm) apart, just before putting it into the oven to bake.

The Vienna Loaf

Also called a Lemon Loaf because of its final shape, this loaf is made like a Bloomer, the only difference being that there is one long, lengthways slash down the centre.

The Cottage Brick

This is like a square Cottage Loaf and is mentioned by Elizabeth David as being more popular in London than the round Cottage. Divide the dough into two square pieces of about one third and two thirds. Put the smaller one on top of the larger. Make a hole through the centre with the handle of a wooden spoon and gradually insert your hand flat, vertically down through the loaf, to make a lengthways slit along the length of the top. This type of Cottage Loaf is not slashed or scored.

The Long Crusty

Make the basic cylinder shape and lay it on a floured baking sheet. Take a sharp pair of scissors and make diagonal cuts all along the top of the loaf, about 1 inch (2.5 cm) deep and 1½ inches (4 cm) long, meeting at the points to make a zig-zag pattern. Leave the loaf to prove before baking.

The Baguette

This is the long loaf originating in France, but well-known all over the world. Make a cylinder of dough and leave it to rest for about 10 minutes. On a floured surface, gradually roll the dough backwards and forwards, continually returning your hands to the centre and gradually moving them outwards. Lay the loaf on a baking sheet and slash the top before proving. The four slashes in a Baguette are diagonal, but only just so, making them very long and overlapping each other.

The Spiral

This is another version of the round loaf, but it is made by first making a long, thin cylinder and then coiling it round from the centre outwards – to form a spiral.

The Plait

Divide the dough into three equal parts and roll them into long, thin cylinders. Lay them parallel to each other. To make an even shape, begin plaiting from the centre outwards. As you near the end, stretch the tips slightly and press them downwards and together. To complete the plait, turn the unfinished ends towards you. Finish as for the first half of the plait.

The Epi

This comes from France and its name means 'ear of wheat' as that is what it resembles. Make a long cylinder and lay it on a floured baking sheet. With a razor blade, make flattened diagonal cuts three quarters of the way through the dough and about 2 inches (5 cm) apart all along the length. Pull the pieces to alternate sides.

The Pain Brie

This is a speciality of the Calvados region of France and is usually made with yeast. To make the shape, form a tapered cylinder as for the Bloomer and leave it to prove. Just before baking, make parallel slashes down the whole length.

The Polka

Another French pattern, this is an elongated cylinder, longer than the Bloomer but thicker and shorter than the Baguette. Its surface is scored into a diagonal chequerboard pattern after proving.

Flat Breads

The types of dough used for breads such as Pitta bread, Naan bread and other flat Middle Eastern types are very similar to a basic white bread dough. They are very springy and bouncy and sometimes seem to have a mind of their own. Nevertheless, they must be rolled. Use a wooden cylindrical rolling pin and flour both it and the work surface well. Roll out the dough after the second kneading. If, halfway through, you find it keeps springing back into its original thickness, cover it with a cloth and leave it to rest for a few minutes before continuing. This type of bread should in no way be stretched.

Instructions for a variety of flat breads will be found in specific recipes throughout this book.

Pizzas and Pies

Dough for pizzas and pies has to be rolled out very thinly and not stretched. Depending on the springiness of the dough, you may have to do this in several stages, letting the dough rest for a few minutes in between.

Breads Baked in Tins and Moulds

For a well-shaped loaf, your dough should be shaped to fit your tin before you put it in. Although it sounds obvious, make sure that you have the right-sized container for the amount of dough that you are making. Most recipes will state the size of container required, but a useful guide is that a mould should be twice the size of the volume of the kneaded dough.

Round containers: shape the dough in a round, as above. The top can be slashed in a similar way to the tops of round loaves baked on a sheet.

Long containers: roll the bread into a cylinder of the appropriate size, as above. The top can be slashed diagonally or once straight down the middle. To give a double top effect, the dough can also be divided into two high rectangles which are put into the mould side by side.

Ring Moulds: form the dough into a tapered cylinder that, when formed into a ring, is the same circumference as the mould. Coil it round the mould, overlapping the ends, and push down gently to distribute the dough evenly.

Gugelhupf Moulds: there are two ways of filling these, the first is as for the ring mould. The second is to form the dough into a long cylinder and cut it into crossways slices which are then spread with a filling. These are then put into the mould in overlapping layers and gently pressed down. (See Gugelhupf recipe page 45.)

Brioche Moulds: rich, soft Brioche dough is baked in a similar shape to a Cottage Loaf, but its texture demands that it is cooked in a container. Take about three-quarters of the dough, form it into a round and put it into the mould. Form the other piece of dough into a pear shape, with the thin end tapered. With your fingers, make a hole down through the centre of the dough in the mould to make a well slightly larger than the tapered end of the smaller piece. Insert the smaller piece of dough into the hole so that its rounded end forms a knob on top of the larger piece. (See Brioche recipe page 33.)

Rolls, Buns and Doughnuts

When you are making rolls and buns, cut the dough into even-sized pieces using a sharp knife and then lightly knead each piece separately.

Round Rolls

Roll the dough round and round between your palms to form a ball. Place it on a floured surface, and turn it round several times with your palms to give an even, round shape. Lay the rolls on a baking sheet without flattening them. Round rolls can be left plain or the tops can be slashed with a single line, a circle or a small cross shape after proving.

Clover Leaf

Cut the dough into smaller pieces. Form each into rounds and lay them on the baking sheet, just touching each other, in groups of three.

Cluster

Lay the rolls in a circular pattern on the baking sheet, just touching each other. As they bake, they will join together, but can easily be pulled apart when required.

Long Rolls

Roll the dough between your palms to form a ball, as above. Lay the dough on a floured work surface and roll it backwards and forwards under your hands until it is of the required length and thickness. A long diagonal or lengthways slash can be added on long rolls after proving.

Ring Doughnuts and Bagels

Make the dough into rounds. Push your forefinger down through the centre of each. Enlarge the holes until they cover about one third of the diameter of the dough.

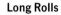

Knots

Form the dough into a ball and then into a long, thin rope by rolling it backwards and forwards under your hands. Make a loose knot, stretching the dough as little as possible.

Parker House Rolls

These are made to give plenty of crust. Roll the dough to a thickness of about ½ inch (1 cm). Using a pastry cutter, cut it into 3½ inch (9 to 10 cm) circles and brush the top surface of

MAKING BREAD

the circles with melted butter. Score down the centre of each circle with a sharp knife and fold the circle in half down the score line. Place them on a baking sheet and gently press them down.

Yeasted Pastries

The dough for yeasted pastries is firmer than for flat breads, but it still needs to be rolled without stretching. It is then cut according to the final pastry shape required. Use a sharp knife or a dough scraper, so that the edges do not become pulled, and a ruler to obtain straight edges and similar sizes. Below are some of the more popular shapes.

Crescent

This shape is used all over the world and is probably most well known as the shape of the French Croissant. Cut equilateral triangles with the sides measuring 6 inches (15 cm). Use a

rolling pin from top to base of each one to slightly elongate them. Slightly pull out the corners of the base so they stick out, and then begin rolling tightly from the base to the tip. Bring the ends round to make a crescent shape and tuck the tip underneath. As the dough expands in the oven the tip should pull itself out again to lie across the top. To make a filled crescent, spread the filling over the bottom half of the triangle before rolling.

Pinwheels

Cut the dough into 6 inch (15 cm) squares. Cut a line from each corner to within ½ inch (1.3 cm) of the centre. Put a portion of the filling in the centre. Fold one bottom corner of each cut section to the centre with the tips overlapping slightly. Seal by pressing down in the centre.

Cockscombs

Cut the dough into 8 inch (20 cm) wide rectangles and spread half with a filling. Fold

over the other half and then cut the folded dough into 4 inch (10 cm) squares. Make three cuts in the folded side of the dough from the fold to within ½ inch (1 cm) of the opposite side. After laying the pastries on a floured baking sheet, gently spread out the sections.

Snails

Cut the dough into a rectangle 8 × 16 inches (20 × 40 cms). Spread it evenly with filling. Roll up the dough along one long side and cut into 1 inch (2.5 cm) thick slices. Lay these flat.

Finishes

Various toppings and glazes can improve the appearance of your bread.

Glazes give the finished loaf a shiny surface. The simplest is a plain beaten egg. You can also use egg beaten with a little water or milk.

For sweet buns you can use milk, sweetened by being warmed with a little sugar – 2 teaspoons to 5 fl oz (150 ml).

Most loaves are glazed immediately after shaping.

The topping on a loaf adds to the appearance and also, to some extent, to the final flavour. It is sprinkled on after glazing but before slashing, so that the slashes will show up plainly. The following are ingredients that are used most frequently: poppy seeds, sesame seeds, caraway seeds, cracked wheat (on whole-wheat breads only), flaked almonds and chopped nuts (the latter two mainly on sweet breads).

THE HISTORY OF BREAD

The story of bread begins around 10,000 BC, after the last ice age. As the earth warmed up, grasses with seeds began to grow, and the nomadic hunters of the world discovered that they could harvest, dry and grind them to produce a coarse, gritty flour.
Wild wheat and barley grasses grew most abundantly in the Eastern Mediterranean. Strong, hot winds scattered the wild seeds as soon as they ripened, so that local people had to react fast, when the time was right, to gather-in what they could before it blew away. Because there was no organized cultivation, the rest was left to seed itself for the following year.

THE HISTORY OF BREAD

By 9000 BC, the people of the Middle East had established themselves in villages near to the best wild crops, and from this time onwards, they started to select, domesticate and cultivate the wild animals and grasses around them.

The first primitive breads appeared at this time. The toasted and ground grains were first mixed with water, then kneaded into a thick paste or dough. The resulting unleavened, stone- or ash-baked Hearth Cakes became a staple food. Middle Eastern Lavash, Indian Chapatis, Mexican Tortillas, Ethiopian Injera and Scottish Oatcakes all evolved. Nowadays some of these are eaten cold, but originally, because of the type and coarseness of the grain, they were really only palatable when hot. Although a few attempts were made to improve bread during the Neolithic period, such as sprouting the grain before it was toasted, soaking it in water, and simmering it, the real improvement in quality came with the development of a better grain.

In 6000 BC, the Natufian race, living around the Persian Gulf, began to develop the first real farming methods. They dug the soil and scattered the seeds by hand, instead of leaving it to the wind. They threshed their grain by driving animals over it, and winnowed it by throwing handfuls into the air, a process which continued in Europe until the nineteenth century. In the hope of better harvests and more palatable bread, the Natufians also developed new strains of wheat.

At around the same time, fermented liquids were discovered, perhaps because someone left some honey-sweetened water by a fire. This was the beginning of yeast, and its inclusion in wheat-flour doughs was found to make bread rise. The ancient Egyptians, whose farming communities grew up along the Nile before 5000 BC, certainly knew about and ate leavened bread, although it was usually reserved for the rich. The majority of the people ate flat breads, made from a mixture of coarse-grained flours, and a kind of sourdough bread, known as Ta, which was made from wheat and barley.

By 4000 BC, many countries in Europe were farming countries. Peoples from northern France and Belgium took various types of cereals and domesticated animals to Britain, where they settled, mainly in the south and south west. New types of wheat were developed in different European countries and by the Iron Age (c. 1000 BC), the main types of grain were spelt and club wheat.

The first ovens in Europe were called pot ovens – domed iron pots which were placed over hot hearth-stones. Steam trapped inside them made the bread softer and, even though no leaven was added, encouraged it to rise slightly. Rotary hand querns, for grinding, first appeared in Spain and spread across Europe in the first century AD. At around the same time, Celts in Gaul began to sift their ground grain through a hair sieve, to make it finer, and also found a way of using beer as a leaven. All these developments vastly improved the quality of bread.

By about 1000 BC, the ancient Greeks had devised the first primitive mills to grind the wheat and barley which was grown all over the country. They were made from two horizontally-placed rectangular stones. The top stone had a slit through which the grain was poured, and was worked backwards and forwards using a system of pulleys. The Greeks are also reputed to have invented the donkey-powered mill. Greek bread, raised with a leaven made by soaking millet flour in grape juice, which was subsequently kneaded and left to ferment, was far closer to modern bread than its predecessors.

Despite conquering vast areas of the world, the Romans' expertise did not at first extend to baking. The staple food of the Roman soldiers was puls, or pulmentum, a thick porridge made from millet, spelt or chick-pea flour; or small cakes baked from crushed grains (still known as Haver Cakes in parts of England, because they were once carried in a soldier's haversack). It took a long time for them to switch to ready-made bread because at first it was so coarse and therefore heavy to carry.

However, with the Roman invention of a new type of mill, which used circular revolving millstones, flour was made finer than it had ever been before. Yeast was subsequently imported from Gaul, and Egyptian slaves were brought in to mix the two into bread. The first bakeries were established and with them greater distinctions between bread for the rich and for the poor.

The Roman aristocracy insisted upon fine, white bread, a preference which spread throughout the then known world and which has persisted until late into the twentieth century. Wheat bread was preferred to barley bread and there were all kinds of variations. The Romans probably had the first Baps and Croissants, and they encouraged variation by adding honey, poppy seeds and cheese to their basic bread mixture. Bread was baked in shops and sold on the premises, and also on market stalls.

Very little has been recorded about the development of bread between the end of the Roman world and the beginning of the Medieval period. We do know that the watermill was developed in Europe during the fifth century. The first one ever to appear in British records was one in Kent, mentioned in a charter of the year AD 762. By the time the Domesday Book was written in 1086, there were 5,624 watermills in England alone.

In the sixth century AD, the Slavs in the north east of Europe had developed the forerunner of the moldboard plough, which made it possible to bring large areas of hitherto untouched land into cultivation. And as more grain was grown and fewer people starved, the population increased.

By the time William the Conqueror invaded England in AD 1066, the growing and milling of grain in Europe had established a pattern that was to change very little in the next four hundred years. Mills were often owned by the lords of particular villages, and poor inhabitants were bound to bring their own grain to the lord's mill and pay for the privilege of having it ground. Ploughs, too, were not owned by individuals, but communally, so grain growing was a community project. This fairly loose arrangement was seized upon by Medieval lords and rigidly enforced so that the growing and milling of grain helped to confirm the hierarchical nature of the feudal system.

Tremendous amounts of bread were consumed by Medieval households. At the tables of the poor, bread often had to be a meal in itself, or was served with a thin pottage of vegetables and pulses. In rich households, bread was often the only accompaniment to roasted or stewed meats and was essential in the winter, when most of the meat and fish was brined, to counteract the saltiness of the diet. Despite this, very few plain bread recipes were written down. Apprentices learned them from master bakers, and young girls from their relatives at home.

The regular peasant bread in Medieval Europe was whole-wheat, often containing pieces of chaff as well as the bran and coarsely-ground grain. It was made with a mixture of grains, was dark in colour, heavy in texture and probably had quite a strong flavour. In times of hardship other ingredients were added to increase the amount of flour. Pea and bean flours were common, acorns, ground root vegetables and sawdust could be found in Swiss bread, and in Scandinavia they used tree bark.

Dark whole-wheat bread had quite another use in the homes of rich Normans – namely, to make trenchers (after the French, *tranche*, meaning slice) – a custom since the time of Charlemagne. Trenchers were used as plates, and were cut from large, square loaves that had been turned during baking to give them an even shape. Stewed meat was placed on them before being eaten with the fingers. Trenchers soaked up the gravy so as to make the process as polite as possible, but were rarely eaten themselves during the course of a meal. Instead they were collected in baskets and given to the servants or dogs, or distributed to the poor.

The best-quality bread in the Medieval period was wheat bread, made with flour that had been bolted several times through wool and linen cloths to make it as white and bran-free as possible. It was demanded by the rich and longed for by the poor. The English called it Wastel, from the Norman 'guastel' meaning cake, and similar to Wastel were Pandemain; Mayne bread; and Manchet bread, which was made up into small, bun-sized loaves. Other breads, such as Cocket, in England, were less expensive, because the flour for them was less finely ground. There was a coarse, whole-wheat type called Cheat, Chet, Bis or Treet, which was made from unbolted wheat flour; various maslin and mixed grain breads; and Horse-bread, which consisted of a large proportion of pea and bean flours.

In Scandinavia there were long-keeping Crispbreads and hard, round loaves that were strung on poles and hung in the rafters; while in Italy, although pasta was the staple, and bread was expensive, two special breads *were* devised in the Middle Ages, the Colomba and Panettone (see page 54). In the Middle East, at the same time, there was the white flour bread, Al Khobz al Huwmara, and the coarse flour bread, Al Khobz al Khashkar. Both were glazed with borax which was imported from Armenia.

As towns grew larger, there were more and more commercial bakers who not only made bread for sale, but also took in dough from ordinary house-holders for baking. As with all trades in Medieval London, the bakery business in England was controlled by the guilds, and there were separate guilds for white and brown bread bakers, which existed until the seventeenth century.

Bakers sent their servants and apprentices into the streets with trays of bread, ringing handbells to attract custom. Competition was fierce, with the result that price cutting and reduction in the size of loaves were common practices. In 1277, the first full version of the Assize of Bread was therefore drawn up, to establish sizes and weights according to the quality of the bread. The laws were complicated and it was small wonder that one of the commonest crimes of all in Medieval England was selling underweight bread. For this, and the crime of stealing another baker's dough, the offender's punishment was to be dragged on a sledge through the dirtiest streets of the town with a loaf tied around his neck. After a second offence he would be put in the pillory and after a third, banished from trading forever.

Paris bakers were also organizing themselves into guilds at about this time. They formed the Corporation des Boulangers, and the rights and duties of master bakers, apprentices, and servants were clearly set out. The price of bread was fixed, but the size of loaves depended on the price of wheat.

During the sixteenth and seventeenth centuries bread changed very little. Rye, maslin and barley bread were still made. White wheat bread remained the food of the rich, whilst the poor made do with coarser varieties. The finest bread in English cities was still Manchet, which was sometimes baked without leaven, giving it a very close texture. It was a creamy colour and sometimes enriched with butter and eggs. Cheat bread was more or less the equivalent of present-day whole-wheat, and 'brown bread' was the term used for the coarsest and most branny of all. In sixteenth-century France, however, there was a new kind of fine wheat bread called 'le Pain de Chapitre' but it was not until 1650 that sifted flour became commonly available in Paris.

In Roman times, the French had been famous for using brewer's yeast as a leaven, but this method had virtually died out, and most bread was risen by the sourdough process. In 1665, however, a brewer's yeast leaven was reintroduced by the Flemish. The new bread received court honours and Marie de Medici called it 'Pain à la Reine.' In 1668, however, the French Faculté de Médecine declared that it was made from rotten barley and therefore injurious to health. Furious arguments ensued, but in the end the lovers of good bread won, and the use of brewer's yeast was authorized in 1670. Until then, French bread had had a thin crust and a close, compact crumb. Large loaves weighing 16 lb (7.2 kg) or more had been made at home to last the family a week. The new bread was light and airy with a hard crust, but it did not keep. Consequently, housewives not wishing to bake at home every day, relied on a daily visit to the baker.

The discovery of new countries has made a great contribution to culinary history, and bread is no exception. Not only were these new lands for wheat growing, but they also provided new ingredients for bread making. At the end of the fifteenth century, Columbus discovered America and the Caribbean islands and there he found something that the native Indians called 'may-ees'. It was a decorative grass with huge ears. The Europeans named it maize, or sweet corn. Eaten with beans and vegetables it was the staple food of the Aztecs and Mayans, who used it to make the flat breads that the Spaniards christened Tortillas. In North America and what was to become Canada, when the first harvests of the European settlers were unsuccessful, it was the American Indians who taught them to make the maize-based Johnny Cake (see page 123), also known as Hoe Cake, Ash Cake or Corn Pone.

Maize seeds were taken back to Spain and from there to the rest of southern Europe and eventually the Philippines and even China. Corn breads and the thick corn porridge called polenta, so like the Roman puls, became popular in Italy.

Maize bread was not the only new bread to be discovered. In the Bahamas lived the Taino tribes, who made flat hearth cakes from the stem pulp of the zamia plant. This discovery may have had little effect on the rest of the world, but the discovery of manioc in Cuba did. The roots of the plant were grated and peeled and the bitter juices squeezed out before the pulp was sieved, made into flat cakes and cooked. This was known as Cassava bread and, surprisingly, it was very much liked by the Spanish and the French. In the sixteenth century, manioc (a source of tapioca) was taken to Africa by the Portuguese where it became a principal food.

In return, wheat was taken to the New World. A colony founded by Sir

Walter Raleigh planted the first crop on Roanoke Island, off North Carolina; the Pilgrim fathers planted wheat and rye beside the local corn; and Bartholomew Gosnold, the discoverer of Cape Cod, grew wheat on Elizabeth Island, Massachusetts, in 1602. Many acres of virgin land were put under the plough, but nevertheless it was two hundred years before wheat bread ceased to be a luxury. The first watermill, however, was erected in 1634 and the prosperity and importance of New York was established at this time through its being the centre of the grain trade in the east. Meanwhile, both French and English were settling in Canada, and in southern Africa, in 1652, the Dutch, led by Jan van Riebeek, established a supply port at the Cape from which the voortrekkers set out to establish farms and wheatlands.

The eighteenth century saw the improvement of agricultural methods throughout the whole of Europe and in the newly-settled areas of America. Jethro Tull invented the seed drill and a four-coultered plough, whilst Thomas Coke brought in his threshing machine. In England a four year crop rotation system was devised, whilst Holland vastly improved Europe's grain yields with a seven year system. Steam-powered mills were introduced in both Britain and America to cope with the increasingly abundant crops. Wheat flour became more available everywhere. The people had more bread, and, as a result, the population of Europe increased by 48 million to 188 million between 1750 and 1800.

In France, bread making was reaching perfection. Brewer's yeast was replaced by a special baking yeast, imported from Holland and Austria, and there was a great deal of research and discussion into what made a good loaf. In 1778 the basic ingredients and methods were agreed and the Ecole de Boulangerie was established in Paris in 1780, although it lasted for only thirteen years. By then nearly every baker was a master of his craft.

There were several really poor harvests in England towards the end of the eighteenth century but, although wheat became scarce, it did not lose its popularity. In times of great shortage the government sponsored a 'standard loaf' made of coarse, dark wheat flour, containing a large proportion of bran; but the people wanted white bread and the result was bread doctored with chalk, alum, beanmeal and even bonemeal. Even the poorest demanded white bread, and in 1795 the recently introduced poor relief system was calculated on its price.

During the nineteenth century, agricultural methods continued to increase wheat yields in both Britain and North America. By this time, land in Australia was being farmed – the climate of the south west, in particular, being ideally suited to the growing of wheat.

The reaping machine was invented by a Scots preacher called the Reverend Patrick Bell. While the British resented change to a method of harvesting that had been the same since the first wheat was planted, the Americans thought it a great idea and eventually used one patented in their own country. John Deere of Illinois invented a lightweight plough, and a binding machine was

● *Harvesting, Palouse, Washington state*

introduced, first in America, and later perfected in Britain. Australian farmers came up with the idea of a combine harvester that would cut and thresh in one go.

New types of wheat were also being developed, such as Red Fife, a good, hard, bread-making wheat that was taken west by the pioneers; and Maquis wheat, which could be sown in the spring and cropped early.

America became the world's largest grain producer – the new railways ensured transport across the country – and in 1884 Canada actually exported wheat back to Britain. Despite all the developments, however, there was widespread adulteration of bread by bakers, and soaring costs. It was these factors that induced two British writers to encourage every housewife to bake their own.

William Cobbett produced his *Cottage Economy* in 1823, giving instructions on all aspects of country housekeeping and smallholding. 'How wasteful,' he says, 'how shameful, for a labourer's wife to go the the baker's shop; and how negligent, how criminally careless of the welfare of his family, must the labourer be, who permits so scandalous a use of the proceeds of his labour.' But in praise of home-baked bread: 'Here is cut and come again. Here is bread always for the table. Bread to carry afield, always a hunch of bread to put into the hand of a hungry child.'

Eliza Acton wrote her *English Bread Book* in 1857 because she disliked the unhygienic conditions in commercial bakeries and the fact that bread was still adulterated.

In America, Fannie Farmer wrote *The Original Boston Cooking School Book* in 1896, into which she put twenty pages of bread recipes. 'The study of bread making,' she said, 'is of no slight importance and deserves more attention than it receives.'

But no matter how housewives were urged to bake their own bread, more and more was being made commercially and the process became increasingly mechanized. The first kneading machine was invented in the late nineteenth century, but in both Britain and Europe it was disregarded until after the upheavals of the First World War, during which bread was rationed and was made of whatever grains there were available. Also at the end of the nineteenth century, the first roller mills were introduced.

Between the two World Wars, the Chorleywood baking process (involving the addition of improvers to the flour and intensive mechanical kneading) was devised in England. This method could produce uniform, mass-produced bread, and large-scale bakeries in many parts of the world use a similar process today.

Nowadays, sophisticated city supermarkets stock a large range of breads in addition to the ubiquitous white-sliced loaf. However, commercialization takes little account of the amazing variety of local shapes and flavours to be found all around the world. This book aims to bring just such regional diversity to a wider audience.

FRANCE

*Bread is extremely important in the French diet, as the main accompaniment to every
meal – from a simple salad to a rich blanquette or ragout. Where the British choose potatoes,
the Chinese rice, and the Italians pasta, the French will have bread.
Bread is dunked into hot chocolate, covered in nourishing soup, used to mop up gravies and
sauces, and is, of course, eaten with ripe local cheese.
French families shop for bread daily, and the joy of this is that there is at least one craftsman
baker to be found in every village to satisfy the demand.*

Boulangeries were traditionally opened six days a week, closing on Mondays, but now they often stagger their working days so that there is always at least one local shop open every day. Each shop sells a vast selection of different shapes and sizes of loaves, including some specific to the locality.

France has been famous for its bread since Roman times when, unusually for the age, it was risen with brewer's yeast. With the fall of Rome, however, refinements slipped, and the common French diet reverted to a cereal porridge, supplemented occasionally by bread made in the home. This bread was either unleavened or started by a sourdough method, and typically made from a mixture of coarsely ground and unsieved grains including rye, wheat, buckwheat, barley and oats.

By the eleventh century, however, bread had become a mainstay of the French diet. The bread of the ordinary people was still very coarse, often made from mixed cereals, but, as in the rest of Europe, finer wheaten breads were produced for the rich. Many windmills and watermills were built at this time and communal bakehouses were set up in every village, where bread prepared at home could be taken for baking.

Using the sourdough method to make all types of bread, generally called Pain au Levain, was common practice throughout France. One of the most famous breads, from the thirteenth century to the Revolution, was the Pain de Gonesse – a fine wheat bread, highly praised by Henry IV and later by Marie de Medici. Both brown and white types were sold in the Paris markets. In the fifteenth and sixteenth centuries there were Pain de Chailli, a quality

Put in the loaves and bake them for 1 hour, brushing the surfaces well with more cold water every 15 minutes. This seems like a very long baking time, but regular brushing with water will prevent the loaves from drying out or burning. If they look as if they are going to colour too quickly, cover them with aluminium foil.

When the loaves are done, lift them on to wire racks to cool. Eat them slightly warm or as soon as they are cool, and certainly on the day that you make them.

This basic dough is made into many different shapes, some standard throughout France and others particular to a region, town or even shop where a *boulanger* has a speciality. The same dough can taste different depending on the size and shape of the finished loaf.

The Flûte is a longer and thinner version of a Baguette, and the Ficelle, meaning 'string', even thinner. The Opéra or Restaurant is shorter and fatter; the Petit Parisien, shorter, fatter and usually softer in the middle; the Pain d'Alsacienne like a short Bloomer with lengthways scores; and the Pain Espagnol similar, with very pointed ends. It is said that the Epi was made for the person who, sent out to buy the loaf, was tempted to break off and eat the crusty end before reaching home. Cut to resemble an ear of wheat (see page 19), it has many such crusty knobs for pulling off – so everyone can have a share. Like several other breads, the Epi has been made, over the years, for both pagan and Christian festivals. Other examples include the Couronne, formed into a wreath, and the Couronne Sartoise, formed into a spiralled horseshoe. The Palette is like an oval paddle; the Pain Collier like a horse collar; the Tabatière like an open snuff box; and the Champignon like a mushroom.

The Pain de Campagne, however, is the most popular of the speciality breads, and it can be found all over France, in small bakers and in hypermarkets. It is made with wheat flour or a mixture of wheat and rye, using the sourdough method which makes it moist, pleasantly acidic, and long keeping. The Pain de Campagne is usually round with cross cuts on the top that divide it into six sections – in other words, a Miche (see page 16). Sometimes it was made almost as big as a cartwheel, in order to last a family for a week. Cartloads of such loaves were taken each week to outlying districts and left at the side of the road for families to collect.

The most popular of the enriched breads, brought about by the taxes of the nineteenth century, is the Pain Viennois, which looks like a Baguette, and is semi-sweet with a fluffy-textured crumb. The dough is enriched with malted flour, sugar and milk powder.

The Petits Pains, literally 'small breads', are shaped rather like outsize rolls, some with diagonal slashes and others with one slash lengthways. They are made of white wheat flour (Petits Pains Ordinaire), with rye flour, or with a mixture, and the dough can be plain or enriched with milk, eggs or butter.

The following recipe is for semi-sweet rolls made with milk and egg. In the area around Paris they are called Fougasses, which can be confusing since this is also the name of a different bread, made in Normandy.

Petits Pains au Lait

To make sixteen buns:

1 oz (25 g) fresh yeast or 1 tablespoon dried
8 fl oz (225 ml) warm milk, plus 2 tablespoons
1 lb (450 g) strong plain flour
1 teaspoon salt
1½ oz (40 g) sugar, plus 1 oz (25 g)
1 egg
2 oz (50 g) butter, softened

Dissolve the yeast in a little of the warm milk and leave to stand – five minutes for fresh yeast and 15 for dried. Place the flour in a bowl and toss in the salt and 1½ oz (40 g) sugar. Make a well in the centre, pour in the yeast and the remaining milk and add the egg. Mix everything to a dough and knead it on a floured board until it is smooth. Knead in the butter. Place the dough in a bowl, cover it with a cloth and leave in a warm place for 1 hour.

Heat the oven to 400°F/200°C/gas 6. Knead the dough again and divide it into sixteen equal pieces. Form them into round rolls and place them on a floured baking sheet. Leave the buns to prove for 20 minutes and bake them for 15 minutes. Cool them on a wire rack.

To glaze the Fougasses, dissolve 1 oz (25 g) sugar in 2 tablespoons milk and brush over the hot buns.

A visit to the *boulangerie* on the way to school is a treat for many French children, and bakers in different areas bake certain small rolls for them. These rolls are eaten with chocolate during the first break of the day. To give the right blend of bread and semi-soft chocolate, the rolls can be split open and left with pieces of chocolate in them near a heater, or even sat upon for a short time! Some bakers actually bake the chocolate inside the rolls and this really is the most delicious combination. When eaten, they are still warm, the chocolate is soft, but not runny enough

● *The Baguette*

to be messy. Even after cooling, when the chocolate has solidified again, they still make an excellent sweet snack. You can even serve them as a dessert with cream.

Petits Pains au Chocolat

To make eight buns:

½ quantity basic bread dough (see page 12), made with milk, or 8 oz (225 g) dough as for Petit Pains au Lait

7 oz (200 g) bar of plain chocolate that can be broken into 8 rectangles

Make up the dough and leave it to rise in the usual way. Preheat the oven to 400°F/200°C/gas 6.

Knead the dough on a floured board, divide it into eight pieces and roll each one into a rectangle about 4 × 6 inches (10 × 15 cm). Break the chocolate into eight rectangles. Lay a piece of chocolate on one of the rolled pieces of dough. Fold over the ends of the dough and then the sides, to enclose the chocolate completely.

Place the finished parcel, with the joins of the dough underneath, on a floured baking sheet. Continue to make the rest of the buns in the same way.

Leave the buns to prove for 20 minutes. Bake them for 15 minutes or until they are golden brown. Cool them on a wire rack and eat them warm or cold.

Flat, flavoured breads are popular in France. They are ideal snacks and, when accompanied by a salad, make a complete meal. The Forron is the simplest of all these. It comes from the Dauphiné region of south east France and is made of an oil-enriched dough pressed into a tart tin and topped with cream cheese made from either cow's or goat's milk. Walnuts and onions are used to top another flat bread called Le Sale de Bugey.

When making a savoury tart, French housewives often use a bread dough in place of pastry. They may well buy the dough ready-made from the local baker and knead in a little oil themselves.

The following two recipes are examples of tarts made with bread bases: one with a Quiche Lorraine filling and the other with a simple béchamel sauce flavoured with Gruyère cheese. They are very simple to make and lift out of the tins so easily that you will never want to make a pastry tart again. Both are best eaten warm, with a salad.

Tarte Lorraine

To make one 10 inch (25.5 cm) diameter tart:

½ quantity basic bread dough (see page 12), plus 2 tablespoons olive oil, risen for 1 hour

2 rashers streaky bacon

1 small onion

½ oz (15 g) butter

1 egg

1 egg yolk

5 fl oz (150 ml) creamy milk

1 oz (25 g) Cheddar or Gruyère cheese, grated

Preheat the oven to 400°F/200°C/gas 6. Dice the bacon and thinly slice the onion. Cook them in a frying pan in the butter, until the onion is golden and the bacon is just cooked through.

Knead the dough on a floured board and roll it out to line a 10 inch (25.5 cm) diameter tart tin. Prick it in several places with a fork. Spread the bacon and onion over the dough. Beat together the egg, egg yolk, milk and cheese. Pour them over the bacon and onion. Leave the tart for 20 minutes. You will find that the edges of the dough begin to rise and the filling forms a wide well in the middle.

Bake the tart for 25 minutes, or until the edges are golden brown. Push the loaf out of the tin and serve.

Cheese and Tomato Tart

To make one 10 inch (25.5 cm) diameter tart:

½ quantity basic bread dough (see page 12) plus 2 tablespoons olive oil, risen for 1 hour

1 oz (25 g) butter

1 small onion, thinly sliced

2 tablespoons strong plain flour

10 fl oz (275 ml) milk

4 oz (110 g) Gruyère cheese, grated

3 ripe tomatoes

Line a 10 inch (25.5 cm) tart tin as for Tarte Lorraine above. In a saucepan, over a medium heat, gently cook the onion in the butter until it turns golden. Stir in the flour and milk and cook, stirring, until you have a thick sauce. Take the pan from the heat and beat in the cheese. Cool the sauce and pour it over the dough that lines the tart tin. Slice the tomatoes and lay the slices on top. Prove and bake as for Tarte Lorraine.

In Normandy there is a Fougasse containing eggs and butter, which is rolled into a rectangle with leaf shapes incised into it. Cheese or anchovies are scattered over the top, and it is folded in half to make a shape that resembles a bagpipe.

The Pissaladière is the Niçoise equivalent of the pizza, made with oil-enriched dough, rolled flat and topped with anchovies and in some cases a fresh tomato salad. Anchovies are also used a lot in Provence and the following recipe comes from that area. It is not a flat bread, but a round dome of moist, flavoursome dough made using a sourdough leaven. It is wonderful with butter (although not traditionally served with it) and also with tomato soup or a stew.

La Pompe aux Anchois

To make one 1 lb (450 g) loaf:

½ quantity basic bread dough (see page 12), put into a large bowl, covered with clingfilm and kept in a warm place for 2 days
2 × 1¾ oz (45 g) tins anchovy fillets
2 oz (50 g) butter, softened
2 eggs, beaten
8 oz (225 g) strong plain flour

Take five of the anchovy fillets, cut them in half lengthways and then into pieces about 5 inches (5.5 cms) long. Crush the remaining fillets to a paste.

With the fermented dough still in the bowl, knead in the crushed anchovies, the butter and then the eggs, a little at a time. At first it will look impossible for all the egg to be absorbed, but this will happen after about 10 minutes and you will be left with a smooth, very soft dough. Knead in the flour and then turn the dough on to a floured work surface for a final kneading to make it smooth and elastic. Return the dough to the bowl, cover it and leave it in a warm place for 1 hour or until it has doubled in size.

Preheat the oven to 400°F/200°C/gas 6. Knead the dough again, form it into a ball and place on a floured baking sheet. Put the pieces of anchovy on top, pressing down lightly. Leave the dough in a warm place to prove for 20 minutes.

Bake the loaf for 25 minutes, or until it is golden brown and sounds hollow when tapped. Cool on a wire rack.

The richest of all breads in France is the Brioche, made with white flour, eggs and large amounts of butter. The crumb is light, moist and truly golden in colour, and the crust is thin and crisp. A Brioche is best when it is still warm from the oven, but it will keep well in a plastic bag and also makes excellent toast.

Brioches are made in the traditional fluted tin, narrower at the base than at

● *La Pompe aux Anchois*

● *A plain Brioche*

the top, with a standard capacity of about 1¼ pints (725 ml). They can also be made in ordinary round cake tins, loaf tins, ring moulds, Gugelhupf moulds or small dariole moulds. Brioche dough is put into the refrigerator to chill for at least 30 minutes and preferably eight hours. This firms the butter and makes the dough easier to handle.

Brioche

To make three large or eighteen small loaves:

1 oz (25 g) fresh yeast or 1 tablespoon dried
3 fl oz (90 ml) warm water
1 lb (450 g) strong plain flour
1 tablespoon sugar
1 teaspoon salt
4 eggs
8 oz (225 g) butter, softened
1 egg yolk, beaten with 1 teaspoon water
(for Cheese Brioche, add 4 oz (125 g) Gruyère cheese, grated)

Dissolve the yeast in the warm water and leave it to stand – five minutes for fresh yeast, and 15 for dried. Place the flour in a bowl and toss in the sugar and salt. Make a well in the centre. Pour in the yeast mixture and break in the eggs. Mix everything to a dough and knead it in the bowl for about 5 minutes. Turn it on to a floured board and knead it until it is smooth. Punch it out flat and dot it with one third of the butter. Knead this well in. Repeat this twice, with the remaining butter. This process may well take 20 minutes or so. When you have finished you should be able to form it into a ball and coat it with flour. Place the dough in a bowl, cover it and leave it in a warm place for 1 hour.

Punch the dough down and knead it again. Return it to the bowl and chill it for at least 30 minutes. At this point the dough can be left in the refrigerator for up to eight hours, in fact the longer you leave it, the more workable it becomes.

Preheat the oven to 400°F/200°C/gas 6. Grease any tins that are not non-stick. Knead the dough again, lightly. If you are making a Cheese Brioche, knead in the grated cheese at this point. Divide the dough into the right number of portions for your tins. To shape a Brioche, divide each piece again into portions of about two thirds and one third. Put the larger piece into the tin and make a hole in the centre. Shape the smaller piece into a plug and insert it in the hole so that it makes a small round, sitting on top of the first piece.

Leave the Brioche for 30 minutes, or until the base has risen to the edge of the tin. Brush with egg and water glaze. Bake the large Brioches for 25 minutes and the small ones for 10 minutes. They should be golden brown. Turn them on to wire racks to cool.

A fresh Brioche can be served with jam or other preserves to accompany tea or coffee, or with patés or hors d'oeuvre. The tops of the small ones can easily be pulled away, giving space for a sweet or savoury filling.

Brioche dough can also be used for wrapping other ingredients such as beef for boeuf-en-croûte, a salmon filling for a koulibiaca, or a spicy garlic sausage. For these recipes you can halve the amount of butter to make the dough more workable, if preferred.

Sausage Brioche

To make one 14 inch (35 cm) long loaf:

Brioche dough (see above) made with 8 oz (225 g) flour, risen and chilled
12 oz (350 g) French garlic sausage, in one piece, skinned if necessary
egg and water glaze, as for Brioche

Preheat the oven to 375°F/190°C/gas 5. Roll the dough into a rectangle, large enough to cover the sausage completely. Lay the sausage on top. Fold the dough over the sausage. Place the Brioche on a floured baking sheet with the join on the underside. Leave it to prove for 20 minutes and brush with the glaze. Bake the Brioche for 30 to 35 minutes, or until golden brown. Serve hot, or cool on a wire rack.

Cheese Brioche Plait

To make one 15 inch (38 cm) long plait:

Brioche dough (see above) made with 1 lb (450 g) flour, risen and chilled
6 oz (175 g) Gruyère cheese
egg and water glaze, as for Brioche

Preheat the oven to 400°F/200°C/gas 6. Divide the dough into three pieces. Roll them into sausage shapes about 1½ inches (4 cms) thick and then flatten them. Cut the cheese into thin sticks and lay a line of sticks down the centre of each piece of dough. Bring the edges of the dough together to re-form the sausage shapes. Plait them (see page 18). Lay the plait on a floured baking sheet, prove it for 20 minutes and brush it with the glaze.

Bake the plait for 30 minutes, or until it is golden brown. Cool it on a wire rack and serve it warm or cold.

Croissants came to France from Austria, but in many countries they are deemed typically French. When Croissants are expertly made they can be a delight, slightly crisp on the outside and soft and buttery in the middle. There are sadly, however, many very poor imitations on the market. Well made, and rich but not sweet, Croissants are good at any time of day. They have come to typify the continental breakfast, and are excellent with morning coffee.

Croissants are most often made quite plain, but various fillings can be rolled up inside them such as marzipan, apple purée, mixtures of nuts and honey, dried fruits or candied peel or, for a savoury bake, grated cheese.

They are not difficult to make, but the ten-minute chilling periods make them fairly time consuming. They are made in this way in order to keep the butter firm and the dough therefore easier to handle. In France, many bakers have special chilling cabinets for Croissants, which change temperature at measured intervals. Hard wheat flour is essential for making successful Croissants, so the French use imported flours.

● *Croissants*

water. Mix everything to a dough and knead it on a floured work surface until it is smooth. Return the dough to the bowl, cover it with clingfilm and put it into the refrigerator for approximately 1 hour.

Preheat the oven to 400°F/200°C/gas 6. Put the remaining butter in between two pieces of clingfilm and bang it with a rolling pin until it is a flat rectangle about 9 × 5 inches (23 × 13 cms). Knead the dough again and roll it into a rectangle of about 18 × 10 inches (46 × 25.5 cms). Lay the rectangle of butter in the centre of the rectangle of dough. Fold over the ends of the dough and then the sides. Roll this parcel lengthways into a rectangle and then fold it into three. Wrap the folded dough in clingfilm and put it in the refrigerator for 10 minutes. Repeat this rolling and chilling process three more times.

After chilling for the final time, roll the dough into a square ¼ inch (5mm) thick. Cut it into 6 inch (15 cm) equilateral triangles and form them into crescent shapes (see page 21).

Lay the crescents on floured baking sheets and leave them to prove for about 30 minutes. Glaze the Croissants before baking, by brushing them with the beaten egg. Bake them for approximately 15 minutes, or until they are golden brown. Cool them on wire racks and serve them warm.

Croissants

To make about twenty Croissants:

6 fl oz (175 ml) warm water
8 fl oz (225 ml) warm milk
1 oz (25 g) fresh yeast or 1 tablespoon dried
1 lb 4 oz (560 g) strong plain flour
2 tablespoons sugar
1 teaspoon salt
10 oz (275 g) butter, chilled
1 egg, beaten

Mix together the water and milk. Dissolve the yeast in a little of the mixture and leave to stand – five minutes for fresh yeast and 15 for dried.

Place the flour in a bowl and toss in the sugar and salt. Rub in 2 oz (50 g) of the butter. Make a well in the centre and pour in the yeast mixture plus the remainder of the milk and

The French make many different kinds of sweet breads and yeasted cakes. There is the small oval Empereur, the Cassadière Corse – like a large Croissant with cherries in the centre – and in Alsace, a migrant from Austria, the Gugelhupf (see page 45). There is the Solilemme, a rich, egg bread made in a Brioche or Gugelhupf mould and the simple Breton Kouing-aman which consists of a basic dough into which are kneaded butter and sugar.

Walnuts and prunes are favourite ingredients of many sweet breads. The Pain aux Noix from Périgord-Noir is a sweet milk dough containing chopped walnuts. Raisins, walnuts, butter, eggs, sugar and lemon rind are all ingredients in small buns traditionally served at funerals in Corsica. For festivals and christenings in the area around Lyons there are Pognons aux Peurniaux, Brioche-shaped loaves made from basic dough into which are kneaded prunes, eggs, sugar and butter.

The richest and most delicious of all these sweet fruit breads is the Birewecke, made at Christmas time in Alsace. Large pieces of dried fruit, soaked in kirsch, together with chopped nuts, peel and raisins, are kneaded into a basic bread dough. When you look at the amazing amount of fruit in comparison with the small amount of bread dough, you may be alarmed, but keep mixing with your hand inside the bowl and eventually everything will come together. The Birewecke is not the most attractive of loaves, but if you like large pieces of dried fruit packed tightly together with nuts, you will love it. You will see that there is no sugar in the recipe. The dried fruits give plenty of natural sweetness.

Birewecke

To make two 7 inch (17.5 cm) diameter loaves:

6 oz (175 g) dried pears
2 oz (50 g) dried apple rings
4 oz (110 g) prunes
4 oz (110 g) dried figs
2 oz (50 g) candied peel, chopped
3 oz (75 g) raisins
3 fl oz (90 ml) kirsch
½ quantity bread dough (see page 12), kneaded and risen for 30 minutes
4 oz (110 g) walnuts, chopped
2 oz (50 g) almonds, chopped
2 oz (50 g) hazelnuts, chopped
¼ teaspoon ground cloves
2 teaspoons ground cinnamon
grated rind 1 lemon
1 egg yolk, beaten with 2 tablespoons water

Place the pears, apple rings, prunes and figs in a saucepan and just cover them with water. Bring them to the boil, simmer them for 5 minutes and cool them for 10 minutes in the liquid. Drain and cut the fruit into large pieces, stoning the prunes. Place them all in a bowl with the candied peel and raisins. Pour the kirsch over them and leave them overnight.

Place the bread dough in a mixing bowl and knead in the fruits and all the remaining ingredients except the beaten egg. This will take some time. Aim at getting everything evenly mixed. Leave the dough in the bowl in a warm place for 1½ hours for it to begin to rise. With this large amount of fruit in the dough it will not double in size.

Preheat the oven to 400°F/200°C/gas 6.

Knead the dough again and form it into two round loaves. Place them on floured baking sheets and leave them to prove for 30 minutes. Brush them with the egg yolk and water glaze. Bake them for 30 minutes or until a skewer inserted in the centre comes out clean. Lift the loaves on to wire racks to cool.

There are very few unleavened or baking-powder risen breads in France. One, called la Foncée, is made in Normandy. It consists of flour mixed with eggs, butter and double cream, glazed with egg yolks and baked in a flat round. It is very similar to some types of flat bread made in Scandinavia.

A bread, very similar to the English gingerbread and parkin, is Pain d'Epice, which is made around Reims, Dijon and Orléans. The large amount of honey produces a very sweet bread with a delicious chewy texture. It is more of a sweetmeat than a bread and very good for picnics and lunch-boxes.

Pain d'Epice

To make one 10-inch (25.5 cm) square loaf:

1 lb (450 g) rye flour
1 teaspoon baking soda
1 lb (450 g) honey
4 oz (110 g) sugar
2 oz (50 g) slivered almonds
2 oz (50 g) candied peel, finely chopped
1 teaspoon ground cinnamon
1 teaspoon ground cloves
½ teaspoon ground aniseed
¼ teaspoon nutmeg, grated
grated rind ½ lemon
4 tablespoons milk, heated with 2 tablespoons sugar

Place the flour in a bowl. Heat the honey to a pouring consistency, skim it if necessary and pour it over the flour. Mix the two together to make a stiff paste. Form the paste into a ball in the bowl, cover it with a clean, dry cloth and leave it for 1 hour.

Preheat the oven to 350°F/180°C/gas 4. Knead all the remaining ingredients into the flour and honey paste and then knead on a floured work surface until you have an even mixture. Roll out the dough to a 10 inch (25.5 cm) square about 1 inch (2.5 cm) thick and lay it on a floured baking sheet.

Bake for 35 minutes or until the top is brown, but not dark brown, and a skewer inserted in the centre comes out clean. Lift the bread on to a wire rack to cool.

GERMANY AND AUSTRIA

*Since the time rye was first planted in central Europe, in around 2000 BC, bread has been
a staple food of the German peoples, and it is now linked inextricably with the economy,
religion and folklore of the area.*

*Austria has traditionally sat, politically, between East and West, and for several centuries
was part of the much larger Austro-Hungarian Empire – which included present day Austria
and Hungary, and the countries which became Czechoslovakia and Yugoslavia,
as well as part of Romania.*

*Long famous for its baking, it could well have supplied enough recipes for a chapter on its
own – its sweet yeast cakes providing a frivolous contrast to the plainer breads of its
neighbour, Germany.*

GERMANY

In Germany, the word Brot (bread) refers only to wheat or rye bread. Breads made of other grains such as oats, maize or barley, are called after the grains themselves, for example Maisbrot (maize-bread).

The history of bread in Germany is similar to that in other parts of Europe. It gradually developed from hard, hearth-baked flat cakes to risen loaves. It differs, however, from more Western breads, in that the sourdough method of raising has remained popular ever since it was first introduced from the Middle East, via Greece, in about 800 BC.

During the Middle Ages, as in other countries, there was a distinction between the white bread for the rich and the dark for the poor, and rural bakers were forbidden by law to make anything but the dark rye loaves. In the years of poor harvest many holy men and women are said to have travelled through the country distributing bread to the poor. Two of these, Saint Antonius von Padua and Elizabeth von Thüringen, who went to Germany in the famine of 1226, became patron saints both of bakers and the hungry.

Baking very quickly transferred from the home to the communal bakehouse and village baker. Most villages consisted of small houses, built close together for protection against enemies. There was no room for an oven in every house and, besides, there was a restriction on fuel. Bread was either home-mixed and baked in a central oven, or it was bought direct from the owner of the oven, the local baker.

The same Medieval-style communal ovens were used well into the twentieth century and the bread from each village had its own characteristic qualities, the result not only of local recipes but of the individual effect of each oven. Called Holzofen-Bauernbrot (wood-oven farm-bread) it was made from various grades of rye flour, either used alone or mixed with wheat flour, and was always raised with a sourdough starter.

Sourdough bread, wherever it is baked, has a thick crust, a spongy crumb, and a characteristic sour-sweet flavour. It is excellent spread thickly with butter or eaten with German cheeses, pickles and smoked sausage. There are many different recipes, using a variety of starters and mixtures of fine and coarse rye and wheat flours. They are simple to make, but the rising times are long, and necessitate a little forward planning.

The first recipe below, for Feines Gesauertes Roggenbrot, is one of the simplest, using only rye flour. It is dark in colour with a strong flavour. Sausages, strong cheeses and pickles are the best accompaniments for this type of bread.

The second recipe, Schwarzbrot, is not really *schwarz* (black) at all, but a rich golden brown colour with a sweet flavour and light texture. You either love or hate caraway seeds, so miss them out if you prefer. Because it is not as tangy as the Roggenbrot, Schwarzbrot can be served with mild cheese or sweet preserves.

● *Traditional German breads on sale*

Feines Gesauertes Roggenbrot

To make one 2 lb (1 kg) loaf:
¼ rye sourdough starter (see page 11)
1 lb (450 g) whole rye flour
10 fl oz (275 ml) warm water or warm buttermilk
2 teaspoons salt

To make this Fine Sourdough Rye Loaf, first place the starter in a small bowl. Mix in 2 oz (50 g) of flour and 5 fl oz (140 ml) of the water or buttermilk. Sprinkle on 2 tablespoons more of the flour and leave the mixture for 12 hours in a warm place to make a risen, bubbling sponge.

In a large bowl, mix together the remaining flour and the salt. Add the starter and the rest of the water or buttermilk. On a floured surface, knead the mixture thoroughly for about 15 minutes, so that the dough becomes smooth. Shape it into a long loaf, place it on a floured baking sheet and leave it in a warm place to rise for 2 to 3 hours or until a finger pressed lightly into it leaves a dent.

Preheat the oven to 400°F/200°C/gas 6. Bake the loaf for 1 hour, or until it is dark brown and sounds hollow when tapped. This sounds rather a long baking time, but if you take the loaf out after the normal time of about 40 minutes you will find that the middle is still soggy. After 1 hour, the crust will be fairly thick but the middle will have a soft, moist crumb.

After baking, cool the loaf on a wire rack.

Schwarzbrot

To make two 2 lb (1 kg) loaves:
1 lb (450 g) whole-wheat flour
1 lb (450 g) rye flour
¼ rye sourdough starter (see page 11)
15 fl oz (425 ml) water, warmed
1 tablespoon salt
2 tablespoons caraway seeds, optional
2 medium potatoes, peeled, cooked and mashed

For this Black Bread, mix the two types of flour together. Take 8 oz (225 g) of the mixed flour and, in a large bowl, mix it into the starter together with 5 fl oz (150 ml) of the water. Cover the mixture with a clean dry cloth and leave it in a warm, draught-free place for 12 hours. When you look at it again it should be bubbling.

Stir in the remaining water, the caraway seeds and half the remaining flour. Mix in the potatoes and finally the salt and the rest of the flour. Knead the dough well. It will be very lumpy at first, but after 10 to 15 minutes should become silky smooth. Return it to the bowl and make a cross-cut in the top. Cover it with a clean, dry cloth and leave it for 4 hours in a warm place until it has expanded. It should have approximately doubled in size.

Oil two 2 lb (1 kg) bread tins. Knead the dough again and divide it between the tins. Cover the loaves and leave them for 1 hour in a warm place so they rise to the level of the top of the tins.

Preheat the oven to 400°F/200°C/gas 6. Bake the loaves for 45 minutes, or until the tops are golden brown and they sound hollow when tapped. Transfer the loaves to wire racks and brush the tops with water while they are still hot, to give them a soft crust.

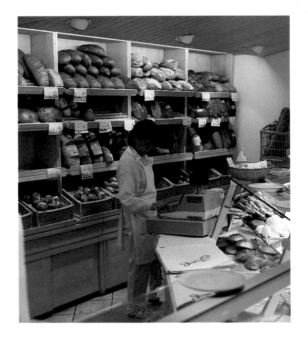

● *A choice of scored and floured brown and white rolls at a bread shop in Wangen, Germany*

The sourdough process has been adapted to commercial use and is used for most rye, rye mixture and whole-wheat loaves. There are about two hundred types of bread produced commercially in Germany, so it would be impossible to describe them all. There are also many speciality breads such as the Pumpernickel types, as well as small rolls and crackers.

The German everyday bread is the Landbrot, sometimes called the Berliner Landbrot. It has a dark crust and a light brown crumb, and is usually made entirely from rye flour. Landbrot is a Krustenbrot or crusty bread. Krustenbrot is baked on trays at high temperatures for a relatively short time. The surfaces can be left plain, or are floured, scattered with grains, or slashed, and the loaves can be round, oval or long. There is a large selection of Krustenbrot, made with mixtures of wheat and rye – Roggenmischbrot (those with more rye than wheat) and Weizenmischbrot (those with more wheat than rye). A relatively new addition to these commercially-baked crusty mixed breads is the Zwiebelbrot or Onion bread, for which chopped cooked onions are mixed into the dough. Onions are often used in the home as a starter for sourdough (see page 11) and their flavour goes well with the sour flavour of rye bread. Caraway seeds are another favourite addition. There are also crusty loaves made with white flour, called Weizenbrot, but all such wheaten loaves are risen with yeast instead of using the sourdough process.

There are also loaves baked in tins – the standard, long rectangle shape with a risen, crusty top. These include white, mixed and wholemeal loaves and specialities such as the Grahambrot (using the American Graham flour), the fibre-rich, sweetly aromatic Schluterbrot, and the mixed flour Paderborner Brot which has a pattern of holes on its browned top.

The other large category of breads consists of those that are baked in steam chambers at low temperatures for up to twenty hours. The dough is completely enclosed in tins, round or square, to give little or no crust and the bread is consequently called Kastenbrot, box-bread. Very often whole grains are used in addition to whole-wheat flour, together with a sourdough starter. The result is a rich, dark, moist bread with a sour-sweet flavour. It can be cut into thin slices and keeps for a long time. The bread is often sold ready-sliced in vacuum packs and probably the best known in other countries is Pumpernickel. There are, however, many other varieties such as Sonnenblumenbrot, made completely with rye flour with the addition of sunflower seeds; Leinsamenbrot with linseeds; Kümmelbrot with caraway seeds; and Fünfcornbrot made with five different types of grain.

Then, of course, there is the vast array of Kleinegebäck, literally meaning 'little-bakes' – plain or rye flour bread rolls decorated and shaped in many ways. Most Kleinegebäck are made from white wheat flour, but those with the enchanting name of Roggelchen (little-rye), are made completely from rye flour. There are regional specialities from all over Germany; they can be long or round, plaits, knots or crescents. Some are plain, some have a pattern slashed in the top, some are glazed, and some are scattered with poppy, caraway or sesame seeds or with salt.

The most well-known of the Kleinegebäck outside Germany is the Pretzel, although few people realize that they are made from bread dough. Fresh and homemade they are absolutely delicious.

There are two ways of cooking Pretzels. If they are poached before baking they will remain slim and after cooking they will be very crisp with an outside that is glossy and smooth. Pretzels cooked in this way make excellent snacks and are good with dips. If you leave out the poaching, Pretzels will rise more and take on the texture of very crisp bread. They are excellent eaten with soup or cheese. Both types of Pretzels should be eaten on the day that they are made as they soon lose their initial crispness.

● *Salzbrezeln*

Salzbrezeln

To make about sixteen Pretzels:

½ oz (15 g) fresh yeast or 2 teaspoons dried
pinch of sugar
7 fl oz (200 ml) warm water
1 lb (450 g) strong plain flour
1 teaspoon fine salt
¾ oz (20 g) butter, softened
¼ pint milk, warmed
2 tablespoons coarse salt
1 egg, beaten

In a small bowl, dissolve the yeast and a pinch of sugar in the water. Leave in a warm place until it begins to froth. Place the flour and the fine salt in a bowl. Make a well in the centre and pour in the yeast mixture. Stir to draw in a little flour from the edges of the bowl. Cover and leave for 10 minutes in a warm place, until the yeast begins to foam again.

Warm the butter and milk together so that the butter melts. Pour them into the well in the flour and mix well. Knead the mixture in the bowl (see page 13) until the dough no longer sticks to the sides. Cover the dough and leave it to rise in a warm place for 1 hour or until it doubles in size.

Knead the dough on a floured work surface for 10 minutes. Cut it into 16 pieces.

To shape the Pretzels, first roll each piece backwards and forwards

39

under your hands to the thickness of a pencil and about 12 inches (30 cm) long, tapering at the ends. Place one piece sideways along the work surface. Bring the ends towards you to make a horseshoe shape. Lift up the ends and cross them over. Press them lightly backwards on to the curve of the horseshoe.

Lay the shaped Pretzel on a floured baking sheet and shape the rest in the same way. Cover the Pretzels with a clean dry cloth and leave them to prove for approximately 10 minutes, or until they are beginning to rise and look rounded.

Preheat the oven to 450°F/230°C/gas 8.

For very simply baked Pretzels, brush them with beaten egg after proving and salt them (see below). Place them in the oven, reduce the heat to 400°F/200°C/gas 6 and bake them for 20 minutes, or until they are golden brown.

Cool them on a wire rack.

To poach the Pretzels before baking, fill a saucepan with 5 pints (2.75 l) water, add 2 tablespoons of salt and bring it to the boil. Cover your work surface with a double layer of kitchen paper. Place the Pretzels, two at a time, in the boiling water and leave them for 15 seconds. Remove them with a slotted spoon and drain them on the paper towels. You will find that they are very easy to handle as the poaching process makes the dough firm and almost impossible to damage. Lay them on floured baking sheets, brush them with beaten egg and salt them (see below). Bake as above: put the Pretzels into the oven, reduce the temperature to 400°F/200°C/gas 6 and bake them for 20 minutes, or until they are golden brown.

Cool them on a wire rack.

To salt Pretzels, either 1) scatter them with coarse salt after brushing them with the beaten egg; or 2) after brushing with the egg, make a slit in the knot of the Pretzel with a sharp knife. Fill the slit with about ¼ teaspoon coarse salt and leave the rest of the Pretzel plain.

Besides all these plainer, everyday breads, there are white wheat flour breads made into special shapes for special occasions. They are called Gebildrote or picture breads. These are descendants of the ritual and sacrificial breads made in pagan times, whose meanings have been long since forgotten. You can find horns, stars and suns, fish, serpents, flowers, sheaves of wheat and whole scenes – such as one depicting the Garden of Eden. If you have ever tried to shape dough and found it rising in all directions but the right one, you will appreciate just how much skill it takes to achieve so much detail.

Bread has always been important at German weddings. A bridegroom at one time passed bread in front of the church altar, signifying his commitment to feed and care for his bride and his future family. A bride carried a wheat-sheaf instead of flowers – the tightly-packed wheat ears showing her wish for their lasting relationship to be as close as the grains in the ear. Even today,

bread plaits decorate the Church at weddings and the first things taken into the house of a newly married couple are bread and salt, with the words 'Brot und salz sollen nie in eurem Hause fehlen' (Bread and salt shall not fail in your house).

Godparents still give their godchildren bread, sometimes in the shape of people, or sometimes baked with small coins inside, for luck. For harvest festivals, crowns of bread are made. At Easter time you may find bread in the shape of a hare with a coloured egg under its tail. For St. Nicholas' Day (6th December) and Christmas there is bread in the shape of St. Nicholas himself or made into wreaths or stars.

There is also the Stollen, a rich fruit bread dusted with icing sugar. I have no German relations or connections, but I always make a Stollen at Christmas. It is rich and sweet, but not as much so as, say, the traditional English fruit cake. Whereas it takes several days after the Christmas dinner to think about fruit cake, a slice of Stollen after apples and cheese makes an excellent snack for supper on Christmas night.

If you want to make it in advance, the Stollen freezes well and will simply defrost itself at room temperature during Christmas Day. Fresh or recently thawed, it will keep for up to four days at room temperature, wrapped in foil or in a plastic bag.

Dresdner Stollen

To make one 14 inch (35 cm) loaf:

2 oz (50 g) seedless raisins
2 oz (50 g) currants
2 oz (50 g) mixed candied citrus peel
1 oz (25 g) angelica, diced
2 oz (50 g) glacé cherries, halved
4 tablespoons rum
¾ oz (20 g) fresh yeast or ¾ tablespoon dried
3 oz (75 g) sugar
1½ tablespoons warm water
1 lb (450 g) strong plain flour
1½ oz (40 g) slivered almonds
4 fl oz (120 ml) milk
¼ teaspoon almond essence
grated rind ½ lemon
½ teaspoon salt
1 egg, beaten
5 oz (150 g) butter, 3 oz (100 g) diced and softened, 2 oz (50 g) melted
½ oz (15 g) icing sugar

● *Dresdner Stollen*

Place the fruits in a bowl with the rum, and soak them for at least 1 hour.

In a small bowl, stir the yeast and 1 teaspoon of the sugar into the water. Leave this five minutes for fresh yeast and 15 for dried.

Sprinkle 1½ tablespoons of the flour into the fruit together with the almonds. Stir until the flour is completely absorbed.

Warm the milk until it is lukewarm and stir in the remaining sugar until it has dissolved. Stir in the almond essence and lemon rind.

Place all but 2 oz (50 g) of the flour in a large bowl with the salt and make a well in the centre. Pour in the yeast mixture and stir in a little of the flour from the edges of the well. Add the egg and the milk and sugar mixture. Beat in the softened butter. Mix everything to a dough, turn it on to a floured work surface and knead it, using the rest of the flour, for 15 minutes or until it is no longer sticky. Knead in the fruit and almonds, 4 tablespoons at a time. Clean and dry the bowl and brush the inside with 1 tablespoon of the melted butter. Brush the top of the dough with another 2 teaspoons of the melted butter and place it in the bowl. Cover the dough with a clean cloth and leave it for 2 hours, or until it has doubled in size.

Punch down the dough and let it rest for 10 minutes. Roll it out into a rectangle 12 × 8 inches (30 × 20 cms). Brush it with the remaining melted butter. Bring one long side to the centre of the rectangle and press it down lightly. Fold the other long side across it, overlapping the centre seam by about 1 inch (2.5 cm). Press the edge gently to keep it in place. With floured hands, taper the ends of the loaf slightly and push the sides gently together to mound it in the centre. The finished loaf should be about 3½ inches (9 cms) wide and 14 inches (35 cms) long.

Place the loaf on a floured baking sheet and brush it with any remaining melted butter. Leave it in a warm place for 1 hour or until it has doubled in size.

Preheat oven to 375°F/190°C/gas 5.

Bake the Stollen for 45 minutes, or until it is golden and crusty. Cool it on a wire rack. Just before serving the Stollen, sift the icing sugar over the top.

Bread plays an important part in almost every meal in Germany. Breakfast may be hot crisp rolls served with butter and fruit preserves, with eggs or, particularly in northern Germany, with thin slices of cheese or cold meats. At 9.00 or 10.00 o'clock there may be a Zweites Frühstuck (second breakfast). The main meal is often eaten in the middle of the day and bread may accompany a stew or a soup. In the afternoon there is Kaffee (afternoon coffee) with yeasted cakes or small sandwiches. In the evening there is Abendbrot or supper (literally translated as bread of the evening). This will consist of dark breads as open sandwiches or simply accompanying cheeses, meats and pickles.

Bread can also be made into a complete meal. In country districts cubes of cheese are put into bread mixtures. The onion cake below, based on a white bread dough is traditionally eaten with new wine. It is absolutely huge, wonderfully tasty, risen and golden and perfect for picnics and informal lunch parties.

Zwiebelkuchen

To make one 10 inch (25.5 cm) cake:

1 oz (25 g) fresh yeast or 1 tablespoon dried
8 fl oz (225 ml) warm water
pinch of sugar
2 teaspoons salt
1 lb (450 g) strong plain flour
6 oz (175 g) lard or butter
3 egg yolks, beaten
2 lb (1 kg) onions, finely chopped
7 oz (200 g) lean bacon, finely chopped
3 eggs, beaten
4 fl oz (120 ml) sour cream
½ teaspoon caraway seeds, optional, or to taste

In a small bowl, dissolve the yeast in half the water, add the sugar and leave it five minutes for fresh yeast and 15 for dried. Dissolve the salt in the remaining water. Place the flour in a large bowl, make a well in the centre and pour in the yeast. Mix in a little of the flour from the edges of the bowl, add the salt water and mix in a little more flour. Melt 4 oz (110 g) of the lard or butter and put it into the well together with the egg yolks. Mix to make a dough and knead it in the bowl (see page 13) until it is smooth. Cut a cross in the top, cover the dough with a clean dry cloth and leave it in a warm place for 1 hour, or until it has doubled in size.

Over a low heat, fry the onions in the remaining lard or butter until they are transparent. Add three quarters of the bacon and continue to fry it gently until it is cooked through.

Preheat the oven to 375°F/190°C/gas 5. Knead the dough again. Roll it into a round 12 inches (30 cms) across and lay it on a floured baking sheet. Fold over 1 inch (2.5 cm) all the way round to make a raised rim about ¾ inch (2 cm) high. Leave the dough to prove for 10 minutes.

Beat the eggs with the sour cream. Put the onions and bacon on top of the round of dough and pour the egg mixture over them. Sprinkle with the remaining bacon and the caraway seeds. Bake the cake for 30 minutes or until the filling is set and the edges are golden.

AUSTRIA

Austria is the land of afternoon coffee and sweet yeasted cakes. The Viennese in particular have loved bread and pastries for over five hundred years and it is said that the country's sweet tooth developed in the eleventh and twelfth centuries when returning Crusaders stopped in Vienna, bringing with them spices and sugar cane from the East.

In 1488, Vienna gave its name to the Vienna roll, a small plain bread roll made with a dough enriched with milk and butter. Emperor Frederick V ordered a batch of rolls which were to be stamped with his likeness to be distributed to poor and needy children. The rolls were originally called Kaiser-semmeln (Emperor rolls) but, when the portrait of the Emperor was dropped, they became plain Vienna rolls. Today they are usually made round, with the top slashed into four sections.

The golden age of Vienna began in the early seventeenth century, the Baroque era, when the eating habits of the rich became more than extravagant. Many different baking guilds existed at that time, each specializing in a particular delicacy. There were the sugar bakers, chocolate makers, marzipan makers, cake bakers and sweet bakers; and the bread bakers were divided into ordinary bread bakers, roll bakers and luxury bakers.

One of the favourite shapes into which sweet yeasted cakes and breads were moulded was the crescent. On Christmas Day 1217 the bakers of Vienna paid homage to Duke Leopold of Babenburg with an offering of crescent-shaped rolls and again in Vienna in 1683, crescent rolls said to be in the shape of the Mohammedan crescent were baked to celebrate the victory over the Turks. Crescents are easy to make (see page 21) and the ones below, made with rich but unsweetened dough, have a surprise of sweet dried fruits and peel in the centre. These are literally 'crescents to accompany coffee'.

Kaffeekipfeln

To make about 20 crescents:

1 oz (25 g) fresh yeast or 1 tablespoon dried
6 fl oz (175 ml) milk, warmed
7 oz (200 g) butter, cut into small pieces
1 lb (450 g) strong plain flour
pinch of salt
2 egg yolks
2 tablespoons double cream
1 egg, lightly beaten

Filling:

3 oz (75 g) walnuts, chopped
3 oz (75 g) raisins
3 oz (75 g) candied peel, finely chopped
⅛ teaspoon ground ginger

Mix the yeast with half the milk and leave it to stand – five minutes for fresh yeast and 15 for dried. Rub the butter into the flour as though you were making pastry. Add the salt, the egg yolks, cream, yeast mixture and the remaining milk. Mix everything to a stiff dough and knead it for a few minutes.

● *Immature wheat fields*

● *Gugelhupf*

Roll the dough into a rectangle, three times as long as it is wide and fold the short sides across to fold it into three. Repeat the rolling and folding four times, each time having the length of the rolling pin going across the fold. After the final fold, put the dough on to a floured board or baking sheet. Cover it and leave it in a warm place for about 1 hour or until it doubles in size. Knock it back by kneading the dough again. Roll it out to about ¼ inch (5 mm) thick and cut it into 6 inch (15 cm) equilateral triangles.

Mix all the filling ingredients together. Shape the triangles as on page 21 and place about 2 teaspoons of the filling at the centre of the base of each one. Roll the triangles into crescent shapes (see page 21, again) and lay them on floured baking sheets and leave them to prove for 20 to 30 minutes or until they have risen by about half as much again.

Preheat the oven to 400°F/200°C/gas 6. Brush the crescents with the beaten egg and bake them for 20 minutes or until they are golden brown.

Gugelhupf

To make one 8 inch (20 cm) Gugelhupf:

1 oz (25 g) fresh yeast or 1 tablespoon dried
¼ pint (150 ml) milk, warmed
6 oz (75 g) sugar
12 oz (350 g) strong plain flour
4 oz (110 g) butter
1 egg
2 egg yolks
pinch of salt
3 oz (75 g) sultanas
2 oz (50 g) slivered almonds
2 tablespoons caster sugar, or vanilla sugar, if available

The Gugelhupf (also called gugelhopf and kugelhopf in other countries) is another Viennese speciality. It is a sweet yeasted cake baked in a fluted, spiral-patterned mould. If you do not have such a mould an ordinary ring mould will do quite well. These type of yeasted cakes have a close texture, rather like a cross between bread and sponge cake. They are sweet but not over-sweet and excellent with tea or coffee in the afternoon or in the middle of the morning. Try to eat a Gugelhupf on the same day that it is made as they tend to go stale very quickly. When first baked they are a dream, light in the centre and crisp on the outside.

The first recipe below is plain and simple, very much like that made by the actress Katherina Schratt for her lover, Emperor Franz Joseph I, who called at her house at 4.30 every afternoon when he knew the Gugelhupf would be coming out of the oven. (Gugelhupf, incidentally, was a favourite with Marie Antoinette, whose mother, Maria Theresa was Austrian.)

For a richer Gugelhupf, try making a Pattzerlgugelhupf. The same basic Gugelhupf mixture is first cut into slices which are spread with a sweet filling. When the slices are layered in the mould they produce a marbled sweetness throughout the finished cake. Instead of the nut filling in the recipe that follows, you can use apricot or another jam or preserve, or a purée of cooked fruit such as apples.

The name Pattzerlgugelhupf comes from the pattzerln, or slices, into which the dough is cut.

Mix the yeast with the milk, 1 teaspoon of the sugar and 3 oz (75 g) of the flour. Leave the mixture for 20 minutes to make a frothy sponge.

Cream together the butter, the rest of the sugar, the egg and egg yolks. Place the rest of the flour in a large bowl with the salt and 2 oz (50 g) sultanas. Make a well in the centre. Add the yeast sponge and the butter and egg mixture.

Mix everything to a dough and knead it on a floured work surface for about 10 minutes, or until it is smooth and elastic. Return it to the bowl, cover it with a clean dry cloth and leave it to rise in a warm place until it has doubled in size, about 1½ hours.

Preheat the oven to 400°F/200°C/gas 6.

Butter an 8 inch (20 cm) Gugelhupf mould and sprinkle it with the remaining sultanas, the almonds and a little flour. Knead the dough again and put it into the mould (see page 19). Leave it to prove for 1 hour, or until it almost reaches the rim of the mould.

Bake the Gugelhupf for 40 minutes, or until a skewer comes out clean when pushed into the centre.

Turn the Gugelhupf on to a wire rack, sprinkle it with caster or vanilla sugar and leave it to cool before you cut it.

● *A bread stall at Linz Market, Austria*

Pattzerlgugelhupf

To make one 8 inch (20 cm) Pattzerlgugelhupf:

1 oz (25 g) fresh yeast or 1 tablespoon dried
3 fl oz (90 ml) milk, warmed
12 oz (350 g) strong plain flour
3 oz (75 g) sugar
1 teaspoon salt
2 eggs, beaten
2 tablespoons rum
grated rind ½ lemon
3 oz (75 g) unsalted butter, in small pieces
2 tablespoons icing sugar, sieved

Filling:

3 oz (75 g) walnuts, finely chopped
¼ teaspoon ground ginger
grated rind ½ lemon
2 tablespoons milk
1 oz (25 g) sugar
½ oz (15 g) butter
2 tablespoons rum

In a small bowl, dissolve the yeast in the milk. Leave it to stand – five minutes for fresh yeast and 15 for dried. Place the flour, sugar and salt in a bowl and toss them with your fingertips to mix them. Make a well in the centre and add the yeast, eggs, rum and lemon rind. Mix everything to a dough. Turn it on to a floured work surface and knead it vigorously for 10 minutes. Punch it down. Place one third of the butter pieces over the surface and knead them in. Do this twice more. Put the dough into a bowl and make a cross-cut in the top. Cover it and leave it to rise in a warm place until it has doubled in size, about 1½ hours.

To make the filling, mix the walnuts with the ginger and lemon rind. Warm the milk, add the sugar and butter and stir until they have dissolved. Pour the mixture over the walnuts. Cool to lukewarm and add the rum.

Butter an 8 inch (20 cm) Gugelhupf mould and dust it with flour. On a floured surface, roll the dough into a thick sausage shape, about 3 inches (7.5 cm) in diameter. Slice it into pieces about ⅜ inch (1 cm) thick. Divide the filling between the slices, spreading it out and pressing it well down into the dough. Cover the bottom of the mould with the slices, filling side up. Add another layer of slices, arranging them across the gaps in the first layer. The top layer should be put

in with the filling side down. Cover the dough with a clean dry cloth and leave it for about 1 hour, or until the dough has almost risen to the rim of the mould.

Preheat the oven to 350°F/180°C/gas 4. Bake the Gugelhupf for 45 to 50 minutes or until the dough has slightly shrunk away from the sides of the mould and the top is browned. Leave the Gugelhupf to cool in the mould for a few minutes. Turn it on to a wire rack and dust it with sugar.

The following two recipes use an ordinary white bread dough, made with milk, into which are kneaded butter or lard and sugar. They are basic, no-nonsense recipes, the kind any housewife appreciates, and wonderful for feeding a hungry family after a day out in the open air. The Kletzenbrot, Dried Fruit Buns, are folded packets of light dough round a rich fruit and nut filling. These kind of recipes are intended to make use of whatever is in the store cupboard so if, for example, you do not have any pears or prunes, try whole dried apricots.

Kletzenbrot

To make sixteen buns:

1 lb (450 g) basic bread dough (see page 12) made with milk instead of water
2 oz (50 g) butter or lard, softened
1 oz (25 g) sugar

Filling:

12 oz (350 g) dried pears or prunes
4 oz (110 g) walnuts or hazelnuts, finely chopped
2 oz (50 g) sugar
1 egg, beaten

After mixing and kneading the dough for the first time, press it down flat. Spread it with half the butter or lard and sprinkle it with half the sugar. Knead these in well and then repeat with the remaining butter and sugar. Place the dough in a bowl, make a cross-cut in the top, cover it and leave it in a warm place for 1½ hours to double in size.

Soak the fruits in water to cover for 1½ hours. Drain and chop them finely, stoning the prunes. Use a food processor for a fine, even mix, if you like. Mix in the nuts, sugar and egg.

Knead the dough. Cut it into sixteen pieces and roll each piece into a thin (about 1 inch (2.5 cm) thick) 5-6 inch (15-15 cm) square. Place a portion of the filling on each square. Wet the edges of the dough and fold them over the filling. Turn the buns over so the joins are underneath. Place them on a floured baking sheet and leave them to prove for 30 minutes.

Preheat the oven to 350°F/180°C/gas 4.

Bake the buns for 30 minutes until they are puffed up and golden brown.

Zwetschkenfleck

To make one 13 inch (32.5 cm) tart:

1 lb (450 g) basic bread dough (see page 12) made with milk instead of water
2 oz (50 g) butter or lard, softened
1 oz (25 g) sugar

Topping:

2 lb (1 kg) gooseberries or other fruit such as rhubarb, plums, red or white currants, blackcurrants or blackberries
4 oz (110 g) sugar

Prepare the dough as for the Kletzenbrot and leave it to rise for 1½ hours or until it has doubled in size. Preheat the oven to 400°F/200°C/gas 6.

Knead the dough and roll it into a thin 15 inch (38 cm) square. Place it on a floured baking sheet and turn in 1 inch (2.5 cm) all round to make a thickened edge.

Plums should be stoned without being cut right through, and placed stalk end down on the dough, tightly packed. Cut rhubarb into ¾ inch (2 cm) lengths and put them end up on the dough. Gooseberries should be placed end up but the currants and blackberries can simply be scattered over the top. Sprinkle the fruit with sugar. Leave the tart to prove in a warm place for 20 minutes. The dough should rise slightly round the fruit to hold it in place.

Bake the tart for 25 to 30 minutes, or until the fruit is cooked and the edges are risen and golden.

This fruit tart is wonderful – golden and puffy round the edges and moist, sweet and juicy in the middle. Again, make it with any fruit in season. It being springtime when I first made it, I used rhubarb which gave the whole centre a rosy pink tinge. Another very popular filling, however, are gooseberries – sweetened to taste.

● *Zwetschkenfleck*

ITALY

From its borders with Austria, Switzerland and France, to its southern tip – surrounded by the Tyrrhenian and Ionian seas and the islands of Sicily and Sardinia – Italy is a country of distinct regions. Each has its own culinary traditions and styles that have not blurred even to the present day. Think of Italian food and you think of pasta, herbs, vegetables, seafood, cheese, smoked ham and pizza. Pizza is the only bread-based Italian speciality that has become famous worldwide. It would be easy to imagine that bread has taken a poor second place to pasta all over Italy for hundreds of years, but this really is not so.

Bread has been so important that there is a saying in the country: 'Senza il pane tutto diventa orfano' (without bread, one is deprived of everything). A generous, loving and warm-hearted person is described as 'buono come il pane' (as good as bread), but someone who takes advantage of his fellows is 'uno che mangia pane a ufo' (someone who eats another's bread but never gives in return). Young children in Italy are told to finish up their bread, or their job in the next life will be to go around picking up all the small pieces that other children have thrown away.

Bread has been made in Italy since ancient times. The cooking of early Italy was influenced by Greek and Etruscan ideas, developed and improved by the Romans. It is said that the Romans themselves were never excellent bakers. In early times their staple dish was called puls or pulmentum, a kind of porridge made from coarsely ground millet, spelt (a primitive wheat) or chickpea flour. Each Roman soldier was given a ration of about 2 lb (1 kg) of this grain which he roasted on a hot stone and then mixed with water. The resulting porridge was either eaten as gruel or made into small, flat hearth-cakes. In early Roman houses, the process was much the same.

The Greeks influenced the Romans in the baking of bread as we know it today, for it was Greek slaves who worked in the first bakeries, set up in around 170 BC, using wheat which was grown in Sicily and Sardinia and imported from Egypt. Even though wealthy Roman ladies could afford to buy the best white flour to powder their faces, white wheat bread remained out of reach for all but the rich and, as in all European countries, this state of affairs remained the same until at least the seventeenth century.

Italy was one of the first Western countries to plant and use maize, and in the eighteenth and nineteenth centuries, polenta (a maize dish very similar to the early Roman gruel) took the place of bread in northern Italy. However, good though it might be as an occasional alternative to wheat or rye bread, its general consumption caused bad outbreaks of pellagra and wheat once more became the staple grain. Polenta is still widely eaten in northern Italy, but as part of a mixed and balanced diet which includes other grain products.

During the 1950s and '60s there was a plethora in Italy, as in other European countries, of white, commercially-baked, nondescript bread, but regional specialities did not disappear and have, over the past twenty years, been undergoing a revival. This was helped by the Confraternita Amanti del Pane (the Brotherhood of Breadlovers) who formed in 1971 in order to promote real bread. In 1983, a museum of bread was opened in a thirteenth-century building in Bassa Lombardia, which displays one hundred varieties of grain and many different bread shapes from all the regions and villages of Italy.

There are said to exist a thousand or more different bread shapes in the country, some only to be found in a certain region or even in only one baker's shop in a small village. Much Italian bread is now made by small family bakers. In a large town or city the baker's shop is called a *Panetteria* and it will sell standard loaves, the specialities of the town or region plus cakes and pies, pizzas and Brioches. In the villages, the baker's shop is known as the *forno*. Very often the *forno* will look from the outside like an ordinary house, but as you enter, there will be a wooden counter, racks of loaves and a large brick oven which takes up one wall. Village women still take their cakes, pies, roasts and stews to the *forno* to be cooked in the oven after the bread has been removed to the shelves.

Most Italian bread is made from white wheat flour. Despite the shift towards whole-wheat breads in some European countries, 'pane integrale' (whole-wheat) still has the stigma of 'bread for the poor' and it makes up only 2% of total consumption. When made, it is usually shaped like a sandwich loaf or made into rolls.

Yeast is the main leavening for bread in Italy and it is still called 'lievito di birra' (brewer's yeast), from the yeast that was imported by the Romans from Gaul, where it was used to make beer. Dried yeast is also available and occasionally a piece of dough is kept moistened with water and used as a starter for the next batch. This 'lievito naturale' (natural leavening, or sourdough) is only used when the distinct sourdough flavour is required, such as in this rich cheese bread which is made at Easter time.

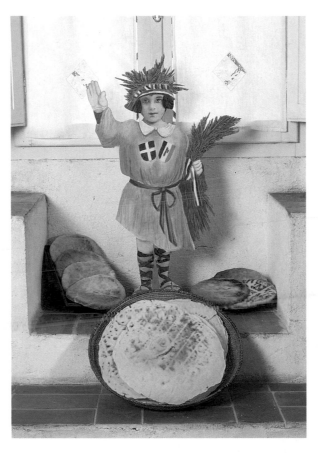

Although the process is lengthy, like all sourdough breads it really takes very little work-time, apart from the adding of the final ingredients. Forward planning, however, is essential. The bread is light textured, moist and yellow-coloured with a golden crust, rather like a savoury Panettone (see page 54). The cheese flavour is strong, but not overpowering and, especially when the loaf is fresh, the slices need no butter.

The dough is very soft, even after the final kneading, so handle it lightly. It will rise only to the top of the tin while it is proving, but more as it bakes.

● *Carte da Musica, Sardinia*

Crescia di Pasqua con Formaggio

To make a 2 lb (1 kg) loaf:
1 lb (450 g) strong plain flour
¾ oz (20 g) fresh yeast or ¾ tablespoon dried
5 fl oz (150 ml) warm water
4 fl oz (125 ml) warm milk
1½ oz (40 g) butter, softened
1 teaspoon salt
2 eggs, beaten
2 oz (50 g) Parmesan cheese, grated
4 oz (110 g) Gruyère cheese, grated

Make this Easter Bread with Cheese over two days. On the first day, make the sourdough. Place 4 oz (110 g) of the flour in a bowl. Dissolve one third of the yeast in the water and leave to stand – five minutes for fresh yeast and 15 for dried. Gradually stir it into the flour. Stir in half the milk to make a creamy-textured batter. Cover it and leave it in a warm place for 24 hours.

On the second day, place 8 oz (225 g) flour in a large mixing bowl and make a well in the centre. Add the sourdough and mix it into the flour, gradually taking flour from the sides of the well. The dough will be very moist at first but should soon become dry and spongy. Form the dough into a ball and leave it in the bowl. Cover it with clingfilm, to prevent a crust from forming on the top, and leave it for 12 hours.

Dissolve the rest of the yeast in the remaining milk. While the dough is still in the bowl, knead in the yeast mixture (see page 13). The dough will be very wet and slippery at first, but the liquid will gradually work itself in to make the dough smooth. Knead in the butter, in small pieces, together with the salt, and then the eggs, in exactly the same way as you did the yeast mixture. This will take about 15 minutes. Knead in the cheeses and then a further 2 oz (50 g) flour. Turn the dough on to a floured work surface and, using the remaining flour, knead it until it is smooth. It will still be very soft and quite difficult to shape. Place the dough in a greased, 2 lb (1 kg) bread tin and leave it in a warm place to prove until it reaches the top of the tin (about 1 hour).

Preheat the oven to 400°F/200°C/gas 6. Bake the loaf for 40 minutes, or until it is golden brown and risen.

Although bread shapes and types are highly regional, there are some that are made nationally. The two best known are the Biova and the Michetta. The Biova came originally from Piedmont. It is cylindrical, with pointed ends, very crusty and so highly-leavened that the inside is almost hollow. The smaller version, the Biovetta, is still popular mainly in the north. The Michetta, which came from Milan, is a small roll, also extremely light and crusty, delicious to eat, but with very short keeping qualities. It is said that it should be eaten within an hour of coming out of the oven.

Focaccia bread also seems to be made in every region of Italy, mainly in country districts. Focaccia is a flat bread, made with a plain white flour dough which may or may not be enriched with a little olive oil. It has a topping of

● *Bread baked in wood-fired ovens*

● *Focaccia (see page 52)*

coarse salt and olive oil. The oil on top gently seeps into the top layer of the bread, making it moist and springy. Traditionally, Focaccia bread was baked in large copper baking tins in a brick oven.

Toppings for Focaccia bread vary. The oil and coarse salt are compulsory. The other ingredients may be as simple as a sprinkling of basil or oregano leaves, but can also consist of olives, onions, prosciutto ham, a local cheese, anchovies or pieces of salami, alone or in any combination, but all in moderation. The same ingredients can also be kneaded into the bread. There are many local specialities and it is easy to devise your own. For the recipe below, the blue cheese topping is the more traditional, the herb and cheese topping is the result of my own saunter round the herb garden and experimenting.

Focaccia

To make one 10 inch (25.5 cm) square loaf:

1 lb (450 g) strong plain flour
1 oz (25 g) fresh yeast or 1 tablespoon dried
10 fl oz (275 ml) warm water
2 teaspoons fine salt
2 tablespoons olive oil

Onion and Blue Cheese Topping:

2 medium onions
2 tablespoons coarse salt
1 tablespoon chopped fresh sage leaves, or 1 teaspoon crumbled dried sage
4 oz (110 g) Dolcelatte cheese
4 tablespoons olive oil

Herb and Cheese Topping:

5 tablespoons freshly chopped mixed herbs (about half of it parsley)
1 clove garlic, finely chopped
2 teaspoons coarse salt
4 oz (110 g) Provolone or Gruyère cheese, grated
4 tablespoons olive oil

Place the flour in a bowl and make a well in the centre. Sprinkle the yeast into half the water – leave it five minutes for fresh yeast and 15 for dried. Pour the yeast mixture into the flour and mix in a little of the flour from the edges of the well. Dissolve the salt in the remaining water and mix it into the flour, together with the olive oil. Mix everything to a dough, knead it well and leave it in a warm place for up to 1 hour to double in size.

If you are using the onion and blue cheese topping, thinly slice the onions and place them in a bowl with all but 2 teaspoons of the coarse salt. Just before returning to the dough, drain the onions, rinse them with cold water, drain them again and dry them on paper towels.

Preheat the oven to 400°F/200°C/gas 6. Knead the dough again, roll it out into a 10 inch (25.5 cm) square and place it on a floured baking sheet.

For the onion and blue cheese topping, arrange the drained onion slices evenly over the dough. Sprinkle it with the remaining salt and the sage. Cut the cheese into small dice and scatter them over the onions. Drizzle the olive oil over the top.

For the herb and cheese topping, scatter the herbs evenly over the surface of the dough. Sprinkle over the garlic, then the salt. Cover the herbs with the grated cheese and drizzle the olive oil over the top.

Leave the dough in a warm place for about 20 minutes, or until it has risen and thickened. Bake the loaf for 30 minutes. Eat it warm or turn it on to a wire rack to cool.

In some regions, the Focaccia dough is divided and the two pieces rolled out and baked with a filling in between. In a village near Genoa, for example, it is filled with formagetta, a local soft cheese. In other areas it is made into a Tortino, or vegetable pie, which can be a meal in itself or which can be an accompaniment to cheese or cold meats or fish. It is excellent for picnics. Rolled very thinly the bread dough becomes light, rich and crisp with a moist layer of filling.

Endive, courgettes, artichokes, French beans, aubergines or cardoons are all used in Tortino fillings, plus pine kernels, almonds, cheese or eggs.

Tortino con Spinaci e Olive

To make one 10 inch (25.5 cm) round filled loaf:

1 lb (450 g) strong plain flour
1 oz (25 g) fresh yeast or 1 tablespoon dried
10 fl oz (275 ml) warm water
2 teaspoons salt
3 oz (75 g) butter, softened
1 egg, beaten

Filling:

12 oz (350 g) fresh spinach, washed and tough stems removed
1 small onion
12 black olives
1 oz (25 g) butter
2 oz (50 g) pine kernels
4 tablespoons chopped fresh parsley

Place the flour in a bowl and make a well in the centre. Sprinkle the yeast into half the water. Leave it to stand – five minutes for fresh yeast and 15 for dried. Pour the yeast into the well and mix in a little flour from the edges. Dissolve the salt in the remaining water, pour it into the well and mix everything to a dough.

Knead the dough on a floured surface, punch it down and spread it with one third of the butter. Knead in the butter and repeat the process two times more. Return the dough to the bowl, cover it and leave it in a warm place to double in size, for about 1 hour.

Finely chop the spinach and the onion. Halve and stone the olives. Melt the butter in a large frying pan over a high heat. Add the onion and cook it, stirring, for 1 minute. Add the spinach, lower the heat to medium and cook until the spinach has wilted and softened. Add the pine kernels and stir until they begin to brown. Take the pan from the heat and mix in the olives and parsley. Let the mixture cool.

Preheat the oven to 400°F/200°C/gas 6.

Knead the dough again and divide it into two equal pieces. Roll each of them into 10 inch (25.5 cm) rounds. Lay one round on a floured baking sheet and spread it with all the filling. Lay the other dough round on top and pinch the edges together to seal them. Brush with the beaten egg.

Leave the loaf in a warm place for 20 minutes. Bake it for 30 minutes, or until the top is golden brown and the loaf sounds hollow when tapped.

Eat the Tortino warm or cool it on a wire rack.

● *Tortino con Spinaci e Olive*

53

The breads of Italy are so many and varied that it is best to go on a gastronomic tour to discover them all. Italy has northern borders with France, Switzerland, Austria and Slovenia.

The northernmost region and also the smallest, Valle d'Aosta, has borders with both France and Switzerland. It is a mountainous area, and bread and hearty soups form a large part of the diet. The bread here is, unusually for Italy, made from a mixture of wheat and rye flour and the soups themselves often contain bread, particularly one called Valpellinentze whose other ingredients are cabbage and the local fontina cheese.

The area of Valle d'Aosta borders on the region that is called Piemonte, or Piedmont. The town of Torino or Turin, in the centre of this region, has given to the world one of Italy's most famous types of bread, Grissini, or bread sticks, which Napoleon called 'les petits batons de Turin'. The ones bought in other areas of Italy, and those that are exported, are factory made, but around Turin you can still buy handmade Grissini, long and irregular in shape, lightly dusted with flour and with a crisp, crumbly texture. In Piedmont they are often served with *bagna cauda*, a rich anchovy dip that is accompanied by raw vegetables.

Tucked away to the south of Piedmont is the small, coastal region of Liguria in the centre of which is the city of Genoa. Liguria boasts an excellent Focaccia bread and the best toppings are either made with the local soft cheese or with olive pulp left from the first pressing of oil. A special, sweet bread, called Pan Dolce, comes from Genoa. It is a shallow dome shape with a triangle cut into the top, and its mixture includes dried and candied fruits, nuts and spices. Traditionally it is served at Christmas, brought to the table with a sprig of bay on top and cut by the youngest member of the family.

Next to Piedmont in the east, bordering on Switzerland, is Lombardy, famous for its dairy products, rice and polenta. Lombardy has its own bread stick. Called the Francesina, it is much larger than the Grissini, weighing about 4 oz (110 g). The dough is only partly leavened and so it has a hard crust and compact crumb. In addition to this, Lombardy has given Italy one of its richest and most delicious breads, the Panettone.

Go to Milan, the main city of Lombardy, and you will find the Panettone in every food shop. They are sold in restaurants and cafés and even at the windows of trains. The exact shape of the Panettone varies according to the baker. Some are made in cylindrical tins, a practice that only began in the 1920s, others are baked in the traditional round tins that are wider and flatter, but there will always be a dome-shaped top, said to resemble the cupolas of Lombardy churches.

There is a delightful story which explains the origins of the Panettone. The name comes from Pan de Tonio, Tony's bread. Tony was a baker who lived in the fifteenth century in the Milanese quarter of Borogo delle Grazie. He was poor, but he had a beautiful daughter by the name of Adalgisa. A young man of rich and noble family, one Ughetto della Tela, fell in love with Adalgisa but, old-fashioned values being what they were, was not allowed to marry one so poor and of such humble birth. Ughetto knew that his own family valued wealth above everything, so just before Christmas he sold his hunting falcons to buy the finest flour, eggs and butter. These he gave to Tony to make traditional cakes, but he added in some ideas of his own – plump sultanas and lemons with which to make candied peel. Tony set to work and produced the best cakes that Milan had ever seen. His fame and fortune were made and Ughetto's family allowed him to marry the daughter of the once poor baker.

The Panettone is still tremendously popular and the two main producers, Motta and Alemagna, make over 24 million kg (53 million lb) every year, with a good proportion of this sold around Christmas time. No wonder, for the Panettone is a culinary delight, rich and golden yellow in the middle and with a thin, crisp brown crust. It is sweet, but not over-sweet with just enough candied peel and sultanas to make it interesting. Although few are made at home, the recipe is not too difficult and well worth attempting.

The Panettone is equally good with mid-morning coffee or after-dinner drinks. Serve it cut into wedges.

Panettone

To make one 8 inch (20 cm) round loaf:

1¹/₂ oz (40 g) fresh yeast or 1¹/₂ tablespoons dried
3 tablespoons warm water
6 egg yolks
1 teaspoon vanilla essence
grated rind ¹/₂ lemon
¹/₂ teaspoon salt
2 oz (50 g) caster sugar
12 oz (350 g) strong plain flour
butter, 5 oz (150 g) softened, 1 oz (25 g) melted
2 oz (50 g) candied citrus peel, chopped
2 oz (50 g) sultanas
2 oz (50 g) raisins

In a large mixing bowl, mix the yeast with the water and leave it in a warm place – five minutes for fresh yeast and 15 for dried. Stir in the egg yolks, vanilla essence, lemon rind and sugar.

Using your hand, mix in 8 oz (225 g) of the flour, one third at a time, adding the salt as you do so. Gather the dough into a ball, but keep it in the bowl. Knead in the butter, in small pieces, about one third at a time. Knead in 2 oz (50 g) more flour, a little at a time, still keeping the dough in the bowl. Take the dough out of the bowl and knead it for a short time on a work surface, using as much of the remaining flour as necessary to make it smooth and elastic. Shape it into a ball, put it into a large, clean bowl and sprinkle the surface with a little flour. Cover it and leave it in a warm place for about one hour, or until it has doubled in size.

Preheat the oven to 400°F/200°C/gas 6.

Butter an 8 inch (20 cm) cake tin.

Punch down the dough and knead in the candied peel, sultanas and raisins. Do this quickly so that the dough does not discolour. Shape the dough into a ball and place it in the cake tin. There should be a gap of about 1 inch (2.5 cm) all round. Leave the dough for 30 minutes, or until it has doubled in size. Brush the top with half the melted butter. Bake for 10 minutes and then brush with the remaining butter. Reduce the oven temperature to 350°F/180°C/gas 4 and return the loaf to the oven for a further 30 to 35 minutes, or until the top is golden brown and crisp and a skewer stuck in the centre comes out clean.

Cool the Panettone on a wire rack.

At Easter time, a similar mixture to that for Panettone, without sultanas but with the addition of toasted almonds, is baked in the shape of a dove and called a Colomba. The custom goes back to 1176 when two doves landed near the Milanese army standards during the battle of Legano. The Milanese saw this as a sign of protection, and their forces of the Lombard League went on to defeat the army of the Holy Roman Emperor, Frederick Barbarossa. The Colomba has been baked ever since to commemorate the event.

Also at this time of year, on St. George's Day, in April, a flat, round Brioche called a Pan di Miglio, is served in Milan. It is made from yeast-leavened wheat and corn flour, butter, egg yolks and sugar, and is flavoured with vanilla. Its accompaniments are cream, sugar and a garnish of elderflower.

The region of Trentino-Alto Adige to the north of Lombardy has one long border with Austria. It is really two small regions fused together. The cooking of Trentino is influenced by that of Lombardy, but Alto-Adige takes its styles and its names from Austria. There are two main types of bread in the area, Schuttelbrot and Schlagbrot, and both are made from a mixture of wheat and the rye that is grown in the local valleys. Schuttelbrot takes the form of large, round loaves, which are so hard that they can only be eaten if they are soaked in one of the many local soups. Schlaghrot, on the other hand, is soft and light.

Bread forms the basis of the local dumplings called Canderli. The bread is soaked in milk and mixed with eggs, flour, smoked pork fat, onion and herbs. The dumplings are the size of an orange and are cooked in soup or served with melted butter and herbs or with gravy. A variation of this is the Schwarzplentene which are made from rye and buckwheat bread and served with sauerkraut and tomato sauce. Leftover bread is also made into a sweet pudding with figs.

Another speciality of the area is Krapfen, or doughnuts. In Trentino-Alto Adige they are, typically, round and contain a blob of jam in the centre. In other parts of Italy they are fried, but in Alto Adige they are baked.

● *Sticks and Coburgs for sale, Rome*

Moving on to Veneto, in which are the cities of Venice, Verona, and Padua, the bread specialities are sweet and frivolous. On New Year's Eve in Venice, you may be served with the Vaneziana, a large, sweet bun, made with a dough similar to that of the Panettone (above), without fruits, nuts or peel, but flavoured simply with orange and lemon rind and with a top covered with white sugar crystals. Also from Venice is the Fugassa, or Fugazza, a kind of sweet Focaccia. It is raised with bicarbonate of soda and contains butter milk, rum and lemon peel. From Vicenza comes the Focaccia Vicentina, which is made with a similar dough, baked in dove shapes with a hard-boiled egg in the centre. Verona has its own Christmas cake, the Pan Doro, or golden bread, so called because of its colour. Risen with yeast and enriched with butter and eggs, it is baked in a star-shape and covered with icing sugar. Even the local bread pudding is a luxurious one. Instead of being soaked in milk, as it is in other Italian regions, the stale bread is soaked in wine and mixed with eggs, spices, candied peel, nuts and sometimes slivers of bitter chocolate. It is known as Torta di Pane Ubriaca, drunken cake.

Emilia-Romagna, the region that lies centrally in the north, boasts sausages, pasta, parma hams, wheat, butter and cheeses and the richest style of cooking in Italy. Bologna, the chief city, is known as Bologna la grassa (the fat). The area around the city of Ferrara, particularly the small town of Porto Garibaldi, is well known for its excellent bread. The local loaves are rounded, with the crust drawn up into four points at the top, forming a crown.

Everywhere bread is enriched with, or fried in, butter or lard. The local flat bread in Modena is known as Stria and it is brushed or dotted with lard before being baked in a hot oven.

Piadini were once called 'the national dish of the Romagnoli'. They are small pieces of dough enriched with pork fat, rolled round and flat. They were once cooked on an earthenware disc called a *testo*, but now a cast-iron pan or griddle is used. The rounds of dough are cooked quickly over a high heat until they are slightly charred; smoked pork fat, salami or local cheese is laid on one half while the other half is folded over to make a substantial, easy to eat snack. Once the food of peasants, Piadini have become fashionable in modern bars.

Gnocchi Fritti from Modena, and Crescentine from Bologna are the deep fried specialities. Gnocchi Fritti are made with bread dough, again enriched with rendered pork fat, that are cut into diamond shapes and deep fried either in more pork fat or in olive oil. They are eaten hot with salami, ham, or cheese. Crescentine are enriched with lard or pork crackling and sometimes pieces of prosciutto ham. They are cut into rounds or diamond shapes and can be either baked or deep fried.

On New Year's Eve around the city of Ferraro, the traditional dessert is the Pan Pepato di Cioccolato. Pan Pepato, also called Pampepato, is a sweet Brioche-type bread which originated in the Middle Ages and which contains pepper as a flavouring. The Ferrarese Pan Pepato is flavoured with butter, cocoa powder, honey, spices, almonds and lemon peel, and is covered with chocolate icing and sprinkled with hundreds and thousands. It was once eaten at any time between the week before Christmas and Twelfth Night and the bakers of Ferraro would send the cakes as presents to local rulers and also to the Pope.

South of Emilia-Romagna lies Tuscany, where the cooking must be amongst the healthiest in all Italy. It relies on the best of fresh ingredients cooked extremely simply. Admittedly this was the home of the Medicis, whose banquets were anything but simple, and also the headquarters of the first cooking academy, the Compagnia del Paiolo (the Company of the Cauldron), whose twelve members each had to produce an elaborate dish of their own invention at every meeting. For the ordinary people, however, 'simple and good' has always been the principle of their cooking, and bread, vegetables and fresh fruit, or simply bread and soup have traditionally formed the substantial part of a meal.

The favourite Tuscan bread is Pan Sciocco, which is unsalted because the Tuscans believe that salt interferes with the flavour of other foods. It accompanies most meals and goes particularly well with delicacies such as salty ewe's-milk cheeses and salami made from wild boar. Tuscan soups, typically rich with vegetables and herbs, are always ladled over Pan Sciocco.

Another Tuscan bread dish is Panzanella, a salad based on bread, vegetables and anchovies. In the traditional version, two-day old Pan Sciocco is soaked in water, squeezed and mixed with sweet peppers, cucumber, tomato and onion in a dressing of oil, vinegar, crushed anchovies and capers. In more modern versions, the bread is made into croutons before being added to the same ingredients.

Pane di Rosmarino, Rosemary Bread, is served at Easter time. In Florence the dough is made into small rolls and elsewhere in Tuscany into long or round loaves. The bread is subtly flavoured by simmering raisins in oil with a rosemary sprig. The rosemary flavours both oil and raisins, enabling it to gently permeate the bread, which is soft and moist in the centre with a thin shiny brown crust. It is a semi-sweet bread and can be eaten with or without butter.

Rosemary Bread

To make one large loaf or sixteen rolls:

basic bread dough (see page 12) made with 1 lb (450 g) strong plain flour
2 rosemary sprigs
6 oz (175 g) raisins
4 tablespoons olive oil
1 teaspoon salt
1 tablespoon caster sugar
2 tablespoons sugar, dissolved in warm water

Gently simmer the raisins and rosemary in the oil for 10 minutes, without allowing the raisins to brown or harden. Discard the rosemary. After the dough has been kneaded for the first time, gradually knead in the cooled oil and raisins, the salt and the caster sugar. Place the dough in a bowl, cover it and leave it to rise for 30 minutes.

Preheat the oven to 400°F/200°C/gas 6. Knead the dough again and either shape it into one loaf or into sixteen rolls. Place them on a floured baking sheet and leave them for 20 minutes. Bake the loaf for 30 to 35 minutes and the rolls for 20 minutes, brushing the tops with the sweetened water halfway through. Cool on wire racks.

From Tuscany we come to the regions around Rome, which are Latium, Umbria and the Marches. Here the cooking is plain but hearty. Since Roman times, the best loved foods have been bread, cheese, olives and fresh vegetables. One of the most popular breads in the area today is the Ciriola, a light, crusty roll that is made with a highly-leavened dough so that it is light and airy inside with a crisp, golden crust. A speciality of Rome itself are Maritozzi, sweet rolls containing pine nuts, sultanas and candied peel, and coated with icing sugar.

All over central Italy, the standard loaf is the Pagnotta. It is round with a double cross slashed in the top and weighs anything from 1 to 2½ lbs (450-1 kg). It was once traditionally sliced by the man of the house at table. He held it in the crook of his arm, moving the knife towards himself across the bread.

An ancient Roman inscription on a wall in Fara, in Sabina, makes reference to a Crustulum, an oil-soaked cake that was given out by the authorities to the townspeople on important civil or religious feast days, mainly during December and January. The Bruschetta, served today in Latium, Umbria and Tuscany, is a direct descendant. The Bruschetta is a coarse, flat bun, soaked in olive oil, flavoured with garlic and toasted, preferably over hot coals. Once the food of the poor, the Bruschetta is now a popular snack in cafés and bars.

Another Roman favourite is the Crostini alla Provatura, where slices of bread topped with provatura cheese are put into the oven for the cheese to melt and cover the bread completely.

On the middle of the eastern Italian coast is Abruzzi, where pasta and polenta complement the seafood, pork, lamb and vegetables. The favourite bread here is the Spaccatina, a round flat loaf with a deep cut in the centre, its top brushed thickly with lard, rendered pork fat or olive oil.

Passing through the small region of Molise, we come to Campania and the city of Naples, home of the pizza that has spread across the world, changing almost beyond recognition as it turns up in specialist restaurants and frozen food cabinets.

In Campania, as in other regions of southern Italy, cooks know how to make simple, cheap ingredients into robust and colourful dishes. Plain bread is made into garlands and shapes of fruit, flowers or religious symbols and given simple flavourings, such as the pepper in the following recipe. These pepper wreaths are beautiful to look at besides being rich and crisp. They also keep for a long time. In Campania they would be made with freshly-made lard. If you don't fancy using the commercial kind, or if you are a vegetarian, use butter instead. The unusually low cooking temperature gives the wreaths their crispness.

Taralli a Sugna e Pepe

To make eight small wreaths:

basic bread dough (see page 12) made with 1 lb (450 g) strong plain flour with 1 teaspoon freshly ground black pepper added to the flour before mixing

5 oz (150 g) lard, softened and in small pieces

1 teaspoon salt

Flatten out the dough and dot it with one third of the pieces of lard and sprinkle on the salt. Knead these in. Repeat twice, with the remaining lard.

Knead the dough again on a floured board, and divide it into sixteen pieces. Roll each one into a long sausage shape about ⅜ inch (1 cm) thick. Take two pieces of dough. Starting from the centres, twist them together. Bring the ends together and join them in a circle.

Lay the wreath on a floured baking sheet, and make the others in the same way. Leave them in a warm place for 1 hour.

Preheat the oven to 350°F/180°C/gas 4.

Bake the wreaths for 40 minutes, or until they are golden brown and crisp. Cool them on a wire rack.

● *Pizza Napoletana*

57

So what about the pizza? Where did it come from and what are its real ingredients. The name pizza actually means a pie and is also, to confuse matters, used to refer to fruit tarts and some cakes. However, the pizza, as we know it, goes back to Roman times, when it was a thin, flat bread, baked on a hot stone, with a topping of olive oil, herbs and sometimes honey. When tomatoes arrived from the New World, the small, sweet varieties were found to grow so well in the southern Italian sun, that they were used in almost every dish. Huge batches were stewed down in cauldrons to make a thick purée that has been poured over meats and poultry, used as the basis of soup and, inevitably, spread over Italian flat bread. It was not until the eighteenth century that the present day pizza was developed around Naples. Despite the menus that you may read in world-wide pizza restaurants, the authentic topping should be a simple one: tomato sauce, mozzarella cheese, and either basil or oregano – red, white and green, the colours of the Italian flag.

The dough for the pizza base is a plain bread dough made with strong white flour, yeast and water. I always add a little olive oil which adds to the crispness of the edges. If I were in Naples, however, I might very well go to buy the basic dough from the local *forno*.

Basic Pizza Dough

To make one 10 inch (25 cm) pizza or four 7 inch (17.5 cm) pizzas:

8 oz (225 g) strong plain flour
1/2 oz (15 g) fresh yeast or 2 teaspoons dried
5 fl oz (150 ml) warm water
1 teaspoon salt
1 tablespoon olive oil

Make up the dough as for the basic bread dough on page 12, adding the olive oil with the salt water. Knead it and leave it to rise in the usual way.

To make the base for a large Pizza, roll the dough into a large round, about 11 inches (28 cm) in diameter, then fold over 1/2 inch (1.3 cm) all the way round. To make individual Pizzas, divide the dough into four and roll each piece thinly to a diameter of about 8 inches (20 cm).

Pizzas can be baked in special Pizza plates or tins, but you will always get the crispest texture and the best degree of rising by laying the Pizza on a floured baking sheet.

Pizzas should always be eaten hot, straight from the oven. Not only is the base at its crispest, but the mozzarella cheese is perfect when melted.

The tomato sauce for a Pizza topping can be made while the dough is rising. You can also make it in advance and store it in a covered container in the refrigerator for up to three days. The onions and garlic are optional.

Tomato Sauce for Pizza

Enough for one 10 inch (25.5 cm) pizza:

1 lb (450 g) ripe red tomatoes
2 tablespoons olive oil
1 small onion, finely chopped
1 clove garlic, finely chopped

Scald, skin and chop the tomatoes. Gently soften the onions and garlic in the oil in a frying pan over a low heat. Add the tomatoes and simmer, stirring frequently, for 50 minutes, or until you have a thick purée.

Leave it to cool.

Pizza Napoletana

Pizza dough, as above
tomato sauce, as above
6 oz (175 g) mozzarella cheese, thinly sliced
1 teaspoon chopped basil or about 15 whole oregano leaves

Roll the dough into a circle and fold the edge as above. Lay it on a floured sheet. Spread the tomato sauce over the top. Lay the slices of mozzarella over the tomato sauce and scatter the herbs over that. Leave the pizza in a warm place for 20 minutes to prove.

Preheat the oven to 400°F/200°C/gas 6. Bake the Pizza for 15 to 20 minutes or until the edges are crisp, but not browned, and the cheese has melted.

Sardiniara

Pizza dough, as above
tomato sauce, as above
12 black olives, halved and stoned
2 × 1¾ oz (16 g) tins anchovy fillets

This is a Pizza with an anchovy topping which really comes from the small northern region of Liguria. It is rich and delicious.

Prepare the Pizza base and spread it with tomato sauce. Put the olive halves on top. Cut the anchovy fillets in half lengthways and again crossways. Lay the pieces, haphazard fashion, over the top of the tomato sauce. Prove and bake as above.

● *Harvested grain field*

The Calzone is a Pizza which is made into a packet and deep fried. The simplest filling for a Calzone is a slice of prosciutto ham topped with thin slices of mozzarella cheese. Others have ricotta, diced mozzarella and grated parmesan or pecorino cheese, and sometimes beaten egg mixed together with the ham or, as an alternative, salami, in thin strips. The following recipe is the perfect combination. You still have the melting slices of mozzarella and whole pieces of ham, but underneath is a soft bed of ricotta and parmesan. The Calzone should be eaten while it is hot and crisp and, accompanied only by a green salad, it makes a very substantial meal.

In Italy, the Calzone is fried in olive oil. In most other countries, this would be a very expensive exercise. Olive oil also has a low burning temperature and flash-point. I have therefore used sunflower oil, which is cheaper and more tolerant of high temperatures.

Calzone

To make four 8 inch (20 cm) Calzones:

basic Pizza dough (see page 58) made with 8 oz (225 g) flour
sunflower oil for frying

Filling:

4 oz (110 g) ricotta cheese
1 oz (25 g) parmesan cheese, grated
4 thin slices prosciutto ham
4 oz (110 g) mozzarella cheese, cut into 8 slices

Cut the dough in four pieces and roll each one into a round about 8 inches (20 cm) in diameter. Lay them flat on the work surface. Mix together the ricotta and parmesan cheeses.

Take one dough round and spread one quarter of the ricotta mixture over half of it, leaving about ½ inch (1 cm) round the edge. Lay a slice of ham on top and two slices of mozzarella on top of that. Fold over the other half of the dough and seal the edges. Lay the Calzone on a floured baking sheet while you make the others in the same way.

For frying, choose a saucepan or casserole that will easily take the calzone lying flat. An oval-shaped one is ideal. Add sunflower oil to the depth of about 1½ inches (4 cm) and heat it over a high heat.

Fry the first calzone in the oil until the underside is golden brown, about 1½ minutes. Turn it over and brown the other side. Lift out the calzone with a slotted spoon and place it in a shallow dish lined with paper towels.

Cook the others in the same way and serve them hot, as soon as possible.

The other regions of the south, with a similar, colourful, sunblessed cuisine to Campania, are Apulia, Basilicata and Calabria. All over the area, the traditional loaves are large.

The local bread of the Apulia region is called Schiacciata. It is made by the sourdough method of keeping back a batch of the previous week's baking, and each round loaf weighs up to 4½ lb (2 kg). Home baking is still popular in Apulia. Once a housewife has shaped her loaf she marks it with her own particular brand, called a *marca di pane*, which may show the family crest or initials. Some of the old wooden brands are so beautiful that they are now family heirlooms or collectors' items. The loaves are then taken to the local *forno* for baking.

Bread in Basilicata was also traditionally made at home and taken to the *forno*, but now it is mostly bought. The traditional loaf, made from coarse wheat flour, is called a Panella and it can be as large as a cartwheel. One loaf would at one time last a family all week.

There are also two offshore islands, Sicily and Sardinia. The cookery of Sicily was learned from the Greeks and that of Sardinia from the Phoenicians. After each absorbed a little more from the Arabs, they influenced the Romans and so the whole of Italy. Both islands, throughout the Roman period, supplied the mainland with wheat.

The typical Sicilian bread is large and cartwheel-shaped, and traditionally it was made in the home and baked in the small, dome-shaped oven that was built near the fireplace in most Sicilian kitchens. There are also lozenge-shaped loaves, sandwich rolls and flat buns, and a flat, unleavened bread that is soaked in oil and served with salt fish. As Sicily is so close to Campania, it is not surprising that Pizzas are popular on the island. The Pizzas of Sicily are called Sfinciuni, and they are sold in bakers' shops and also from the carts of itinerant salesmen. There are two types. One is a round of dough, thicker than that for Pizza Napoletana, covered with the local cacciacavallo cheese, tomatoes, onions, anchovies, breadcrumbs and oil. The second, called Sfinciuni di San Vito, consists of a stuffing of minced pork, local sausage and breadcrumbs, sandwiched between two thin sheets of dough.

Other traditional loaves are the Vasteddi, of which there are two types: the Vasteddi Maritati, or married vasteddi, which has a filling of meat and cheese, and the Vasteddi Schietti, which is plainer. I have not been able to find an original recipe for either but they sounded so good that I wanted to have a try. From the description, I have worked out the following ingredients for Vasteddi Maritati. I didn't have any pork spleen, so I used a lean pork chop instead. It is a wonderful loaf for a picnic and the special touch is the topping of cumin seeds that gives the bread an inbuilt spice.

Vasteddi Maritati

To make one 8 inch (20 cm) round:

basic bread dough (see page 12) made with 1 lb (450 g) strong plain flour plus 2 tablespoons olive oil
1 lean loin pork chop
3 tablespoons olive oil
2 rashers back bacon
4 oz (110 g) ricotta cheese
8 thin slices Italian salami
2 teaspoons cumin seeds

Make the bread dough and leave it, covered, in a warm place for 1 hour. Cut the pork chop into thin strips and fry them quickly in the olive oil until they are just cooked through. Remove them. Cook the bacon rashers in the oil until they are only just done. Remove them and cut off the rinds.

Preheat the oven to 400°F/200°C/gas 6. Knead the bread dough on a floured board, divide it into two equal pieces and roll one to a round of 8 inches (20 cm) in diameter. Lay one piece on a floured baking sheet. Spread the ricotta cheese over the top, leaving an edge of about ½ inch (1.3 cm). Lay the pork strips on top of the cheese, then the salami and finally the whole bacon rashers. Lay the second round of dough on top and press the edges together to secure them. Scatter the cumin seeds over the top and press them down slightly.

Leave the loaf in a warm place for 30 minutes and then bake it for 40 minutes, or until it is risen and golden. Cool it on a wire rack.

Sardinia is a rolling island of low hills whose lamb, beef, pork and vegetables are made into plain but hearty meals, often accompanied by bread. Sardinia boasts the largest loaf in Italy, the Civraxiu, which can weigh as much as 9 lb (4 kg). It is a speciality of Cagliari, the capital of the island, and is made with semolina rather than finely-milled flour.

The tradition in Sardinia is that the women make the bread while the men cook the meat. The meat speciality is the *caraxiu* – whole kid, lamb or piglet cooked in a deep enclosed pit with aromatic woods and herbs. To go with this succulent, flavoursome meat, the women make *Carte da Musica*, or sheets of music. They are in fact thin, round sheets of flat bread, about 12 inches (35 cm) in diameter, with the proper name of Pane Carasau. When cooked they crackle into lined patterns like the ruled staffs of music paper. Delicious with roasted meats, they are also highly portable and have been taken as the herdsman's lunch for centuries.

Bread is so important in Sardinia, that huge, decorative loaves are baked for festivals and important occasions. There are flowers and garlands for weddings and special shapes for Easter, Christmas and harvest-time.

● *Vasteddi Maritati*

SPAIN AND PORTUGAL

Bread has long been held in the greatest of esteem in the Spanish peninsula and the art and skill of the baker have always been recognized.
The Romans praised Spanish bread, describing it as white, fine-textured, full of flavour and aroma. Conquering Arabs, in the tenth century, improved the country's agriculture by building waterwheels and channelling water into the fields. Wheat growing flourished, thus ensuring that bread would always be one of Spain's important foods. Wheat is the main product of La Mancha in central Spain, where the old windmills made famous by Cervantes' 'Don Quixote' have been preserved as honoured relics of the past.

SPAIN

Spanish bread today, at least that made in the country, is similar in nature to the bread of Roman times – crusty on the outside and soft and sweet-tasting inside. There are variations as to ingredients and methods of baking, but the essential character of the loaf is the same throughout Spain – rich, crusty and white. From the plain Peasant Bread to the sweet Panettone, Spain offers a wealth of treats for the bread-lover.

Common throughout Spain is the rounded cushion-shaped loaf made by tucking the edges of the kneaded dough underneath and baking on an open tray, but there are also regional variations. In the North, tear-shaped loaves are popular, while in Andalusia you will find oblong loaves which are slashed along the top. The size of loaves also varies, depending on who they are intended to feed.

The time spent 'working the yeast' coupled with the usual rising time, gives this bread a rich, sweet flavour. It has a crispy crust and soft crumb and stays fresh for up to two days.

Spanish Peasant Bread

To make two large loaves:

3 lb (1.4 kg) strong plain flour
1½ pints (900 ml) warm water
3 tablespoons milk
1½ oz (40 g) fresh yeast or 1½ tablespoons dried
1½ tablespoons salt

Place the flour in a bowl, reserving one handful. If it is a cold day, warm it slightly by setting it near a radiator or on top of a stove with the oven switched on.

Pour ¼ pint (150 ml) of the water into a small bowl, add the milk and sprinkle in the yeast. Leave fresh yeast for five minutes and dried for 15 minutes. Make a well in the flour. First stir the mixture, and then pour it into the flour – but do not mix it in. Scatter the reserved handful of flour over the top.

Leave the flour and yeast in a warm, draught-free place, to stand for one hour. After this time the yeast should be bubbling well.

Using your hand, begin to draw the flour into the yeast from the edges of the well. When the centre feels dry, sprinkle in the salt. Now gradually add the remaining water, still bringing flour from the edges of the bowl to the centre. When all the water has been added, continue kneading until the dough begins to feel smooth.

Turn the dough on to a floured work surface and knead it well for about ten minutes until it feels soft, very workable and not at all sticky. Form it into a round cushion shape, tucking the sides underneath, and return it to the bowl, rounded side up. Cover the bowl with a clean dry cloth and leave it in a warm place for 1 hour for the dough to double in size.

Preheat the oven to 400°F/200°C/gas 6. Knead the dough again and divide it into two. Form each piece into a round cushion shape as before, folding the sides underneath to obtain a smooth, rounded top. Place the loaves on floured baking sheets and bake them for 40 to 45 minutes, or until they are lightly browned and sound hollow when tapped. Cool them on wire racks.

● *Broa (left) and Spanish Peasant Bread (right)*

Bread appears with nearly every meal in Spain. Potatoes are seldom used and rice is only popular in mixed dishes like paella. Bread is the filling part of the meal and is essential for mopping up the rich sauces and gravies which are a part of many Spanish dishes.

Castilian bread has a harder crust and is said to be ideal for scooping and mopping up the succulent *cocido madrileno*, a mixed meat, chicken and vegetable stew. Pieces of bread are also put on the plate to be mashed with the fattier pieces of meat. Typical of Aragon are chilindron sauces, made with tomatoes, onions, garlic, serrano ham and toasted sweet peppers, to accompany meat and vegetables, and always mopped up with a thick crust of Aragonese bread. From Madrid and the Basque areas comes *olla podrida*, containing five kinds of meat and spiced sausage and a mixture of vegetables and dried beans. Its only accompaniments are bread and red wine.

La Pringa, a bread snack served in tapas bars, probably has its origins in the eating of bread with rich stews. It consists of a mixture of salted and fresh meats, cooked together for a long time and mashed to a paste which is then spread into half-cooked rolls before they are returned to the oven. The result is a delicious combination of hot, crusty bread and spiced, salty meats.

● *Panaderia in Madrid*

Add the onion and garlic and soften them. Stir in the paprika and cayenne pepper and cook them for 1 minute, stirring. Mix in the diced sausage. Add the meats and coat them in the mixture. Pour in the stock and bring it to the boil. Cover and simmer gently for 2½ hours or until the meats are very tender and the stock has almost evaporated.

Take out the meats and the cubes of sausage. Dice the meats, removing the bones from the pork belly. In Spanish kitchens, the meats are probably mashed and pounded by hand, which you may do if you wish. However, it works equally well if you put the meats and sausage into a food processor and work them to a coarse paste.

Meanwhile, make the bread dough and let it rise in the usual way. Preheat the oven to 400°F/200°C/gas 6. Form the dough into twenty small, round buns. Lay them on floured baking sheets and leave them for 20 minutes to prove. Bake them for 10 minutes. Take them out of the oven and, with a sharp knife, quickly slit each one almost in half crossways. Fill the buns with the meat paste and close them up again. Return them to the oven for a further 10 minutes.

They are delicious eaten hot, straight from the oven, but are also excellent cold.

La Pringa

To make twenty buns:
1 lb (450 g) fresh belly of pork
1 lb (450 g) collar of bacon, in one piece
3 tablespoons olive oil
1 large onion, thinly sliced
1 clove garlic, finely chopped
1 tablespoon paprika
1 teaspoon cayenne pepper
4 oz (110 g) chorizo sausage, in one piece
1 pint (570 ml) stock
half quantity of Spanish Peasant Bread dough

Cut the rinds from the pork and bacon and remove the strip of fat from the underside of the pork (reserve it if you are making the Broas de Torresmos de Souzel (see page 69). Cut the sausage into ⅝ inch (1.5 cm) dice.

Heat the oil in a large, flameproof casserole over a low heat.

Bread is also an essential ingredient of many dishes in Spain. One of the simplest is the simple *pa amb tomatec* (bread and tomatoes) from Catalonia. Thick slices of fresh bread are rubbed with a cut tomato until they turn pink. They are then given a light sprinkling of olive oil, are topped with tomato slices and served either alone or with serrano ham.

Migas are small cubes of fried bread that are eaten as a snack or as a separate course of a meal. Cubes of bread are soaked overnight in a wet, salted cloth and then fried until crisp in garlic-flavoured oil.

Pounded bread and bread cubes are essential ingredients of the cold soup from Andalusia called *gazpacho* and also the hot, garlic soup from Cadiz called *a ajo*. From La Mancha, the huge, dry plateau in Castile in central Spain, comes Pastel de Queso y Bacon (cheese and bacon cake). It is made with the local sheep's milk cheese, bread, milk, eggs and bacon.

Spain also has its sweet breads, and the most well known is the Roscon de Reyes, produced at home and by local bakers for Reyes, the day of the Three Kings, on the 6th January. Spanish children do not have a Santa Claus on the 25th December; their presents are brought by the Three Kings on the night of the 5th January. January the 6th is a holiday on which to visit relations and exchange presents. The celebratory cake is the Roscon de Reyes in which a bean was traditionally hidden. The person who received the bean in their portion was to be king for the day. Nowadays, instead of the bean, a small charm or coin is put in. It is said to bring good luck although, in some families,

● *Harvesting grain by hand in Old Castile, Spain*

the tradition is that the person who gets it has to pay for the Roscon!

The Roscon de Reyes is a rich, sweet, yeasted cake, baked in a ring and decorated with slivered almonds and candied peel. Commercially-baked ones come in a variety of sizes and some are filled with cream or a sweet filling. Many contain a variety of novelties, rather like a box of crackers. This recipe appeared in the *Gourmetour*, a gorgeous, colourful magazine about Spain, its food and wine, which is sent to food writers.

Roscon de Reyes

To make one 10 inch (25.5 cm) ring:

1 oz (25 g) fresh yeast or ½ oz (15 g) dried
4 tablespoons warm milk
8 oz (225 g) sugar
1 lb (450 g) strong plain flour
3 whole eggs
1 egg, separated
1 teaspoon salt
1 tablespoon dark rum
1 tablespoon orange-flower water
grated rind ½ orange
grated rind ½ lemon
4 oz (110 g) butter, softened
2 oz (50 g) slivered almonds
2 oz (50 g) candied peel, bought in the piece and cut into thin slivers

In a small bowl, sprinkle the yeast into the milk and leave it to stand – five minutes for fresh yeast, 15 for dried. Add 1 teaspoon of sugar and gradually sprinkle in enough flour to make a soft dough – about 2 oz (50 g). Place the dough in a bowl, cover it and leave it in a warm place for about 40 minutes, to double in size.

Place the remaining flour in a large bowl and make a well in the centre. Beat the eggs and egg yolk together and pour them into the well. Add the sugar, salt, rum, orange-flower water and grated orange and lemon rinds. Using a wooden spoon, gradually work the flour into the well and beat until everything is well mixed.

Place the ball of yeast dough in the mixture and, using your hands, gradually knead the two together until you have a smooth, soft dough. Knead it lightly on a floured work surface until it is no longer sticky. Divide the dough in four. Flatten each piece out slightly and put one quarter of the butter into the centre of each piece. Work it into the dough and then knead all the pieces together again. Place the dough in a clean bowl and leave it in a warm place for 1 hour to double in size.

Preheat the oven to 350°F/180°C/gas 4. Knead the dough again and put a trinket or coin (nothing plastic that will melt) into it. Form the dough into a cushion shape. Push the rounded handle of a wooden spoon down through the centre and gently pull the dough into a ring-shape. Either lay the ring on a floured baking sheet and fill the centre with a core of aluminium foil, or put it into a 10 inch (25.5 cm) diameter ring mould.

Leave the dough in a warm place for 30 minutes. Brush the top with the egg white and scatter it with the slivered almonds and candied peel. Bake the cake for 40 minutes or until it is golden brown on top and cooked through. Turn it on to a wire rack to cool.

● *Coca de Trampo Mallorcina*

THE BALEARICS

The Balearics are the islands off the coast of Spain which include Mallorca and Minorca. Their plain bread is similar to that from Spain and one of the specialities is the Coca de Trampo. Trampo is the word used for a mixture of aromatic vegetables, such as onions, tomatoes and sweet peppers. The Coca is a flat bread with a rich topping, similar to a pizza. The base for the Coca is made with a quantity of basic bread dough into which olive oil is kneaded. The result is bread with a pastry-like texture. Crisp and flaky on the outside it is soft and creamy in the middle. The rich vegetable topping melts into the base to give it flavour and additional softness. It makes a wonderful vegetarian meal.

Following, is another recipe that can be made with the basic Spanish Peasant Bread dough. The addition of the olive oil makes the cooked dough very rich. The inside is soft and creamy, especially where the vegetable juices have soaked in, and the outside is crisp. Served with a green salad and sprinkled with diced cheese, it makes a delicious, substantial meal.

This is a variation on a recipe from *Las Mejoras Tapas, Ceñas Frias y Platos Combinados*, by Gloria Rossi Callizo.

● *Market stall, Barcelos, Portugal*

Coca de Trampo Mallorcina

To make one 12 inch (30 cm) loaf:

Trampo:

1 lb (450 g) tomatoes
3 tablespoons olive oil
1 sweet green pepper
1 sweet red pepper
1 large onion
1 clove garlic, finely chopped
3 tablespoons chopped parsley

Base:

1/3 quantity Spanish Peasant Bread dough (see page 63)
5 fl oz (150 ml) olive oil

Scald, skin, seed and chop the tomatoes. Heat the oil in a saucepan over a low heat. Mix in the tomatoes, cover and simmer them until they have cooked to a thick purée. Cool them.

Preheat the oven to 350°F/180°C/gas 4.

Let the bread dough rise in the usual way. Knead it on a floured board and then gradually work in the olive oil, tablespoon by tablespoon. This looks impossible at first, but if you have patience, all the oil will eventually be absorbed. Each time you add oil, pull the dough out flat, sprinke 1 to 2 tablespoons of it in the centre and then bring the edges together without letting any oil escape. When you begin kneading, the outside of the dough will be very oily and there will be oil on your work surface, but keep kneading until the dough feels smooth again. The more oil you have added, the longer you will have to knead, but eventually the dough *will* take it all.

Lightly flour the work surface and a rolling pin, and roll the dough into a 12 inch (30 cm) round. Lay it on a floured baking sheet and let it rest for about 5 minutes.

Spread the puréed tomatoes over the surface of the dough, leaving an edge of about 1 inch (2.5 cm) all round.

Cut the peppers into long, thin strips and halve and thinly slice the onion. Arrange them over the tomatoes. Sprinkle the finely-chopped garlic and then the parsley over the peppers and onion and finally dribble the remaining oil over the top.

Bake the Coca de Trampo Mallorcina for 40 to 45 minutes, or until the edges are browned and feel crisp, and the vegetables are cooked. Serve it hot.

PORTUGAL

Bread is just as important in Portugal as it is in Spain. Here, too, the village bakers take pride in their work and besides baking bread for sale, they also bake loaves made by local villagers for their personal consumption. Portuguese bread has a thick crust and is moist and chewy on the inside. Besides the wheat breads, there is also this corn bread, called Broa.

Baked in a round, it remains fairly flat and has a crisp outside and crumbly middle and a strong, characteristic corn flavour. It is traditionally used to dip into the gravies of rich stews. It is also served with Caldo Verde, a kale, potato and spicy sausage soup, and with a mixed dish of peas and sausage which is typically topped with eggs.

● *Broa*

Broa

To make one 9 inch (23 cm) round loaf:

9 oz (250 g) fine cornmeal
1½ teaspoons salt
1 teaspoon sugar
7 fl oz (200 ml) boiling water
2 tablespoons olive oil
½ oz (15 g) fresh or 2 teaspoons dried yeast
3 tablespoons lukewarm water
4 oz (110 g) strong plain flour

Place 6 oz (175 g) of the cornmeal in a mixing bowl with the salt and sugar. Add the boiling water and stir vigorously until the mixture is smooth. Beat in the oil and leave the mixture to cool.

Sprinkle the yeast in the warm water and leave it to begin to work – 5 minutes for fresh yeast and 15 minutes for dried. Stir it into the cornmeal mixture. Beginning with a wooden spoon and finishing with your hand, gradually add the remaining cornmeal and the white flour to the mixture. Form the dough into a ball and knead it. Place it in a bowl, cover it with a clean, dry cloth and leave it in a warm place for 1 hour to rise.

Preheat the oven to 350°F/180°C/gas 4.

Lightly oil an 8 inch (20 cm) diameter flan tin. Knead the dough again and pat it into a round the size of the tin. Put it into the tin and leave it in a warm place for 30 minutes.

Bake the loaf for 40 minutes, or until the top is golden and crisp. Turn it on to a wire rack to cool.

This Portuguese recipe can be made with the plain Spanish bread dough (see page 63). It is known as Crackling Cake, and the result is a rich, dark brown, sweet and spicy bread that should be eaten on its own, without butter, accompanied by coffee, hot chocolate or tea. It is taken from *Cozinha Regional Portuguese* by Maria Odette Cortes Valente, published in 1976.

The best pork fat to use is that which can be found under a belly of pork in a layer about ¼ inch (5 mm) thick. It can be peeled away easily in one piece.

Broas de Torresmos de Souzel

To make one 2 lb loaf:

basic Spanish Peasant Bread dough (see page 63) made with 8 oz (225 g) flour
8 oz (225 g) pork fat
1 tablespoon olive oil
8 oz (225 g) strong plain flour
8 oz (225 g) sugar
2 eggs, beaten
1 teaspoon ground cinnamon
1 teaspoon ground aniseed
3 fl oz (90 ml) brandy
1 egg yolk, lightly beaten

● *Communal oven, Mertola, Portugal*

Make the dough and leave it in a bowl, covered with a clean, dry cloth, for 1 hour or until it has doubled in size.

Cut the pork fat into small dice. Heat the oil in a large frying pan over a low heat. Put in the diced fat and fry it gently, stirring frequently, until the cubes are brown and most of the fat has been rendered from them. Stir in the flour and keep stirring until it browns slightly. Take the pan from the heat and beat in all but two teaspoons of the sugar, with the beaten eggs, spices and brandy. Cool the mixture to lukewarm.

Preheat the oven to 400°F/200°C/gas 6. On a lightly-floured work surface, knead the spiced mixture into the risen dough about one eighth at a time, working each portion in well before adding the next. The dough will feel light and spongy and immensely workable.

Oil a 2 lb (1 lb) loaf tin and lightly press the dough into it. Cover it and leave it in a warm place for 30 minutes or until the dough has risen about ⅜ inch (1 cm) above the rim of the tin. Brush the top of the loaf with the egg yolk and sprinkle it with the remaining sugar.

Bake the loaf for 40 minutes and test to see if the loaf is done by inserting a thin skewer into the centre. The top will be dark brown.

An ancient festival takes place at harvest time in the town of Tomar, in central Portugal. It is called the Festival of Tabuleiros. Tabuleiros means 'tray', the word used to describe the tall crown of bread that is decorated with wheat ears and flowers. Each must be as tall as the young girl who wears it on her head in the procession. The girls are accompanied by a male relative or fiancé who helps to steady the crown. Following behind are musicians, standard bearers and soldiers, oxen with gilded horns and wine carts. In the evening the oxen are slaughtered and there is a blessing of bread, meat and wine in front of the local Church. Then the seventeen best Tabuleiros are chosen. On the next day, the food is distributed to the poor and there are donkey cart races, bull fights, dancing and fireworks.

Sweet bread is also popular in Portugal. This is a plain, sweet bread, traditionally baked in spiral shapes, called Caracois, or, with currants added, in plaits called Tranca a Tricana. When cooked, the lighter parts of the crust are golden yellow and the inside has the texture of a dense, rich Madeira cake. Eat it as a mid-morning or afternoon snack, with coffee, hot chocolate or tea.

Massa Sovada

To make two 8 inch (20 cm) diameter loaves:
1 oz (25 g) fresh or ½ oz (15 g) dried yeast
4 tablespoons warm water
1½ lb (675 g) strong plain flour
8 oz (225 g) sugar
1 teaspoon salt
7 fl oz (200 ml) warm milk
3 eggs
4 oz (110 g) unsalted butter, softened and cut into small pieces

In a small bowl, sprinkle the yeast into the water. Leave fresh yeast for 5 minutes and dried for 15 minutes.

Place 1 lb (450 g) of the flour in a large bowl and toss in the sugar and salt with your fingertips. Make a well in the centre and pour in the yeast mixture and the milk. Add the eggs whole, as though you were making batter. Gradually beat in flour from the edges of the well until everything is well mixed.

Beat in the butter and then the remaining flour, about 1 oz (25 g) at a time. Continue beating until you have a soft dough that can be gathered into a ball. Turn the dough on to a floured work surface and knead it until it feels smooth and elastic. Place it in a lightly-greased bowl and cover it with a clean dry cloth. Leave it in a warm place for one hour to double in size.

Preheat the oven to 350°F/180°C/gas 4.

Flour two 9 inch (23 cm) diameter pie plates.

Knead the dough again and divide it in two. To make the Caracois, form each piece into a sausage shape about 1½ inches (4 cm) in diameter and spiral it round inside one of the pie plates.

For the Tranca a Tricana, knead in 1 oz (25 g) currants after the butter and second amount of flour have been added. Divide the dough in two as before and then each piece in three. Roll these three pieces into sausage shapes and form them into a plait (see page 18). Lay the plaits on floured baking sheets.

Bake the loaves for 40 to 45 minutes or until they are risen and golden brown. Cool them on wire racks.

● *Tomar Festival, Portugal*

● *Massa Sovada*

SWITZERLAND AND THE NETHERLANDS

*Switzerland and The Netherlands may be two of the smaller countries in Europe, but each
has its own definite style of cooking, albeit taking in influences from bordering countries.
The Netherlands is one of the so-called Low Countries, with a long sea coast and borders
with Belgium and Germany. Switzerland, in contrast, is completely land-locked, with high
mountains and borders with France, Germany, Austria and Italy.*

SWITZERLAND

Switzerland is well-known for its sausages and cured meats and its rich milk, which goes into butter, cheese and chocolate. Swiss bread also benefits from these dairy products and they are added in different proportions to give loaves and rolls in a wide variety of shapes, sizes, flavours and textures. There are over two hundred types of bread in Switzerland, some known and baked nationally and some produced only in certain cantons. You will also find Croissants and Brioches from France and Gugelhupf from Austria, all as good as they are in their countries of origin.

Baking in Switzerland goes back thousands of years. Sourdough leaven was first used around 3000 BC and the first commercial bakeries were established just before the Roman occupation. In the early Middle Ages, baking guilds were set up – bakers baked bread for sale and also took in loaves from other people for baking. At that time bread was made of flour of varying grades, and in years of poor harvest, chestnuts, acorns, root vegetables and even sawdust were mixed with whatever coarsely-ground flour was available.

In the sixteenth century, there were three basic sorts of bread, white bread for the very rich, half-white bread for the wealthy and what was known as Graubrot (grey bread) or Ruchbrot (notorious bread) for the majority of people. The main grain for this everyday bread was rye, mixed at different times with spelt, wheat, barley or oats.

Wherever you go in Switzerland today you will notice a wide variety of bread shapes and many of these have ancient origins, both practical and symbolic. The small, ring-shaped breads and rolls go back to the time when small loaves were strung on poles and stored across the rafters. The plait is said to have originated in the ancient custom whereby the newly widowed would cut off their hair as a sacrifice to their dead husband. Some bread shapes were once fertility or harvest symbols, and there are many different versions of the cross, which was symbolic even before Christianity.

Today, there are Normalbrot (everyday bread), Spezialbrot (enriched, sweetened, flavoured, etc.), Kleinbrote (rolls), Gebildbrote (which are the wonderfully elaborate picture breads) and the Kantonsbrote, the specialities of each individual canton.

This plaited bread, following, comes into the category of Spezialbrot. It is enriched with milk, butter and egg to make a bread that is sweet and soft on the inside with a thin, crisp crust. The Swiss plait can be made with four lengths of dough joined together at the top, but the following technique makes for a neater finish.

● *Alpine pastures*

Schweizer Zupfe

To make one plait:
1 oz (25 g) fresh yeast or 1 tablespoon dried
10 fl oz (275 g) warm milk
1 lb (450 g) strong plain flour
2 teaspoons salt
3 oz (75 g) butter, softened
1 egg, beaten
2 tablespoons kirsch (optional)
1 egg, beaten, for glaze

Dissolve the yeast in a little of the milk. Leave this to stand – five minutes for fresh yeast and 15 for dried. Place the flour and salt in a bowl. Make a well in the centre and pour in the yeast mixture and the remaining milk. Add the butter and one beaten egg and any kirsch. Mix everything to a dough and knead it on a floured work surface. Return the dough to the bowl, cover it and leave it for 1 hour, or until it has doubled in size.

Preheat the oven to 400°F/200°C/gas 6. Punch down the dough and knead it again. Divide it into two pieces and roll each piece into a sausage-shape, about 1 inch (2.5 cm) in diameter. Lay one piece on the work surface in a straight line. Lay the other piece across it horizontally, to make a cross with equal-length arms. Take the top part of the first piece and fold it down towards you and slightly to the right (as if at four o'clock). Fold the right-hand side of the horizontal piece left over the piece you have just folded down (as if at five o'clock). Take the left-hand side of the horizontal piece and fold it across over two strands of dough (as if at four-thirty). Take the piece now on the far right and fold it to the left, over one strand. Then take the piece on the far left and fold it to the right over two strands. Continue folding, first over one strand, to the left, and then over two, to the right, until your strands run out. Then turn the whole loaf over and seal the ends together.

Lay the loaf on a floured baking sheet and leave it to prove for 20 minutes. Glaze it with the other beaten egg. Bake the loaf for 35 minutes, or until it is golden brown. Cool it on a wire rack.

● *Birnbrot*

Another special bread is the Birnbrot, or pear bread. There are two ways of making it – the one below, which is rolled up, and another, more complicated method, in which the purée of dried fruits is mixed with rosewater and kirsch and kneaded into bread dough. This fruit dough is then divided into small loaves, each of which is encased in rich pastry before being baked.

This rolled Birnbrot is cut across into slices to reveal spirals of light, sweet dough wrapped around a spicy filling of fruits and nuts. Birnbrot is served in the afternoon, accompanied by hot chocolate.

Birnbrot

1 oz (25 g) fresh yeast or 1 tablespoon dried
3 fl oz (90 ml) warm milk
10 oz (275 g) strong plain flour
1 egg, beaten
2 oz (50 g) butter, softened, plus extra for greasing
2 oz (50 g) sugar
1 teaspoon salt
1 egg, beaten with 1 tablespoon milk

Filling:

8 oz (225 g) dried pears
6 oz (175 g) prunes
juice ½ lemon
5 fl oz (150 ml) dry red wine, plus 3 tablespoons
3 fl oz (90 ml) water
4 oz (110 g) grapes
3 oz (75 g) walnuts, chopped
3 oz (75 g) sugar
2 tablespoons kirsch
grated rind ½ lemon
¼ teaspoon ground cinnamon
¼ teaspoon ground cloves

Dissolve the yeast in the milk. Leave this to stand – five minutes for fresh yeast and 15 for dried. Place 2 oz (50 g) of the flour in a large bowl and mix in the yeast mixture. Beat in the butter, the egg and the sugar. Add the salt to the remaining flour. Work the flour, about 2 oz (50 g) at a time, into the mixture in the bowl, using your fingers towards the end. Knead the dough, place in a buttered bowl, cover it and leave it to rise for 1 hour or until it has doubled in size.

For the filling, coarsely chop the pears, and stone and chop the prunes. Place them in a saucepan with the lemon juice and 5 fl oz (150 ml) of wine, and add extra water to just cover the fruit, if necessary. Bring the fruit to the boil and simmer it for 10 minutes or until it is soft and all the liquid has been absorbed. Mash the fruit to a purée. Chop and seed the grapes. Mix them into the fruit purée together with the walnuts, sugar, kirsch, lemon rind and spices. Add the remaining wine by the tablespoon until you have a spreadable consistency.

Punch down the dough and knead it. Roll it out to a 15 inch (32.5 cm) square, about ¼ inch (6 mm) thick. Spread the fruit purée over the dough, leaving a space of 1 inch (2.5 cm) around the edge. Fold in the edges and then roll up the dough. Lay the roll on a floured baking sheet and prick over the surface with a fork. Leave it for 1 hour.

Preheat the oven to 350°F/180°C/gas 4. Brush the roll with the egg and milk mixture and bake it for 35 minutes, or until the outer layer is crisp and golden. Cool the Birnbrot on a rack and serve it warm or at room temperature.

The Gebildbrote, or picture breads, are made with a plain bread dough which is intricately worked into many forms and patterns.

Switzerland's cantons each have their own special bread recipes, or Kantonsbrote, which have been around for centuries. Some have become larger or smaller over the years, but the basic shapes remain the same – rounds, ovals, knots, rings – with patterns and slashes and other embellishments to characterize them.

Special loaves are baked for weddings, betrothals and births. There are different Gebildbrote for St. Nicholas' Day, Christmas, New Year and Easter, and many old bread customs are associated with the time around Lent. St. Agatha is the patron saint of Swiss bakers and on St. Agatha's Day (February 5th) all bakers once made special ring-shaped loaves called the Agatha-Ringe. These were taken to the Church to be blessed in the early morning and were then hung up in the local houses as a protection against fire. There are also New Year bread customs. In St. Gallen, for example, every child who makes a lantern for the New Year procession is given a small loaf called the Altjahrmann (old year man).

Bread and milk was for many years the typical Swiss breakfast and sometimes midday and evening meal as well. The combination of bread and Swiss cheese is well known in the Swiss fondue, but also appears in another form. Enriched bread dough is used as the base for a tart which contains a mixture of cheese, eggs and cream. The one below is called a Zwiebelwahe or onion tart. With less onions it can be called a Käsewahe or cheese tart. It is similar to the French dough-based tarts, but butter rather than oil is used to enrich the dough. Dough tarts are usually easier to make in the long run than pastry ones. Although you have to wait for them to rise, the mixing and handling of the dough is as quick as for pastry and the tart is easier to get out of the tin.

● *Zwiebelwahe*

Zwiebelwahe

¹/₂ oz (15 g) fresh yeast or 2 teaspoons dried

5 fl oz (150 ml) warm water

1 teaspoon salt

8 oz (225 g) strong plain flour

2 oz (50 g) butter

Filling:

1 oz (25 g) butter

2 medium onions, finely chopped

¹/₂ teaspoon paprika

8 oz (225 g) Emmenthal cheese (or use Gruyère, or half and half)

2 eggs

5 fl oz (150 ml) single cream

¹/₄ nutmeg, freshly grated

Dissolve the yeast in half the water and the salt in the other half. Place the flour in a bowl. Make a well in the centre and add the yeast mixture. Stir in a little flour from the edges of the bowl and add the salt water and the butter, Mix everything to a dough and knead it on a floured work surface. Return it to the bowl, cover it and leave it for 1 hour, or until it has doubled in size.

For the filling, soften the onions in the butter over a low heat, stir in the paprika and let the mixture cool. Grate the cheese. Beat the eggs with the cream and nutmeg.

Preheat the oven to 400°F/200°C/gas 6.

Knead the dough and roll it into a round to fit a 10 inch (25.5 cm) tart tin. Place it in the tin, then cover it with half the cheese and then the onions. Pour in the egg and cream mixture and top everything with the remaining cheese. Leave the tart for 20 minutes in a warm place and then bake for 20 minutes, or until the top of the filling is golden.

Take the tart from the tin as soon as it is cooked and preferably serve it hot or at least while it is still warm.

THE NETHERLANDS

The character of food in Holland has remained unchanged for hundreds of years. The people of Holland have the longest life-expectancy in Europe, a fact almost certainly brought about by their taste in food and, latterly, by their interest in a healthy lifestyle.

The best of ingredients, cooked well and served simply, make up most Dutch meals. Dutch bread too, is wholesome and unfussy. There are very few intricate shapes, but it is of excellent quality. Most is made from white or whole-wheat flour, or a mixture, and most loaves are baked in open rectangular tins and have either a plain rounded top, or one divided by a lengthways slash down the centre. Most everyday breads are made with a basic bread dough (see page 12) and some are enriched with milk, butter and eggs. There are also wholegrain breads, similar to the German Pumpernickel but with a sweeter flavour.

The first three recipes below were given to me by a Dutch friend, now living in England. The Wir Brood (White Bread); is a rich, golden bread, with a thin, crisp brown crust and a crumbly texture like a cross between ordinary bread and Madeira cake. It is semi-sweet and goes as well with cheese, cold meats and pickles as it does with jams and preserves.

Wir Brood

To make a 2 lb (1 kg) loaf:

1 oz (25 g) fresh yeast or 1 tablespoon dried
10 fl oz (275 ml) warm milk
1 lb (450 g) strong plain flour
2 teaspoons salt
1½ oz (40 g) caster sugar
2 egg yolks
3 oz (75 g) butter, softened

Dissolve the yeast in a little of the milk. Leave this to stand – five minutes for fresh yeast and 15 for dried. Place the flour in a bowl and toss in the salt and sugar. Make a well in the centre, add the yeast mixture and mix in a little of the flour from the sides of the well. Add the remaining milk, the egg yolks and butter. Mix everything to a dough and knead it on a floured work surface. Return the dough to the bowl, cover it and leave it in a warm place for 1 hour, or until it has doubled in size.

Preheat the oven to 400°F/200°C/gas 6. Oil a 2 lb (1 kg) loaf tin. Punch down the dough and knead it again. Form it into a cylinder shape and put it into the tin. Leave it in a warm place to prove for 20 minutes. Just before putting the loaf in the oven, make a deep slash lengthways down the centre. Bake the loaf for 35 minutes or until it is golden brown and sounds hollow when tapped.

The Bruin Brood (Brown Bread), made with a mixture of whole-wheat and white flours, is also soft-textured, but is not as rich as the white one. It is an excellent everyday bread. The milk can be replaced wholly, or in part, by water, and you can vary the proportions of the flours. You could use all whole-wheat flour and the recipe also works well if you would rather make a simple white bread instead, using all strong plain flour.

Bruin Brood

To make one 2 lb (1 kg) loaf:

¾ oz (20 g) fresh yeast or 3 teaspoons dried
10 fl oz (275 ml) warm milk
12 oz (350 g) whole-wheat flour
4 oz (110 g) strong plain flour
2 teaspoons salt
½ oz (15 g) butter

Dissolve the yeast in a little of the milk. Leave this to stand – five minutes for fresh yeast and 15 for dried. Place the two types of flour in a bowl with the salt. Toss them together. Make a well in the centre and pour in the yeast mixture. Mix in a little of the flour from the edges of the well and then add the butter and the remaining milk. Mix everything to a dough and knead it on a floured work surface. Return the dough to the bowl, cover it and leave it in a warm place for 1 hour or until it has doubled in size. Knead it again, form it into a ball and place it on a floured baking sheet. Leave it in a warm place for 20 minutes. Knead and prove again in the same way.

Preheat the oven to 400°F/200°C/gas 6. Knead the dough yet again and roll it out to an elongated triangle. To make a rectangle to fit into a 2 lb (1 kg) loaf tin, fold in the corners. Place the loaf in the oiled tin and leave it to prove for a further 20 minutes. Bake the loaf for 40 minutes or until it sounds hollow when tapped. Cool it on a wire rack.

The Dutch are, in the main, very healthy eaters, so this Sugarbread from Friesland must be eaten only as an occasional treat. It is rather like a large Chelsea bun, both in texture and flavour. The sugar melts as it cooks and makes soft, sweet patches in the dough as well as giving it a moist texture. Eat it plain or with butter. Don't be alarmed if the top becomes very dark, this is the effect of the melted sugar. You might have to give your bread tins a good soaking after making sugarbread, as the syrup can run out and set on the edges. Nevertheless, it is well worth it.

Fries Suikerbrood

To make one 2 lb (1 kg) loaf:
basic bread dough (see page 12) made with 1 lb (450 g) strong plain flour
10 oz (275 g) sugar cubes

Make the dough and leave it to rise for 1 hour. Preheat the oven to 400°F/200°C/gas 6. Place the sugar cubes in a plastic bag and bang them with a rolling pin until they are broken into coarse lumps.

Knead the dough and then gradually knead in the sugar. Form the dough into a cylinder shape and put it in an oiled 2 lb (1 kg) bread tin. Leave the loaf in a warm place to prove for 20 minutes.

Bake the loaf for 35 minutes, or until the top is a deep golden brown.

I found the following recipe in Countess Morphy's book, *Recipes of all Nations*, which was published for Selfridges in, I believe, the 1930s. She says: 'This is one of the great national Dutch cakes or "sweet" breads. The best are made at Deventer by the famous firm of Verkade.' The final note is: 'Should it be a little hard, keep it in the bread pan with other breads before using.' The outer crust is hard, but the inside is pleasantly chewy, very spicy and sweet. In many ways this could be described as a true Gingerbread. Serve it plain or with butter.

Boterhamkoek

To make one 2 lb (1 kg) loaf:
1 lb (450 g) ordinary plain flour
3 oz (75 g) Muscovado sugar
2 teaspoons anise seeds
1 teaspoon ground cinnamon
1 teaspoon ground ginger
½ teaspoon ground nutmeg
3 teaspoons baking powder
1 lb (450 g) golden syrup
5 fl oz (150 ml) milk

Preheat the oven to 325°F/170°C/gas 3. Place the flour, sugar, spices and baking powder in a bowl and toss them together with your fingers. Make a well in the centre and pour in the syrup. Using a wooden spoon, begin to beat the syrup into the flour. Beat in the milk, a little at a time, to make a soft, dropping consistency. You will probably find fingers more efficient than a spoon by the end.

Place the mixture in a greased 2 lb (1 kg) bread tin and smooth the top. Bake the loaf for 1 hour, or until a skewer stuck into the centre comes out clean.

Turn it out of the tin and cool it on a wire rack.

● *Fries Suikerbrood*

● *Boterhamkoek*

GREAT BRITAIN

The British Isles have a temperate climate, ideally suited to the growing of grain.
Wheat and barley flourish in the warmer south while the cooler, shorter summers of the
northern and upland areas are ideal for growing oats and rye.
In Britain, bread is occasionally regarded as an accompaniment to a meal, but more
commonly it is a meal in itself. Originally the Bannock (a rough mixture of ground grain
and water, baked on a hot stone) was the staple food; now you have only to look at the
sandwich lunches of office workers to realize that old habits die hard.

The United Kingdom is made up of four countries – England, Northern Ireland, Scotland and Wales. However, these countries have breads and cooking methods in common, ranging from the simple, griddle-cooked Oatcake, to rich buns and loaves full of butter, sugar and dried fruits. Looking at them, you can trace the history of bread-making in all four countries.

Usable grain first came to Britain around 4000 BC. It was ground in a quern and mixed with water to make a kind of porridge. Sometimes this was formed into cakes and baked on a hot stone, but this first bread was fairly unpalatable. Gradually the grain improved and stone-baked cakes became the major part of the diet all over the country. The bakestone was eventually superseded by the cast-iron griddle, but the principle was the same. The griddle has remained in British households ever since. It hung over Saxon, medieval and sixteenth-century fires, beside the cooking pot and the spit, and was eventually placed on iron ranges and ovens. Mine is constantly in use on a wood-burning stove during the winter and frequently on an electric ring in the summer. If guests arrive unexpectedly, out comes the griddle for Scones, Oatcakes, Muffins or Singin' Hinnie (see page 82).

The masters of this type of cooking have to be the Scots. Their Oatcakes and Bannocks are world famous, and rightly so. In her book, *The Scots Kitchen*, published in 1930, F. Marion McNeill lists over twelve types of Bannocks and Oatcakes. The Bannocks are made from a mixture of flours, including barley and maslin (where wheat and rye are grown together). Oatcakes, she says, were made for all occasions, including special ones for Beltane (May Eve) and other Celtic festivals, and a cross-shaped one for Christmas. There was even a special one to give to teething children.

Here are two recipes, one for Oatcakes, which are thin and crisp, and another for Bannocks, which are softer. The bicarbonate of soda is a modern addition which did not arrive until the mid-nineteenth century. It gives a lighter texture.

● *Aerial view of wheat harvesting*

Place the lard and water in a saucepan and set them over a low heat for the lard to melt. Cool them to lukewarm. In a bowl, mix together the oatmeal, bicarbonate of soda and salt. Make a well in the centre and pour in the melted lard and water. Mix everything to a dough.

Place the dough on a floured work surface and knead it lightly. With a rolling pin, flatten it into a round about ¼ inch (5 mm) thick. Trim the edges to neaten them and cut the round into eight wedges. These are called Farls.

Heat a lightly greased griddle over a medium heat and bake the cakes until they begin to curl up at the edges but are not coloured (if they begin to colour, turn down the heat or move them to the sides of the griddle. Turn the Oatcakes over and cook them until the underside is smooth and firm. Cool them on a wire rack.

Bannocks

To make about sixteen Bannocks:
6 oz (175 g) fine or medium oatmeal
2 oz (50 g) whole-wheat or whole-barley flour
2 teaspoons baking powder
1 teaspoon salt
1 oz (25 g) lard or butter
5 fl oz (150 ml) milk

Oatcakes

To make eight Oatcakes:
1 oz (25 g) lard
5 tablespoons water
8 oz (225 g) medium oatmeal
½ teaspoon bicarbonate of soda
¼ teaspoon salt

Place the oatmeal and flour in a mixing bowl with the baking powder and salt. Rub in the butter or lard. Make a well in the centre and pour in the milk.

Mix everything to a dough and roll it out to about ¼ inch (5 mm) thick. With a pastry-cutter, stamp the dough into approximately sixteen 2 inch (5 cm) rounds.

Heat a lightly-greased griddle over a low to medium heat.

Cook the Bannocks for about 10 minutes each side, or until they are firm and are just beginning to brown (if they should start to brown too quickly, turn down the heat a little). Bannocks are at their tastiest when eaten warm.

The griddle was also used frequently in the north of England and Wales. When you buy Oatcakes in the shops in Derbyshire, Lancashire and in some parts of Wales, you may well be surprised to find that, unlike their Scottish counterparts, they are soft and pliable. They are ideal for toasting or for frying.

Soda bread and Scone mixtures, both plain and sweetened, have also been regularly baked on British griddles and some, such as the Selkirk Bannock and the Singin' Hinnie from Northumberland, contain dried fruits. The Singin' Hinnie is so-called because it sizzles as it cooks. You will discover, if you make it, why there was a special implement called 'Singin' Hinnie hands' to turn it over. The operation is quite difficult, best carried out (in the absence of Singin' Hinnie hands) with two fish slices.

The Singin' Hinnie is served hot, straight from the griddle, slit crossways, buttered and cut into wedges. It is a wonderful, easy, hot snack, with which to welcome people on cold winter evenings.

Another name for the griddle is the girdle and so you get Girdle Cakes, also from Northumberland, which are similar to Singin' Hinnie but cut into small rounds.

● *The Black Country Museum bakery, Dudley*

Singin' Hinnie

To make one 10 inch (25.5 cm) flat cake:

12 oz (350 g) ordinary plain flour
1 teaspoon salt
½ teaspoon bicarbonate of soda
1 teaspoon cream of tartar
3 oz (75 g) lard or butter
4 oz (110 g) currants
7 fl oz (200 ml) milk

Place the flour, salt, bicarbonate of soda and cream of tartar in a bowl and rub in the lard or butter. Toss in the currants. Make a well in the centre and mix in the milk. Mix everything to a dough. Knead the dough lightly and roll it into a round about 10 inches (25.5 cm) across and ¾ inch (2 cm) thick.

Heat a lightly-greased griddle over a low heat. Place the dough on the griddle and cook until golden brown on each side and cooked through (about 15 minutes altogether). If you are using an electric ring with a concentrated circle of heat, you may find that you will need to turn it off completely for a time and let the Hinnie cook on heat stored in the ring and the griddle.

Serve the Hinnie hot, split and buttered.

Yeast came quite early to the British Isles. During the Iron Age the Celts discovered how to use ale barm as a leaven for bread and it was used to make bread similar to that we are used to now. This use of brewing yeast was carried on in country households well into the nineteenth century. When a housewife baked bread, she went to the neighbour who had most recently brewed the family beer, returning the favour when she had herself been brewing.

By Saxon times, there were professional bakers, but most bread was made at home. The English word 'lady' comes from the Saxon word 'hlaefdige', meaning kneader of the bread, and 'lord' comes from 'hlaefward', keeper of the bread. As with the stone- and griddle-baked cakes, the content and quality of the flour used at this time varied considerably, according to availability. Mostly it was coarsely ground and contained a mixture of flours – even pea and bean meal when times were hard. If you were rich, your bread may have been made from sifted flour, which had a certain proportion of the bran removed. From late Saxon times, white wheat bread was considered the best for both flavour and health. This attitude continued for centuries and all kinds of additions such as chalk, alum and even bones were put into the flour to make it whiter. The situation became so bad that first William Cobbett, in his *Cottage Economy*, 1823, and then Eliza Acton, in *The English Bread Book*, 1857, urged English housewives to make their own bread and to turn their backs upon the adulterated loaf that was produced so unhygienically in the commercial ovens of the towns.

Country bakers, of course, had always produced excellent bread, and throughout the twentieth century, baking standards improved. During the two World Wars there existed a 'standard loaf'. In the Second World War this contained all the wheat germ and a little of the bran with the result that, despite the general poverty and food rationing, standards of nutrition actually improved.

It was not until the 1960s that nutritional research actually proved that we had been wrong all along. Stoneground, whole-wheat flour was found to be good for us and people began to pay higher prices for what had for centuries been considered poor man's food. Since then, there have been reliable supplies of a wide range of flours; good quality yeast, both fresh and dried; ovens that heat up quickly and maintain an even temperature; and good storage facilities, plus the many bakers and shops which make bread. For home bakers, there are health food shops and specialist food shops which supply not only whole-wheat flour but rye and barley meals as well.

Much British flour, during the past century, has been roller ground, but recently many wind and water mills have been restored and produce their own brands of flour – some of it from organic wheat, of which there is an ever-increasing supply. Many of these mills are open to the public and have their own bakery and restaurant.

Even breads produced by the larger bread companies are improving. It was not so long ago that nearly all white flour in Britain was chemically bleached to make it white instead of the natural creamy colour that it really

● *Singin' Hinnie*

is. When, a few years ago, it was discovered that traces of chemicals remained in the finished loaf, it was banned. Vitamin C, too, was added for a time to facilitate rising, but even that is rarely used now. British bread is now healthier and there is a wider variety to choose from.

Before the greater availability of different grains, the differences between British breads were in their shapes. The Cottage loaf, the Bloomer, and the Tin Loaf were all made to a similar recipe, but characterized by their shapes.

Following, are two examples of breads made from unusual grains: Barley and Maslin bread. The Barley bread needs a little more yeast than normal, as the flour does not have the same rising ability as wheat or rye flours. Barley bread is light in colour, with a sweet, rich flavour. For the Maslin bread, I have used strong plain flour instead of the wholemeal which would have been common in poorer households. The white flour makes the bread lighter. There is a good mix of flavours, with the slightly sour rye complementing the sweet barley. Both breads are made up like the basic bread dough (see page 12), so I have given the ingredients without the method.

Barley Bread

To make one 2 lb (1 kg) loaf:

1½ oz (40 g) fresh yeast or 1½ tablespoons dried
10 to 12 fl oz (275 to 300 ml) warm water (add the 10 fl oz (275 ml) first and the rest if necessary)
1 lb (450 g) barley meal
2 teaspoons salt

Maslin Bread

To make one 2 lb (1 kg) loaf:

1 oz (25 g) fresh yeast or 1 tablespoon dried
10 to 12 fl oz (275 to 300 ml) warm water, as above
10 oz (275 g) strong plain flour
3 oz (75 g) barley meal
3½ oz (100 g) rye meal

The following bread comes from Wales and it was originally adapted by Bobby Freeman from one in *Y Tyr, a'r Teulu* (meaning 'The House, and Domestic Economy') written in 1891. It appears in Bobby Freeman's booklet *Welsh Bread*. Caraway bread was popular in rural Wales as caraway cake was in England. The loaf is light textured and dark brown, with a sweet, nutty flavour. If you do not like the flavour of caraway seeds you can omit them and the loaf will still be good. Serve it with fruit preserves or with cheese.

Bara Caraw

To make one 2 lb (1 kg) loaf:

1 oz (25 g) fresh yeast or 1 tablespoon dried
10 to 12 fl oz (275 to 300 ml) warm water
6 oz (175 g) strong plain flour
6 oz (175 g) whole-wheat flour
4 oz (110 g) rolled oats
1 teaspoon salt
1 teaspoon caraway seeds
2 oz (50 g) dark Muscovado sugar

In a small bowl, sprinkle the yeast over half the water. Leave this to stand – five minutes for fresh yeast and 15 for dried. Put the flours, oats, salt, caraway seeds and sugar in a mixing bowl. Make a well in the centre and pour in the yeast and 5 fl oz (150 ml) of the remaining water. Mix everything to a dough, adding the rest of the water if necessary. Turn the dough on to a floured work surface and knead it. Return it to the bowl, cover it and leave it in a warm place for 1 hour to double in size.

Preheat the oven to 400°F/200°C/gas 6. Knead the dough again and place it in a 2 lb (1 kg) loaf tin. Leave it to prove for 20 minutes. Bake the loaf for 40 minutes and cool it on a wire rack.

A great favourite of the English has always been bread rolls, made with yeasted wheat flour dough. I just had to include the following recipe for Kentish Huffkins, small, slightly enriched rolls, made in a circular shape with an indentation in the middle. This recipe was the first that I ever had published. I always make them with whole-wheat flour, but white flour or a mixture works just as well. Looking for Scottish recipes to put into this chapter, I found Baps or Breakfast Rolls, which are always served fresh, and sometimes warm. The flour is white but the recipe almost identical to that for Huffkins.

Kentish Huffkins

To make sixteen buns:

1 oz (25 g) fresh yeast or 1 tablespoon dried
5 fl oz (150 ml) warm water
1 lb (450 g) whole-wheat flour
2 teaspoons salt
2 oz (50 g) lard
5 fl oz (150 ml) warm milk

In a small bowl, sprinkle the yeast over the water. Leave this to stand – five minutes for fresh yeast and 15 for dried. Place the flour and salt in a mixing bowl and rub in the lard. Make a well in the centre and pour in the yeast mixture and the milk. Mix everything to a dough. Turn it on to a floured board and knead it until it is smooth. Return it to the bowl, cover it and leave it in a warm place for 1 hour to double in size.

Preheat the oven to 400°F/200°C/gas 6.

Knead the dough again and divide it into sixteen equal pieces. Form each piece into a round bun. Push your finger through the centre of each piece of dough and pull out the edges gently to form a ring. Lay the rolls on floured baking sheets and leave them in a warm place for 20 minutes to prove.

Bake them for 20 minutes until they are cooked through but only lightly brown. As they cook, the hole in the centre will close to make a deep indentation. As soon as the rolls come out of the oven wrap them in several clean, dry cloths. This keeps in the steam and gives a soft crust. Leave the rolls until they are quite cool.

Scottish Baps or Breakfast Rolls

To make sixteen Baps:

ingredients as for Kentish Huffkins, using strong plain flour

After the second kneading, divide the dough into sixteen pieces and make them into oval shapes about 3 inches (7.5 cm) long and 2 inches (5 cm) wide. Lay them on floured baking sheets. Brush them with a mixture of milk and water to give a glaze. If you would rather have a floury-textured surface, brush them with flour just after glazing and again after proving.

Leave the rolls for 20 minutes in a warm, draught-free place to prove. Just before they go in the oven, press your finger gently, a little way into the centre of each one.

This will prevent the crusts from blistering as the rolls bake. Bake the baps for 20 minutes and cool them on wire racks.

● *Kentish Huffkins*

The recipe for rolls that follows also comes from Scotland, this time from Aberdeen. They are actually a cross between bread and flaky pastry. They are wonderful when warm and keep exceptionally well for about two days. Serve them with soups and salads or perhaps as part of a savoury table at parties.

Buttery Rowies

To make about 20 rolls:

1 oz (25 g) fresh yeast or 1 tablespoon dried
12 fl oz (350 ml) warm water
1 lb (450 g) strong plain flour
1 tablespoon salt
1 tablespoon sugar
6 oz (175 g) butter, softened
6 oz (175 g) lard, softened

In a small bowl, sprinkle the yeast into half the water and leave it to stand – five minutes for fresh yeast and 15 for dried. Place the flour, salt and sugar in a large mixing bowl and rub in 1 oz (25 g) of the butter. Make a well in the centre, pour in the yeast mixture and the remaining water and mix everything to a dough. Knead it on a floured work surface, return it to the bowl, cover it and leave it in a warm place for 1 hour, or until it has doubled in size. Knock it back, wrap it in clingfilm and put it in the refrigerator for 15 minutes.

Take the dough out of the refrigerator, roll it into a rectangle and dot one third each of the remaining butter and lard on two thirds of the surface. Along its shortest sides, fold the dough into three, wrap it again in clingfilm and chill it for a further 30 minutes. Repeat this twice more. Finally, roll the dough into a rectangle about 10 × 8 inches (25.5 × 20 cm) and cut it into 2 inch (5 cm) squares. Lay the squares on floured baking sheets and leave them in a warm, draught-free place for 20 minutes to prove.

Preheat the oven to 400°F/200°C/gas 6.

Bake the rolls for 20 minutes or until they are puffed up and golden brown.

Cool them on wire racks.

● *Wheat field, Hampshire, England*

Sourdough bread, although rarely mentioned in British cookery or history books, was made throughout Britain, but not frequently. In Ireland, where yeast was less used than elsewhere, potatoes were occasionally used as a leaven. The following recipe comes from Florence Irwin's book, *The Cookin' Woman*, which was published in 1949. It makes a close-textured loaf with a nutty flavour.

Barm Bread

To make two 2 lb (900 g) loaves:

First Day:

3 medium potatoes
1 pint (570 ml) water
4 oz (110 g) whole-wheat or strong plain flour

Second Day:

2 lb (1 kg) wholemeal flour
2 teaspoons salt
5 fl oz (150 ml) warm water

On the first day, boil the potatoes in their skins in the water. Drain them, reserving the water, and peel them. In a medium-sized bowl, mash the potatoes to a purée and mix in the flour and 10 fl oz (275 ml) of the water. Cover the mixture with clingfilm and leave it for 24 hours.

By the next day, the potatoes and flour will have begun to ferment and the mixture will be risen with a cracked surface. When you tip the bowl you will see that the mixture has become stretchy like risen dough.

Place the flour in a large mixing bowl and add the salt. Make a well in the centre and pour in the barm and the warm water. Form the mixture into a dough. Turn it on to a floured board and knead it until it is smooth. Return it to the bowl, make a cross-cut in the top, cover the dough and leave it in a warm place for 5 hours.

Preheat the oven to 400°F/200°C/gas 6.

Knead the dough again and divide it into two. Form each piece into a round loaf and place them on baking sheets. Leave the loaves in a

● *Buttery Rowies*

warm draught-free place for 20 minutes to prove.

Bake the loaves for 40 minutes or until they sound hollow when tapped and the tops are golden brown.

Ireland's speciality is Soda Bread, made either on a griddle or in the oven and risen with bicarbonate of soda and sometimes baking powder. Soda Bread is usually made with wheat flour, either whole-wheat or white, or half and half; or with a mixture of wheat and oatmeal flour. In Ireland there are many variations. During times of famine, cornmeal was sent to Ireland from the United States, and Soda Breads were then made with a mixture of cornmeal and wheat flour. Flour, salt and buttermilk are the main ingredients. Originally, the buttermilk was the liquid left in the churn after the butter had been made, now you can buy commercially-prepared buttermilk which works excellently. You can also use a thin, natural yoghurt, such as a goat's milk yoghurt, or ordinary milk to which you add 1 teaspoon of cream of tartar per 10 fl oz (275 ml).

A little fat, such as butter or lard, was added when it was available and Soda Breads could be sweetened with honey or sugar. Dried fruits, candied peel and spices were added for Sunday tea or special occasions.

Wherever you go in Ireland today you will always be able to buy marvellous Soda Bread, either white or brown. Its texture and flavour varies from baker to baker as real bread should, but whenever you eat it you will be reminded of that wonderful country.

The following is a variation that can be worked upon. To change the flour, use all white or ½ white and ½ oatmeal; or ½ white, ¼ oatmeal and ¼ brown. Add 2 oz (50 g) sugar or honey and/or up to 4 oz (110 g) dried fruits or candied peel. Bake the dough on a baking sheet or griddle.

Soda Bread

To make one 1 lb (450 g) loaf:
8 oz (225 g) whole-wheat flour
1 teaspoon salt
1 teaspoon bicarbonate of soda
½ teaspoon cream of tartar
½ oz (15 g) butter or lard
5 fl oz (150 ml) buttermilk

Preheat the oven to 400°F/200°C/gas 6. Place the flour, salt and bicarbonate of soda in a bowl and rub in the butter or lard. Make a well in the centre and pour in the buttermilk. Mix everything into a dough. Turn it on to a floured board and knead it lightly.

Press or roll the dough into a round about 1½ inches (4 cm) thick. Lay it on a floured baking sheet. Score the top into four sections. Bake the bread for 20 minutes, or until it is just coloured and sounds hollow when tapped. Cool the Soda Bread on a wire rack.

Varieties of Soda Bread are also made in Wales and often baked on the griddle. There is Bakestone bread and Blanc bread, and Welsh cakes which are small and spicy. From Scotland, besides the many Oatcakes, there are Highland Slim Cakes, made with wheat flour and enriched with butter and eggs. In England, a similar mixture is cut into rounds and baked to make Scones.

● *Harvesting*

During the seventeenth century, spices, sugar and dried fruits became more readily available to the general population, along with butter, milk and eggs. As a result, more and more recipes for enriched and sweetened breads appeared. The easiest one to make was Lardy Cake. This required a plain bread dough, homemade lard, and any sugar, spices and dried fruits that were available. Because it called for lard, it was made mainly in the English counties where pigs were kept, and usually as a treat at the end of the day's baking. It was called Lardy Cake in the West Country, Lardy Johns in Sussex, and Dough Cake in Buckinghamshire. In Suffolk there was a similar cake called Fourses Cake, which was eaten in the fields at harvest time at the four o'clock break.

Lardy Cake

To make one 8 inch (20 cm) square cake:

basic bread dough (see page 12) made with 8 oz (225 g) flour, risen for 1 hour
6 oz (175 g) lard
½ teaspoon ground cinnamon
½ nutmeg, freshly grated
2 oz (50 g) sugar
1½ oz (40 g) currants
1½ oz (40 g) sultanas

Preheat the oven to 400°F/200°C/gas 6. Knead the dough and roll it into an oblong about ½ inch (1 cm) thick. Spread 1 oz (25 g) of the lard on two-thirds of it and fold it into three. Roll it out again and spread on one quarter of the lard that is left. Sprinkle it with a quarter of the spices, sugar and fruit. Repeat the rolling, spreading and sprinkling three more times.

The last time the dough is folded, do not roll it. Put it into a greased baking or Swiss-roll tin (not on a baking sheet as some of the fat runs out during cooking). Leave the cake in a warm place for 15 minutes or until it has almost doubled in size.

Bake the cake for 40 minutes or until it is golden brown. Cool it on a wire rack for 10 minutes and eat it warm.

From Cornwall comes Saffron Cake, once made only at Easter time but now available from many Cornish Bakers throughout the year. Saffron was once grown in England, in Saffron Walden in Essex, but there is a story that it first arrived in the country with the Phoenicians who traded it for Cornish tin. It was certainly grown in Cornwall until the eighteenth century.

Saffron Cake

To make either two 1 lb (450 g) loaves or sixteen buns:

large pinch of saffron strands
4 tablespoons boiling water
1 oz (25 g) fresh yeast or 1 tablespoon dried
6 fl oz (175 ml) milk, warmed
1 lb (450 g) strong plain flour
pinch of salt
¼ nutmeg, freshly grated
5 oz (150 g) butter
8 oz (225 g) currants
2 oz (50 g) candied peel, chopped
2 eggs, beaten

Place the saffron in a bowl and pour on the boiling water. Leave it to infuse overnight.

In a small bowl sprinkle the yeast over the milk. Leave this to stand – five minutes for fresh yeast and 15 for dried. Place the flour in a mixing bowl and add the salt and nutmeg. Rub in the butter. Toss in the currants and peel. Make a well in the centre. Pour in the saffron and saffron water, yeast mixture and eggs. Mix everything to a dough. Knead the dough in the bowl. Cover it and leave it in a warm place for 1 hour or until it has doubled in size.

Preheat the oven to 350°F/180°C/gas 4. Knead the dough again. Either divide it in half and put it into two greased 1 lb (450 g) loaf tins, or divide it into sixteen buns and place them on a floured baking sheet. Cover the loaves or buns with a cloth again and leave them in a warm place for 10 minutes, or until the loaves have risen about ½ inch (1.5 cm) above the top of the tins and the buns have almost doubled in size.

Bake the loaves for 1 hour and the buns for 30 minutes. Cool them on wire racks. Eat them plain or buttered.

From Wales comes Bara Brith and from Ireland, Barn Brack. Both names are a derivation of the respective country's names for speckled bread. The breads are similar, containing a variety of currants and other dried fruits, but both are included here as representatives of their various countries.

There are many recipes for Bara Brith, but the best are made with yeast instead of baking powder and recommend the use of tea for soaking the dried fruit. Whole-wheat flour is used in the Bara Brith recipe below, but plain flour is also suitable.

Bara Brith

To make one 2 lb (1 kg) loaf:

6 oz (175 g) raisins

6 oz sultanas

2 oz (50 g) Muscovado sugar

16 fl oz (425 ml) hot black tea

1 oz (25 g) fresh yeast or 1 tablespoon dried

1 lb (450 g) whole-wheat flour

½ teaspoon salt

½ teaspoon ground mixed spice

4 oz (110 g) butter, plus extra for greasing

Place the dried fruits and sugar in a bowl. Pour on the tea and leave them to soak for at least 4 hours. Drain the fruits well, reserving the tea. Measure the tea. If necessary, make it up to 10 fl oz (275 ml) with warm water.

Pour the tea into a small bowl. Sprinkle in the yeast and leave it – five minutes for fresh yeast and 15 for dried. Place the flour, salt and mixed spice in a mixing bowl. Rub in the butter and toss in the fruits. Make a well in the centre and pour in the yeast mixture. Mix everything to a moist dough and knead it in the bowl (see page 13). Cover the dough and leave it in a warm place for 1 hour to double in size.

Preheat the oven to 350°F/180°C/gas 4. Grease a 2 lb (1 kg) loaf tin. Knead the dough again. Place it in the prepared tin. Leave it in a warm place to prove for 20 minutes. Bake the loaf for 1 hour or until a skewer stuck in the centre comes out clean. Turn it on to a wire rack to cool and serve it sliced and buttered.

• *Combine harvesters in Sussex, England*

Barn Brack

To make one 2 lb (1 kg) loaf:

Sponge:

½ oz (15 g) fresh yeast or 2 teaspoons dried
10 fl oz (275 ml) warm milk
4 oz (110 g) strong plain flour

Loaf:

1 egg, beaten
2 oz (50 g) butter, softened
10 oz (275 g) strong plain flour
2 oz (50 g) caster sugar
4 oz (110 g) sultanas
2 oz (50 g) currants
2 oz (50 g) candied peel, chopped
1 tablespoon sugar, melted in 2 tablespoons water

To make the sponge, first place the yeast in a large mixing bowl and pour in the milk. Stir in the 4 oz (110 g) flour. Leave the mixture in a warm, draught-free place for 1 hour or until it is risen and bubbling.

Stir the egg and the butter into the sponge and then the flour, sugar, fruits and peel. Mix everything to a dough. Turn it on to a floured board and knead it until it is smooth. Return the dough to the bowl, cover it and leave it in a warm place for 1 hour.

Preheat the oven to 400°F/200°C/gas 6. Knead the dough again. To form the loaf, bring the edges to the centre, turning the loaf, so the underneath becomes smooth. Turn the dough upside down and roll it out to about 1½ inches (4 cm) thick. Place it on a floured baking sheet and leave it in a warm place for 20 mintues to prove.

Bake the loaf for 30 minutes, or until it is golden and sounds hollow when tapped. Brush it with sugared water and return it to the oven for 1 minute.

Cool it on a wire rack.

● *Scots Black Bun*

The most amazing enriched bread is the Scots Black Bun which is made of a buttery dough, packed full of dried fruits and spices, encased by a plain version of the same dough. It was traditionally served on Twelfth Night, but is now more often a Hogmanay (New Year's Eve) speciality.

Scots Black Bun

To make one 8 inch (20 cm) loaf:

basic bread dough (see page 12) made with 1 lb (450 g) strong plain flour
6 oz (175 g) butter, softened
1½ oz (40 g) flaked almonds
8 oz (225 g) raisins
8 oz (225 g) sultanas
3 oz (75 g) candied peel, chopped
1 teaspoon ground allspice
½ teaspoon ground cloves
1 teaspoon ground ginger
½ nutmeg, grated

Knead the dough for the first time and then knead in the butter. Place the dough in a bowl, cover it and leave it in a warm place for 1 hour or until it has doubled in size.

Preheat the oven to 350°F/180°C/gas 4.

Knead the dough again, cut off about one third and reserve it. Mix the almonds, dried fruits, peel and spices together. Knead them into the larger quantity of dough, a little at a time. You will find that the dough gradually darkens in colour. Form the fruit dough into a ball. Roll the smaller quantity of dough into a flat sheet. Put the ball of fruit dough into the centre and bring the sides of the plain dough to the centre. Pinch them together to seal them. Turn the loaf over so that it has a smooth, unbroken top.

Place the loaf on a floured baking sheet and place an 8 inch (20 cm) metal ring around it. Gently press the dough down so that it almost touches the sides of the ring. Prick the loaf all over with a fork, going right through the outer layer. Leave the loaf for 20 minutes to prove.

Bake the loaf for 1 hour, removing the metal ring after the first 30 minutes. The outside will be golden brown and the loaf will sound hollow when it is tapped. Cool it on a wire rack.

Sweet yeasted buns became popular during the sixteenth century. In books of traditional recipes you will find Belvoir Castle Buns from Nottingham, Cheltenham Buns from Gloucestershire, Bath Buns and Chester Buns. London Buns are long, fat fingers of dough covered with pink or white icing, and Chelsea Buns, first made by Richard Hand at the Old Chelsea Bun House in the Pimlico Road, are made by spreading an enriched dough with butter, spices and fruits, rolling it up and cutting it into whirled slices.

Hot Cross Buns, too, are still made all over Britain around Easter time. At one time, buns with a cross on them were made all through Lent. They were banned by Oliver Cromwell and brought back again at the time of the Restoration. Whole-wheat Hot Cross Buns are becoming more popular each year. This is the marvellous recipe that I always use, with separate short-crust-pastry crosses made for the tops.

● *Hot Cross Buns*

In a small bowl, sprinkle the yeast into half the milk. Leave this to stand – five minutes for fresh yeast and 15 for dried. In another bowl, mix the eggs and butter into the remaining milk. Place the flour in a mixing bowl and add the salt, nutmeg, currants and candied peel. Make a well in the centre and put in the yeast mixture, butter and egg mixture, and honey. Mix everything to a dough and knead it in the bowl (see page 13). Cover it and leave it in a warm place for 1½ hours, or until it has doubled in size.

Preheat the oven to 400°F/200°C/gas 6. Knead the dough again and form it into 16 round buns. Lay them on floured baking sheets. Roll out the pastry and cut it into thin strips. Use these to make the crosses on the buns, hanging them over the dough loosely and letting them touch the baking sheets on each side. This allows for the expansion of the buns. Brush the buns with the beaten egg mixture and leave them in a warm place for 20 minutes to prove. Place a tray of hot water in the bottom of the oven to make it steamy. This gives the buns a thin, soft crust.

Bake the buns for 20 minutes, or until they are golden brown. Cool them on wire racks and serve them split and buttered.

Hot Cross Buns

To make sixteen buns:

1 oz (25 g) fresh yeast or 1 tablespoon dried
10 fl oz (275 ml) warm milk
3 oz (75 g) butter
2 eggs, beaten
1 lb (450 g) whole-wheat flour
½ teaspoon salt
½ nutmeg, freshly grated
6 oz (175 g) currants
2 oz (50 g) candied peel, chopped
3 oz (75 g) honey
1 egg, beaten with 3 fl oz (90 ml) milk

Crosses:

shortcrust pastry made with 4 oz (110 g) whole-wheat flour

Crumpets and Muffins became popular in the eighteenth century and both were traditionally eaten around an open fire at teatime, toasted and dripping with butter. Muffins are made with a bread dough containing milk and butter, cooked on a griddle, toasted, split and buttered. They were originally baked in town ovens and carried on a tray on the head of the 'muffin man' who rang a bell to tell customers of his imminent arrival. At one time, so many Muffins were made that violence regularly broke out between rival sellers looking for trade.

Crumpets are made with a similar but more liquid mixture, rather like a thick batter. To make them you will need two crumpet rings. These are metal rings about 3½ inches (9 cm) in diameter and ⅝ inch (1.5 cm) deep. You only need two, as the rings are removed from the Crumpets half way through cooking. You can begin to make two new Crumpets as the first ones are finishing off.

Your homemade crumpets should not look anything like the rubbery, holey ones that you can buy in the shops; they will bubble as they cook to give the same aerated inside, but the tops and base will be slightly smoother as they are turned over during cooking. When done, they should be a light, golden-brown colour. They are richer and more filling than bought Crumpets and do not have anything of that unpleasant, dry, soda-like taste.

Pikelets are similar to Crumpets, only smaller, and you can make them with the same mixture. The name comes from the Welsh, *Pyclid*, which was a soft griddle cake.

You can also make Scotch Pancakes with the same mixture, by adding a little sugar.

Crumpets

To make eight Crumpets:

½ oz (15 g) fresh yeast or 2 teaspoons dried
10 fl oz (275 ml) warm milk
8 oz (225 g) strong plain flour
1 teaspoon salt
1 egg, beaten
1 oz (25 g) butter, softened, plus extra for greasing

In a small bowl, sprinkle the yeast into half the milk and leave it to stand – five minutes for fresh yeast and 15 for dried. Dissolve the butter in the remaining milk. Place the flour and salt in a mixing bowl and make a well in the centre. Gradually beat in the yeast mixture, milk and butter mixture, and egg, to make a thick batter. Cover the batter and leave it to stand in a warm, draught-free place for about 45 minutes, or until it has bubbled up the sides of the bowl.

Grease a cast-iron griddle and warm it over a low heat. This low heat is important as the Crumpets are quite thick and have to be cooked for a relatively long time. A griddle that is too hot will make them burned on the outside and too soft in the middle.

Lightly grease the crumpet rings and place them on the griddle. Spoon two tablespoons of the batter into each ring. Cook the batter for about 3 minutes on the first side. During cooking the batter will bubble and the base and sides will become firm. The underside should cook to a light, golden brown. Remove the crumpet rings. Remember that they will be hot. They are best removed by slipping a palette knife under the edge of the ring, and then lifting it up. Turn the Crumpets over and cook the second side in the same way. Clean the rings, if necessary, and start two other Crumpets beside the first. Be sure to re-grease the griddle at any point during cooking that it becomes dry.

Cool the Crumpets on a plate.

When you are ready to eat them, toast them lightly on each side so that the outsides become firm and dry. Eat them hot with plenty of butter.

Crumpets are always best eaten on the day that you make them.

Pikelets

Make the mixture as for Crumpets and heat the greased griddle over a low heat. Spoon single tablespoons of the batter on to the griddle, without using the rings, and cook them for about 1½ minutes on each side. They should be oval shaped and golden brown. Pikelets can be eaten straight away or cooled and toasted. As with Crumpets, eat them on the day you make them.

Scotch Pancakes

Make as for Pikelets, using the Crumpet mixture but adding 2 tablespoons of sugar to the batter before leaving it to stand.

One other thing that the British Isles are famous for is their Tea Bread – richer than a bread but less so than a cake. Tea breads are usually baked in a loaf tin and eaten sliced and buttered at teatime. Many contain dried fruits that have been soaked in tea and quite a lot contain golden syrup.

The following recipe for Brown Fadge was given to me by a home economics student from Northern Ireland who was helping me with some recipe testing about ten years ago. It is her mother's recipe.

Brown Fadge can be eaten plain or buttered, and if made in a round tin it can be split like a sponge cake and sandwiched back together with a thick layer of butter.

Brown Fadge

To make one 2 lb (1 kg) loaf:

1 lb (450 g) ordinary plain flour
1 tablespoon baking powder
2 oz (50 g) caster sugar
4 oz (110 g) black treacle
1 egg, beaten
8 fl oz (225 ml) milk

Preheat the oven to 350°F/180°C/gas 4. Place the flour in a mixing bowl. Toss in the baking powder and sugar and make a well in the centre. Put in the treacle and egg and gradually beat in flour from the sides of the well.

Place the mixture in a greased, 8 inch (20 cm) diameter cake tin or 2 lb (1 kg) loaf tin. Bake the cake for 40 minutes or until a skewer inserted into the centre comes out clean.

Turn it on to a wire rack to cool.

EASTERN EUROPE

Throughout all the political boundary drawing and re-drawing of the area, the peoples of Eastern Europe have fiercely maintained their own ethnic characters, traditions, languages and tastes in food. The bread is therefore as varied as its peoples. The main grains are wheat and rye, with some buckwheat and also maize. Dark rye bread is popular in the colder regions and light wheat bread where the climate is warmer. Besides plain breads there are many sweetened wheat breads made for everyday and for special occasions.

Bread has been the most important item of the diet in this area for centuries and it is involved in many ancient customs. In northern Russia, the coming of spring is celebrated at a pre-Lent festival called Maslenitsa. A young girl, dressed as Spring, is offered a loaf and a pot of salt, while a woman, dressed as Winter, is given a decanter of wine as a going away present. Also eaten at this festival are blinis – small yeasted buckwheat pancakes – which, fried in butter until they are golden, were eaten in pre-Christian times as the symbol of the returning sun.

Khlib i sil (bread and salt) are also traditionally given to guests in the Ukraine. Symbolically this means that even if the house cannot afford more than bread and salt, the guest is welcome to share them. In other countries, bread and salt are symbols of prosperity. In Poland, for example, they are traditionally the first gifts given to a newly married couple.

The Eastern Europeans love festivals and celebrations, and in many countries, rich, yeasted cakes are baked for such occasions. Generally these contain liberal amounts of eggs and butter, plus sugar, spices, dried fruits and sometimes nuts. A favourite Russian birthday cake, called a Krendel, is formed in a figure-of-eight shape. The Polish have a festival bread called Babke Wielkanocna, which is made from a rich yeast dough and baked in a large Gugelhupf mould. This is flavoured with lemon and orange rinds and contains nuts and dried fruits. In the days before reliable ovens and standard yeast, the dough for this was treated extremely gently and left to rise on feather pillows. Every housewife had her own recipe for Babke Wielkanocna which was passed down through the family like an heirloom. One of the occasions on which it was baked was Easter, the most important religious festival in Eastern Europe.

Russians, too, have an Easter cake. It is known as Kulich, and is either baked in a round tin or in the shape of a stepped pyramid, said to represent Mount Golgotha. It is traditionally eaten with the moulded cheese dessert known as Pashka.

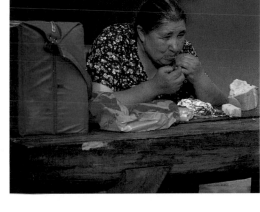

● *Lunchtime in Hungary*

Kulich

To make one 8 inch (20 cm) diameter round or pyramid-shaped loaf:

10 fl oz (275 ml) milk
1 teaspoon saffron strands
1 1/2 oz (40 g) fresh yeast or 1 1/2 tablespoons dried
4 egg yolks
8 oz (225 g) butter, softened
6 oz (175 g) sugar
1 teaspoon vanilla essence
1 lb 8 oz (675 g) strong plain flour
4 cardamom seeds, crushed
1/2 teaspoon salt
grated rind of 1/2 lemon
4 oz (110 g) sultanas
3 oz (75 g) raisins
3 oz (75 g) slivered almonds
1 egg, beaten

Place the milk and saffron in a saucepan. Bring them gently to the boil, stirring, so the milk turns yellow. Strain the milk and cool it to lukewarm. Pour the milk into a large mixing bowl, sprinkle in the yeast and leave it to stand – five minutes for fresh yeast and 15 for dried. Stir in the egg yolks, butter, sugar and vanilla essence. Mix the flour with the cardamom seeds, salt, lemon rind, sultanas, raisins and nuts. Gradually stir these into the yeast mixture to make a dough. Turn it on to a floured work surface and knead it until it is smooth. Return it to the bowl, cover it and leave it for 1 hour, or until it has doubled in size.

Preheat the oven to 425°F/220°C/gas 7.

Knead the dough again and roll it out to a thickness of about 5/8 inch (1.5 cm). Cut a 7 inch (18 cm) circle of dough and lay it on a floured baking sheet. Cut a 6 inch (15 cm) circle and lay it on top. Continue building up circles of dough, down to a 1 inch (2.5 cm) circle, so that you have built up a pyramid shape. Alternatively, form the dough into one large, round loaf and bake it in a round tin or on a baking sheet.

Leave the loaf in a warm place to prove for 30 minutes. Brush it with the beaten egg and bake it for 5 minutes. Turn the heat to 400°F/200°C/gas 6 and cook it for a further 25 minutes, or until it is golden brown and cooked through.

Cool it on a wire rack.

Everyday breads throughout Eastern Europe can be divided into three main types: dark or black breads, usually made from rye meals; unsweetened white bread; and sweetened white bread. There are also several corn breads.

The rye breads are strongly flavoured. They come in a variety of shapes and sizes, such as tin loaves, enormous cartwheels, small ovals and large rounds with slashes across the top. There are Pumpernickel types and lighter-textured loaves sometimes made with a mixture of flours. These dark breads are often served in thick slices and spread with plenty of butter.

In the Ukraine, dark rye breads, called Chernyi Khlib, are the most popular. The really black shiny ones come in pointed oval shapes or large rounds, and the rougher-textured dark brown ones in tin shapes or small rounds. Rye bread is also favoured in the Baltic states. In Latvia there is the almost black, sour Pumpernickel type and a lighter-coloured, lighter-textured one. Here the bakers' shops are identified by a large gold pretzel-shaped pastry hung over the door.

Buckwheat is another type of flour that makes a dark, rich bread. The dough is totally different to that made with any other flour, because it is silky-

• *Kulich (see page 95)*

textured and contains little gluten. It is most commonly used to make Blinis or Pancakes, but is also used in the Baltic states and in Poland to make bread. This recipe from Poland maintains the dark colour and strong flavour of buckwheat bread, but also contains a small amount of strong wheat flour to make the loaf rise and to give it a light texture. It is very crumbly and does not hang together like wheat or rye bread, so be very careful when you are taking it out of the tin. It is good buttered thickly and served with soup or salads.

Pyza z Hreczanej Maki

To make one 10 inch (25 cm) round, flat loaf:

1 oz (25 g) fresh yeast or 1 tablespoon dried
12 fl oz (300 ml) warm water
1 lb (450 g) buckwheat flour
4 oz (110 g) strong plain flour
1 teaspoon salt
8 oz (225 g) lard, melted

In a small bowl, sprinkle the yeast into 5 fl oz (150 ml) of the water. Leave this to stand – five minutes for fresh yeast and 15 for dried. Place the flours and salt in a large mixing bowl, make a well in the centre and pour in the melted lard. Mix it in and add the yeast and remaining warm water. Mix everything to a dough and knead it in the bowl until it is smooth. Cover it and leave it in a warm place for 1 hour, or until it has doubled in size.

Preheat the oven to 350°F/180°C/gas 4. Knead the dough again and press it into a greased 10 inch (25.5 cm) diameter tart tin. Leave it in a warm place for 30 minutes to prove. Bake the loaf for 30 minutes or until it sounds hollow when tapped. Cool it on a wire rack.

Maize is an important crop both in Georgia and Romania. In Georgia there is a saying: 'Better beans and corn bread at home than cake and wine in the land of strangers'. Here, the cornmeal is mixed, uncooked, with water and salt and baked in a pottery dish. The bread is eaten hot or warm as it becomes unpleasantly hard as it cools. The corn bread in Romania, called Mamaliga, is more like the Italian polenta. It is cooked with water first to a thick mush, turned out and cooled to a moist cake which is cut, not with a knife, but by drawing fine string through it. The corn bread from Bulgaria combines the two methods. The cornmeal is first cooked with water to a thick porridge and then baked.

Unsweetened wheat bread is usually made with unbleached white wheat flour and the variety of shapes, textures and flavours is enormous. Some types are heavy and rich and made by the sourdough method and others are light and airy and risen with yeast.

In the Ukraine you will find the Korzh, which is large, flat and round, and the Lalach, which is made in a variety of shapes – long and oval, a Bloomer-type with squared ends, and an enormous rectangle made from four smaller loaves joined together. Then there is the Polianitsa, a large round loaf with one deep slash.

The traditional wheat bread of Georgia was once baked in a brick-lined oven, dug into the ground, called a *tone*. The bread was made from stone-ground wheat, leavened by a sourdough starter. On baking day, a fire was lit in the bottom of the tone, which heated the walls. The oval-shaped loaves were not baked on trays but were literally thrown at the walls of the oven, where they stuck and gently cooked. It sounds easy, but it probably took a great deal of practice to get a throw just right.

In Armenia, the wheat breads show their Middle Eastern ancestry. There is Lavash, thin unleavened sheets which are also baked on the walls of an oven, and Churek, light-leavened flat breads enriched with butter and sprinkled with sesame seeds. Sprinkling them with water before baking gives them a delicious, thin, flaky crust which bubbles slightly in the oven. They are best eaten slightly warm or at least on the day of baking.

Churek

To make five large rounds:

¾ oz (20 g) fresh yeast or 3 teaspoons dried
1½ teaspoons salt
12 oz (350 g) strong plain flour
2 oz (50 g) butter, softened
1 tablespoon white sesame seeds

In a small bowl, sprinkle the yeast into half the water. Leave this to stand – five minutes for fresh yeast and 15 for dried. Dissolve the salt in the remaining water. Place the flour in a bowl and make a well in the centre. Pour in the yeast mixture and salt water and add the butter. Mix everything to a dough. Turn it on to a floured work surface and knead it until it is smooth. Return it to the bowl, cover it and leave it in a warm place for 1 hour or until it has doubled in size.

Preheat the oven to 350°F/180°C/gas 4.

Knead the dough again and divide it into 5 equal pieces. Roll each piece into a thin round, about 7 inches (18 cm) in diameter. Lay the rounds on floured baking sheets. Sprinkle each one with a little cold water and some sesame seeds. Leave the breads for 10 minutes in a warm place. Bake them for 15 to 20 minutes, or until they are a light golden brown.

Cool them on a wire rack.

These flat breads are best eaten warm, but they will keep for several days in an airtight tin and can be gently heated before serving.

A similar type of flat white bread is made in other parts of Eastern Europe. There are several different kinds and many are sold in the streets on market stalls. Most commonly the breads are about 7 inches (18 cm) round with a grid or spiral pattern stamped in the centre. Also to be found in the area, are a variety of small round loaves and leaf-shaped buns.

In the Balkans, Czech Republic and Slovakia, the country bread was made with a white wheat flour and a sourdough starter, giving it a creamy colour, a close texture and rich flavour. In the Balkans, this bread was called Pogaca or farmer's bread. Traditionally, the loaves were made up into flattened 10 inch (25.5 cm) rounds, baked on a heated stone shelf and covered with a dome-shaped lid which had a special ring on top containing hot coals or wood. The finished loaves were cut crossways into long, thin slices and were often served with a fermented cream known as Kajmak.

Caraway seeds and fennel seeds are often used to flavour bread in Eastern Europe. The following recipe comes from Hungary. The light, yeasted, white flour dough contains fennel seeds which give it a sweet, spicy flavour.

In a small bowl, dissolve the yeast in 4 fl oz (120 ml) of the water. Place the flour in a large mixing bowl with the sugar, salt and fennel seeds. Make a well in the centre and pour in the yeast mixture and the remaining water. Mix everything to a dough. Turn it on to a floured work surface and knead it. Return it to the bowl, cover it and leave it in a warm place for 1 hour or until it has doubled in size.

Preheat the oven to 400°F/200°C/gas 6. Knead the dough again and form it into two round loaves. Lay them on floured baking sheets. With a razor blade or sharp knife, make a ¼ inch (5 mm) deep slash across the centre of each one. Leave them in a warm place for 20 minutes to prove. For the glaze, lightly beat the egg yolk with the cream. Brush the loaves with the glaze and sprinkle them with the fennel seeds.

Bake the loaves for 35 minutes, or until they are golden brown and sound hollow when tapped.

Feherkenyer

To make two small round loaves:
1 oz (25 g) fresh yeast or 1 tablespoon dried
12 fl oz (300 ml) warm water
1 lb (450 g) strong plain flour
2 teaspoons sugar
2 teaspoons salt
½ teaspoon fennel seeds
1 egg and 4 tablespoons double cream

Sweet bread is probably served in Eastern Europe far more than cake. Besides the festive varieties mentioned earlier, there are many simpler versions which can be bought throughout the year. The Ukraine is not only famous for its wheat but also for its sugar production. It has an enormous number of sweet breads and rolls that are served mid-morning or in the afternoon, at breakfast time or supper time – in fact, when anyone needs a snack. The Khala are plaited breads which sometimes have a scattering of poppy seeds; Zdoba are small loaves or buns in a variety of shapes, and Perepychka are large and flat, and scored with a ring and a striped pattern in the centre. The Kalach is Bloomer shaped; the Kruchenyk, round with a sun pattern; and the Rizhok, horn shaped. Solomka are small, sweet bread sticks (like sweet Grissini) and Bublyky are ring-shaped rolls.

● *Kirghiz making bread, Central Siberia*

Doughnuts and Rum Babas are popular in Moscow as are sweet Rusks made in a similar way to Scandinavian Crisprolls.

The Poppy Seed Roll is popular throughout Eastern Europe. The version below is a combination of Hungarian and Russian recipes. There is also a version from Poland where the milk is scalded before being poured, still hot, over the flour. The poppy seed filling is sweet and rich and the roll is served, cut into slices, with morning coffee.

Makos es Dios Kalacs

To make one 12 inch (30 cm) long roll:

¾ oz (20 g) fresh yeast or 3 teaspoons dried
4 tablespoons warm water
4 fl oz (120 ml) warm milk
½ teaspoon vanilla essence
grated rind ½ lemon
1 oz (25 g) sugar
2 eggs, beaten
12 oz (350 g) strong plain flour
1 teaspoon salt
3 oz (75 g) butter, softened
1 egg, beaten with 1 tablespoon milk

Filling:

4 oz (110 g) poppy seeds
4 oz (110 g) unsalted butter
2 oz (50 g) honey
2 tablespoons double cream
2 oz (50 g) raisins, chopped
2 oz (50 g) sultanas, chopped
grated rind ½ lemon

In a large mixing bowl, sprinkle the yeast over the water and leave it to stand – five minutes for fresh yeast and 15 for dried. Add the milk, vanilla essence, lemon rind, sugar and eggs. Stir in the flour and salt and add the butter. Mix everything to a dough. Knead it in the bowl (see page 13) until it is smooth. Cover it and leave it in a warm place for 1 hour or until it has doubled in size.

Make the filling. Place the poppy seeds in a coffee grinder or blender and work them to a coarse paste. Beat together the butter and honey and beat in the cream, a little at a time. Fold in the poppy seeds, raisins, sultanas and lemon rind.

Preheat the oven to 350°F/180°C/gas 4.

Knead the dough again and roll it into a rectangle about

9 × 12 inches (23 × 30 cm). Spread the filling over the top, leaving a border of about ¾ inch (2.5 cm) on each long side, but spreading to the edges of the short sides. Roll up the rectangle from one long side and lay it on a floured baking sheet with the overlap underneath. Leave the roll in a warm place for 20 minutes to prove. Glaze it with the egg and milk, and bake it for 40 minutes, or until it is golden brown. Cool it on a wire rack.

Crescent-shaped rolls are just as popular in parts of Eastern Europe as they are in Austria. From Hungary come Sorkifli, salted crescents, made with an unsweetened dough, and sprinkled with caraway seeds and coarse salt. The Balkan Kiflici od Sala, below, are filled with walnuts and are made with suet instead of butter. As you roll the dough, the layers become paper thin and the result is a deliciously flaky pastry rolled round a sweet, nutty filling.

Kiflici od Sala

To make about twenty crescents:

1 oz (25 g) fresh yeast or 1 tablespoon dried
4 fl oz (125 ml) warm milk
2 egg yolks
grated rind 1 lemon
1½ oz (40 g) icing sugar
1 lb (450 g) strong plain flour
1 teaspoon salt
8 oz (225 g) vegetarian suet

Filling:

6 oz (175 g) walnuts, ground
6 oz (175 g) caster sugar
½ teaspoon vanilla essence
4 tablespoons milk

Topping:

2 oz (50 g) walnuts, ground
1 egg yolk, beaten
1½ oz (40 g) caster sugar

In a large mixing bowl, sprinkle the yeast into the milk and leave it to stand – five minutes for fresh yeast and 15 for dried. Stir in the egg yolks, lemon rind, icing sugar, 9 oz (250 g) of the flour and the salt. Mix everything to a dough. Turn it on to a floured board and knead it until it is smooth. Return it to the bowl, cover it and leave it in a warm place for 30 minutes.

Mix the remaining flour with the suet. Roll the dough into a ¼ inch (6 mm) thick rectangle. Sprinkle one third of the suet mixture over two thirds of the dough. Fold the dough and let it stand for 30 minutes. Repeat this twice more, giving the dough a quarter turn each time.

To make the filling, mix together the walnuts, caster sugar and vanilla essence. Bring the milk to the boil, stir it into the walnuts and sugar and leave the mixture until it is cool.

Roll out the dough again and cut it into 6 inch (15 cm) triangles. Roll the triangles into crescent shapes, filling them with the walnut mixture (see page 21). Lay the crescents on floured baking sheets. Brush them with the beaten egg yolk and scatter them with the walnuts. Leave them in a warm place for 20 minutes to prove.

Preheat the oven to 425°F/220°C/gas 7.

Bake the crescents for 15 minutes, or until they are golden brown.

Lift them on to wire racks and dust them with the sugar while they are still warm.

● *A generous slice, Romania*

Remove any rind and bones from the pork belly and dice the meat. Place it in a frying pan and set it on a low heat. Cook it gently for about 30 minutes, stirring frequently, so the pieces become golden brown and crisp. Lift them out with a perforated spoon and drain them on paper towels. Use the fat that is produced as part of the lard to be used in the recipe.

Sprinkle the yeast into half the milk and leave it for 5 minutes. Place the flour in a bowl, make a well in the centre and pour in the yeast mixture and the remaining milk. Add the pork pieces and 2 egg yolks and season well. Mix everything to a dough. Turn it on to a floured work surface and knead it until it is smooth. Return it to the bowl, cover it and leave it in a warm draught-free place for about 1 hour, or until it has doubled in size.

Preheat the oven to 425°F/220°C/gas 7.

Roll out the dough to a 1 inch (2.5 cm) thick square. Spread it with one third of the lard, fold it in half and roll it out again. Repeat this twice more, the last time rolling to a thickness of ¾ inch (2 cm). Cut the dough into 2 inch (5 cm) squares. Place them on a floured baking sheet and cut a shallow, diamond-shaped grid pattern on top of each one.

Brush the squares with the remaining egg yolk. Leave them in a warm place for 10 minutes and bake them for 15 minutes, or until they are golden brown and risen. Serve them hot.

You will find many savoury breads in Eastern Europe. The following buns containing pork pieces are another Balkan recipe. In truth, they are more like a rich, flaky pastry than a bread, but make an excellent lunch and are ideal for picnics.

In some recipes, 3 fl oz (90 ml) of the milk can be replaced by dry white wine, which gives them extra flavour. The use of bacon was my own idea, but it works extremely well. The dough can also be stamped into rounds rather than cut into squares.

Cheese is a popular ingredient in Eastern European savoury breads. Rounds of flat bread layered with the local sirene cheese make up the following Bulgarian recipe. Sirene cheese is a brined goat's cheese, similar to feta, which can be used as a substitute. Serve it warm, while the cheese is still soft, and accompany it with a salad.

Pogacice sa Ovarcima

To make about sixteen flat buns:

12 oz (350 g) pork belly or 8 oz (225 g) unsmoked bacon
½ oz (10 g) fresh yeast or 2 teaspoons dried
5 fl oz (150 ml) warm milk
8 oz (225 g) strong plain flour
3 egg yolks
salt and freshly ground black pepper
4 oz (110 g) lard

Tootmanik s Gotovo Testo

To make one 10 × 8 inch (25.5 cm) loaf:

basic bread dough (see page 12) made with 1 lb (450 g) strong plain flour
5 oz (150 g) butter, melted
8 oz (225 g) feta cheese, grated
1 egg, beaten

● *Tootmanik s Gotovo Testo*

● *Khliab Raiska Ptitsa*

Make the bread dough and leave it to rise. Divide it into nine pieces and roll each piece into an 8 inch (20 cm) diameter circle. Stack the circles in threes, using half the butter to brush between them. Roll each stack into a 10 × 8 inch (25.5 × 20 cm) rectangle.

Brush a 10 × 8 inch (25.5 × 30 cm) baking tin with a little of the butter. Mix the beaten egg into the cheese. Place a sheet of dough in the tin, brush it with the butter and spoon over half the egg and cheese mixture. Place another sheet of dough on top and do the same. Place the remaining sheet of dough on top and brush it with the remaining butter. Leave the loaf in a warm place for 30 minutes or until it has doubled in size.

Preheat the oven to 350°F/180°C/gas 4.

Bake the loaf for 35 minutes or until it is golden brown.

Serve the loaf warm, if possible.

Sirene cheese is also served in a salad with tomatoes and cucumber. It is accompanied by small bread rolls and a bowl of mixed herbs and spices called Ciubritsa, after the local herb, similar to tarragon. Small pieces of bread are broken off, dipped into the Ciubritsa and eaten with the salad.

In Bulgaria, Tootmanik s Gotovo Testo is accompanied by a drink of tea or yoghurt. Another loaf, also from Bulgaria, containing sirene cheese, is the Bird of Paradise Bread, Khliab Raiska Ptitsa, so-called because of its colourful decoration. It is a rich loaf, similar to a Brioche, lightly flavoured with the salty cheese. As before, I have used feta cheese as an alternative.

Khliab Raiska Ptitsa

To make one 8 inch (20 cm) round loaf:

1 oz (25 g) fresh yeast or 1 tablespoon dried
4 tablespoons warm water
1 lb (450 g) strong plain flour
2 teaspoons salt
3 fl oz (90 ml) plain yoghurt
4 eggs
2 oz (50 g) feta cheese, crumbled and sieved

Decoration:

1 egg, beaten
3 tablespoons milk
red pepper cut into a star shape, about 1 inch (2.5 cm) across
4 triangles Munster or Edam cheese about ¼ inch (5 mm) thick
4 × 1 inch (2.5 cm) squares cooked ham, about ¼ inch (5 mm) thick
4 black olives, stoned

In a small bowl, sprinkle the yeast into the water. Leave this to stand – five minutes for fresh yeast and 15 for dried. Place the flour and salt in a bowl and make a well in the centre. Add the yeast mixture, yoghurt, eggs and feta cheese. Mix everything to a dough. Turn it on to a floured work surface and knead it until

● *At a traditional water mill, Armenia*

In a large mixing bowl, sprinkle the yeast into the water and leave it to stand – five minutes for fresh yeast and 15 for dried. Stir in the milk, sugar, cardamom, eggs and butter. Mix the flour with the salt and then gradually beat it into the yeast mixture. Knead the dough in the bowl until it is smooth (see page 13). Cover it and leave it in a warm place for 1½ hours, or until it has doubled in size.

Preheat the oven to 375°F/190°C/gas 4. Knead the dough again and divide it into three equal parts. Form each one into a plait (see page 18). Alternatively, make one long plait and join the ends to make the traditional wreath. You can also make the dough into a crown. Form it into a round and make a hole in the centre using the rounded handle of a knife or a wooden spoon. Then, using your hands, make the hole larger. Using sharp kitchen scissors, cut two thirds of the way into the ring from the outside at 1½ inch (4 cm) intervals all round the edge. Place the loaves on floured baking sheets and leave them for 20 minutes to prove. At this point they will look very flat and moist, but do not worry, they will rise considerably during baking. Brush them with the egg glaze and sprinkle them with the sugar. Bake the loaves for 25 minutes, or until they are lightly browned and sound hollow when tapped. Cool them on wire racks.

Many Christmas or mid-winter breads, like Pulla, have for centuries been baked in the shapes of animals. This goes back to the times when animals were sacrificed to the gods at the darkest time of the year. Small farmers were very poor and often could not spare an animal so, as an alternative, they fashioned them out of dough, and offered them instead.

DENMARK

Denmark is the smallest of the Scandinavian countries, but it is also the most southerly and the greenest, with good pastures producing butter for spreading on to dark rye breads and for making rich yeasted doughs for the famous Danish pastries.

Both barley and rye are grown on the largest, most northern island, but much of the grain for Danish bread is imported. Rye bread was for many centuries the staple of the Danish diet, eaten with herring and sour milk for breakfast or made into a soup with beer and milk for the evening meal. It even formed part of an old-fashioned dessert, which was made by leaving a bowl of milk to sour on a window ledge and serving it sprinkled with sugar and crumbs of sourdough rye bread.

The Swedish smörgåsbord came originally from Denmark where it is called smørrebrød, literally meaning buttered bread. What was originally a simple lunch of buttered bread topped with pickle and herring has become the groaning board that tourists now find. In Denmark, however, the slice of bread topped with something savoury is still a popular lunch. The preferred bread is a sour rye, dark, moist and close-textured. It is well buttered, preventing the bread from becoming soggy or impregnated with other flavours. Cold meats, sliced sausage, marinated fish, seafood or cheese can all be used in the typical open sandwich and these are garnished with a range of salad vegetables and pickles.

The bread below is typical of a Danish rye bread. It is close-textured, dark and strong flavoured, and is excellent for open sandwiches. Its slight sweetness contrasts well with savoury and sharp flavours. Ever since I was given black bread as a child, by our Scandinavian neighbours, I have adored it and been searching for something that resembles it. This is the closest that I have come, although it is slightly lighter in colour.

Rugbrod

To make two small, round loaves:

1 oz (25 g) fresh yeast or 1 tablespoon dried
12 fl oz (300 ml) warm water
8 oz (225 g) rye meal
12 oz (350 g) strong plain flour
2 teaspoons salt
2 tablespoons caraway seeds
2 oz (50 g) molasses
1½ oz (40 g) butter, softened

Place a little of the water in a large bowl and sprinkle in the yeast. Leave it five minutes for fresh yeast and 15 for dried. Mix together the flours, salt and caraway seeds. Add the remaining water, the molasses and the butter to the yeast and gradually add the flours, stirring at first and kneading with your hand towards the end.

Turn the dough on to a floured work surface and knead it until it is smooth. Return it to the bowl, cover it with a clean, dry cloth and leave it in a warm, draught-free place to rise for 1 hour, or until it has doubled in size.

Preheat the oven to 350°F/180°C/gas 4.

Knead the dough again and divide it into two. Form each piece into a small, round loaf and lay it on a floured baking sheet. Bake them for 40 minutes or until they are brown and sound hollow when tapped. Cool them on a wire rack.

● *Danish Pastries (see page 110)*

Pumpernickel-type bread, made commercially by steaming the dough in enclosed containers for long periods, is also much used for open sandwiches and smørrebrød. Crispbreads and Rusks, such as the Swedish ones that follow, are also popular.

The Danes are famous for their pastries, which are now made all over the world. They are called Danish pastries in the English-speaking world, Kopenhagener in Germany and Austria, and, strangely, in Denmark they are called Wienerbrot or Vienna bread. The story attached to them goes some way to explain why. In the sixteenth century, a young French baker called Claudius Gelée was one day making Brioches and forgot to put in the butter. He was just about to knead some into the dough when he was interrupted. Not wishing his mistake to be discovered, he folded the dough over the butter and rolled it out several times. He was surprised to find that the butter did not run all over the place when the dough was in the oven – instead, the finished pastry was light and flaky and tasty. Gelée opened his own bakery in Paris to sell his delicacies, before being invited to Florence by the Italian Mosca brothers. Subsequently they took Gelée's recipe for pasta 'fogliate' or 'dough in layers' to Vienna, where *they* met two Danish bakers. The Danes, in turn, learned the recipe, but added their own finishing touch – a sweet filling – thus making the Danish pastry an early example of European co-operation.

Danish Pastries

To make about thirty pastries:

10 fl oz (275 ml) milk
7 oz (200 g) butter, chilled
1 oz (25 g) sugar
1 egg
1 egg yolk
1½ oz (40 g) fresh yeast or 1½ tablespoons dried
1 lb (450 g) strong plain flour
½ teaspoon salt
¼ teaspoon ground cardamom

Place the milk, 1 oz (25 g) of the butter and the sugar in a saucepan and heat them gently, stirring until the butter has melted and the sugar dissolved. Cool them to lukewarm. Beat in the egg and egg yolk and add the yeast (dried yeast should be dissolved first). Leave to stand – five minutes for fresh yeast and fifteen for dried.

Place the flour in a bowl and toss in the salt and cardamom. Make a well in the centre and pour in the yeast mixture. Mix everything to a dough. Turn it on to a floured work surface and knead it until it is smooth. Form the dough into a cube shape, put it in a plastic bag and chill it in the refrigerator for 20 minutes.

Place the remaining butter between two pieces of clingfilm and bang it with a rolling pin into an 8 × 4 inch (20 × 10 cm) rectangle. Take out the dough and roll it into a rectangle measuring 16 × 8 inches (40 × 20 cms). Lay the butter in the centre and fold the dough over it. Roll out the dough to a rectangle ¾ inch (2 cm) thick. Fold the dough into three. Place it in the bag again and refrigerate for 10 minutes. Repeat this rolling, folding and chilling process three more times.

After the final chilling, roll out the dough and fold it as before. Then cut it crossways into three pieces. You can now make three different types of Danish pastries.

Fruit Snails

1 oz (25 g) butter, softened
1 oz (25 g) caster sugar
1 teaspoon ground cinnamon
1 oz (25 g) sultanas
⅓ recipe Danish Pastry dough, as above

Beat the sugar and cinnamon into the butter and fold in the sultanas. Roll out the dough to a ¼ inch (6 mm) thick rectangle and spread it evenly with the filling. Roll up the dough along one long side and cut it into 1 inch (2.5 cm) thick slices. Lay the slices on a floured baking sheet.

Almond-filled Coxcombs

2 oz (50 g) ground almonds
2 oz (50 g) caster sugar
1 tablespoon beaten egg
3 drops almond essence
⅓ recipe Danish Pastry dough, as above

In a bowl, mix together the ground almonds and sugar. Bind them together with the egg and beat in the almond essence.

Roll the dough into a long, 8 inch (20 cm) wide rectangle. Spread half the width with the filling. Fold over the other half and cut the folded dough into 4 inch (10 cm) squares. Make three cuts in the folded side of the dough, from the fold to within ½ inch (1 cm) of the opposite side. Lay the pastries on a floured baking sheet and gently spread out the sections.

● *The sign of the baker, Copenhagen*

Custard-filled Pinwheels

1 egg yolk
1 tablespoon flour
1 teaspoon cornflour
1 tablespoon sugar
5 fl oz (150 ml) milk
3 drops vanilla essence
1/3 recipe Danish Pastry dough, as above

Beat the egg yolk lightly in a bowl and work in the flour and cornflour and 4 tablespoons of the milk. Pour the remaining milk into a saucepan and heat it to just below boiling point. Gradually stir the hot milk into the yolk mixture. Return everything to the saucepan and stir over a low heat until you have a thick, bubbling sauce. Remove the sauce from the heat and beat in the vanilla essence. Cool the mixture completely.

To make the pinwheels, roll out the dough to a thickness of ¼ inch (5 mm) and cut it into 6 inch (15 cm) squares. Cut from each corner to within ½ inch (1 cm) of the centre. Place a portion of the filling in the centre. Fold alternate sections to the middle so the points slightly overlap, and seal them by gently pressing down in the centre.

Baking

Lay the pastries on floured baking sheets and leave them in a warm place for 20 minutes to prove. Preheat the oven to 400°F/200°C/gas 6. Bake the pastries for 20 minutes or until they are golden brown. Cool them on wire racks.

Finishing

The pastries can be served as they are or drizzled with a simple icing made from 2 oz (50 g) icing sugar and a little water. Halved glacé cherries may be used as a decoration.

The basic Danish Pastry dough can also be made into the Old-fashioned Butter Cake. This is made in a round cake tin and consists of a circle of dough topped with more dough made into circles, spirals or other elaborate shapes. Sometimes a hole is left in the centre and filled with butter, dark brown sugar and raisins.

Old-fashioned Butter Cake

To make one 8 inch (20 cm) diameter cake:
2 oz (50 g) unsalted butter, softened
2 oz (50 g) soft brown sugar
2 teaspoons almond essence
½ quantity Danish pastry dough, as above
8 oz (225 g) icing sugar, ½ oz (15 g) butter or margarine and 2 tablespoons boiling water, for icing

Beat together the butter, sugar and almond essence.

Divide the dough in half and roll one piece into an 8 inch (20 cm) circle. Press it into a shallow, 8 inch (20 cm) diameter cake tin. Roll the remaining piece into a 14 inch (35 cm) square and spread half of it with the butter mixture. Fold the other half of the dough over the top and seal the edges. Cut the folded dough into 2 inch (5 cm) wide strips and roll up each one. Tuck the ends of the strip underneath the roll to prevent them from unwinding in the oven. Place the rolls of dough on top of the round of dough in the tin, evenly spaced and with one in the centre.

Leave the cake for 20 minutes in a warm place to prove.

Preheat the oven to 350°F/180°C/gas 6.

Bake the cake for 45 minutes or until it is golden brown and crisp.

Cool it on a wire rack. Make up icing and drizzle it all over the top before serving.

● *Semla*

anish pastries are eaten at coffee time, alongside other enriched breads such as the Pulla (see page 107) or the Kringle which, besides cardamom, contains raisins, candied peel and almonds.

A similar mixture of nuts and fruits is used to make the Julekage, Christmas Cake.

Julekage

To make one large round loaf or two plaited loaves:

1 oz (25 g) fresh yeast or 1 tablespoon dried
10 fl oz (275 ml) warm milk
2 eggs, beaten
grated rind ½ lemon
6 cardamom seeds, freshly crushed
½ teaspoon ground cinnamon
2 oz (50 g) sugar
½ teaspoon vanilla essence
1 lb (450 g) strong plain flour
½ teaspoon salt
4 oz (110 g) butter, softened
2 oz (50 g) candied fruits, chopped
2 oz (50 g) slivered almonds
2 oz (50 g) sultanas
one egg, beaten

lace half the milk in a large mixing bowl and sprinkle in the yeast. Leave it five minutes for fresh yeast and 15 for dried. Add the remaining milk, the eggs, lemon rind, cardamom and cinnamon, the sugar and vanilla essence. Add the salt to the flour and then gradually mix them into the milk mixture. Knead the dough in the bowl until it is smooth. With it still in the bowl, knead in the butter, candied fruits, almonds and sultanas. Cover the dough and leave it in a warm place for 1½ hours or until it has doubled in size.

Preheat the oven to 350°F/180°C/gas 4. Knead the dough on a floured work surface. Either form it into a ball and put it on to a floured baking sheet or divide it into two and form each piece into a plait (see page 18), again laying the finished loaves on a floured baking sheet. Leave the loaves to prove for 20 minutes in a warm place. Brush them with the beaten egg.

Bake the large loaf for 45 minutes and the smaller ones for 35 minutes. They will be well browned and should sound hollow when tapped. Cool them on a wire rack.

SWEDEN

he Swedes have a wide variety of breads, most of which are based on rye flour or meal. They range from rich Pumpernickel types to the lighter ones made from the finer grades of rye flour. Crispbreads, called Knackebrod, are extremely popular, as are the twice-baked rolls called Rusks or Crisprolls, which are similar to the Kavring from Norway (see page 120).

Traditionally, Swedish bread has a bitter-sweet flavour, the result of a combination of rye flour and molasses, but nowadays, mainly due to a large immigrant population, there is a greater variety of unsweetened bread in the shops. Caraway and fennel seeds are also popular flavourings.

The Swedes have many special-occasion breads. On Shrove Tuesday, the following buns, called Semla or Semlor, are served as a dessert. Traditionally, they should be served in a bowl of milk, but if bread and milk is not to your taste, the milk can be omitted. Without it, they make a delicious teatime treat, rather like English cream buns. The buns themselves are soft and golden, with a thin, crisp crust.

Semla

To make sixteen small round buns:

½ oz (10 g) fresh yeast or 2 teaspoons dried
4 fl oz (120 ml) warm water
1 egg, beaten
6 fl oz (175 ml) warm milk
2 oz (50 g) sugar
4 cardamom seeds, freshly crushed
4 oz (110 g) butter, softened
1 lb (450 g) strong plain flour
½ teaspoon salt
1 egg, beaten

Filling:

4 oz (110 g) ground almonds
4 oz (110 g) caster sugar
2 tablespoons beaten egg
½ teaspoon almond essence
5 fl oz (150 ml) double cream, whipped

Finishing:

2 tablespoons icing sugar for dusting (optional)
hot milk

In a large bowl, dissolve the yeast in the water and leave it for 5 minutes. Beat in the egg, milk, sugar, cardamom and butter. Mix the flour and salt together. Gradually beat the flour into the yeast mixture. Knead the mixture in the bowl until it is smooth and shiny (see page 13). Cover it and leave it in a warm place for 1 hour or until it has doubled in size.

Preheat the oven to 400°F/200°C/gas 6. Knead the dough on a floured work surface, divide it into sixteen pieces and shape each piece into a round bun. Place the buns on floured baking sheets without flattening them. Leave them in a warm place for 20 minutes to prove. Brush the buns with the beaten egg and bake them for 15 minutes or until they are golden brown. Cool them on wire racks.

To make the filling, mix together the almonds, sugar, egg and almond essence. Divide it into sixteen pieces and form each piece into a disc shape.

Slit each bun in half horizontally, leaving one side joined. Place a portion of the almond paste inside and top it with the cream. Sieve icing sugar over the top of the buns if wished.

To serve, spoon hot milk into small dishes and place a filled bun in the centre.

Lussekatter

To make eight cats or one wreath:

1 oz (25 g) fresh yeast or 1 tablespoon dried
4 tablespoons warm water
6 fl oz (175 ml) milk
1 teaspoon saffron threads
4 oz (110 g) butter, softened
4 oz (110 g) sugar
2 eggs, beaten
1 lb (450 g) strong plain flour
4 oz (110 g) sultanas
1 egg, beaten

Decoration

for cats: 24 raisins
for wreath: 2 tablespoons slivered almonds, 2 tablespoons white sugar

Many Swedish speciality breads are made around Christmas time. Prastens Har (priest's hair) is white wheat bread shaped like a curled wig with raisins in the curls. Munkar (monks) are deep-fried yeasted Doughnuts, and Kringlor are twist-shaped buns. Tunnbrod (thin bread) is a thin, round, flat bread that is baked on a griddle and folded or rolled. It used to be made only once a year and piled in stacks for keeping, each stack made from 1½ barrels of flour.

The thirteenth of December is St. Lucia's day, when the oldest girl of each family dresses as the Queen of Light, with a crown of candles on her head, and gives saffron buns to the rest of the household. These buns have been made in many different shapes, but the most popular has always been the cat, and so the buns are now called Lussekatter (Lucy's Cats). The spiral patterns from which the shape is formed are very old, making the probable origin of the buns pre-Christian. The basic spirals can be placed together to make one large loaf, or the dough can be made into a plaited wreath. The buns themselves are soft and sweet and a beautiful yellow colour.

● *Lussekatter*

In a small bowl, add the yeast to the water and leave it to stand – five minutes for fresh yeast and 15 for dried. Place the milk and saffron into a saucepan. Set them on a low heat and bring them slowly to the boil, stirring, so that the milk turns golden. Strain the milk into a large mixing bowl. Stir in the butter and sugar and cool to lukewarm. Stir in the yeast and eggs.

Mix the flour with the salt and beat it into the yeast mixture. Add the sultanas. Knead the dough in the bowl until it is smooth (see page 13). Cover it and leave it in a warm place for 1½ hours, or until it has doubled in size.

Preheat the oven to 375°F/190°C/gas 5. Knead the dough on a floured work surface and divide it into 16 pieces. To make the cats, roll each piece of dough into a sausage shape about 10 inches (25.5cm) long. Form eight of the pieces into an 'S' shape, curling round the ends to make spirals, the top spiral slightly smaller than the bottom one. Form the other eight pieces into reverse 'S' shapes and spiral the ends as before. Cross one forward-facing piece diagonally over one reverse-facing piece, and press lightly down in the centre. Place the formed cats on to floured baking sheets and press three raisins into each one to make the eyes and nose. Leave them in a warm place for 20 minutes to prove.

To make the wreath, take off about one eighth of the dough and reserve it. Divide the rest into three pieces. Roll each one into a rope about 25 inches (62 cm) long and plait them. Form the plait into a ring, joining the ends securely. Roll the reserved piece of dough into a long rope. Loop it over the join and form it into a bow. Place the wreath on a floured baking sheet and leave it in a warm place to prove for 20 minutes. Brush it with the beaten egg and scatter it with the almonds and sugar.

Bake the cats for 20 minutes and the wreath for 35 minutes, or until they are golden brown and sound hollow when tapped.

The traditional dish for serving on Christmas Eve is a home-cooked, lightly-salted ham and the stock in which it is cooked is still saved for the family custom of 'doppa y grytan', dipping in the pot. Sometimes, this is simply a dip into the stockpot to bring good luck and food for the coming year; in other households, the stock is specially made into a clear soup that is served in a large tureen, and surrounded by bread that has been torn into small pieces in readiness for dipping. Once, the bread was always made at home, but now you can go out and buy small round loaves especially made for the Christmas 'dip in the pot', known simply as Doppbrod.

Doppbrod

To make four small, round loaves:
1½ oz (40 g) fresh yeast or 1½ tablespoons dried
3 fl oz (90 ml) warm water
1 lb (450 g) rye meal
10 oz (275 g) strong plain flour
1 tablespoon salt
1 tablespoon fennel seeds
1 tablespoon anise seeds
15 fl oz (425 ml) warm milk
2 tablespoons sugar
1 oz (25 g) butter, softened

In a small bowl, dissolve the yeast in the water and leave it to stand – five minutes for fresh yeast and 15 for dried. In a large bowl, mix together the rye meal and strong flour, salt, and fennel and anise seeds. Make a well in the centre. Pour in the yeast mixture and begin to mix in a little flour from the sides of the well. Add the milk, sugar and butter, and mix everything to a dough. Turn the dough on to a floured work surface and knead it until it is smooth. Return it to the bowl, cover it and leave it in a warm place

● *Flourishing wheat field, Denmark*

for approximately 1 hour, or until it has about doubled in size.

Preheat the oven to 400°F/200°C/gas 5. Knead the dough again and divide it into four equal pieces. Form each piece into a round loaf and place it on a floured baking sheet. Leave the loaves in a warm place to prove for 20 minutes. Bake them for 30 minutes or until they sound hollow when tapped. Cool them on wire racks.

FINLAND

Most of the bread in Finland is made from rye flour. It has been proved to be the most nutritious in the world, and from it the Finnish stamina and strength of character is said to derive.

At one time, all bread was made in the home and there were many regional differences. In the east of the country, for example, bread was made once a week. In the west, baking days were much less frequent and bread could be stored for several months before being eaten.

The following two breads are typical of the Finnish style. The first, Suomalaisleipa, is a leavened rye bread, mid-brown in colour, light in texture, and best eaten when it is fresh.

● *Fertile soil for agriculture*

Turn the dough on to a floured work surface and knead it, using the remaining rye meal. Return the dough to the bowl, cover it and leave it in a warm place for 1 hour, or until it has doubled in size.

Preheat the oven to 375°F/190°C/gas 5. Knead the dough again and form it into a round loaf. Put it on to a floured baking sheet and leave it in a warm place for 20 minutes to prove.

Bake the loaf for 40 minutes, or until it has a hard brown crust and sounds hollow when tapped. Cool it for a while on a wire rack.

The second bread – literally 'Rye-bread rounds' – is of the type that is made into rings and would once have been strung on poles and stored in the rafters of the roof. It is made by a sourdough method with rye meal only, and is close-textured, dark, strong-flavoured, but surprisingly soft, and delicious with butter, cheese and cold smoked meats.

Nowadays it is eaten fresh, but in the old days, during storage, it would have become like a crisp Rusk. Large batches of this type of bread were often made during springtime, before the ice melted, and kept in store for the summertime.

Suomalaisleipa

To make one round loaf:

1 oz (25 g) fresh yeast or 1 tablespoon dried
10 fl oz (275 ml) warm water
1 tablespoon dark Muscovado sugar
½ oz (10 g) butter, softened
8 oz (225 g) strong plain flour
6 oz (175 g) rye meal
1½ teaspoons salt

In a large mixing bowl, sprinkle the yeast into half the water and leave it to stand – five minutes for fresh yeast and 15 for dried. Stir in the remaining water, the sugar, butter, all the plain flour, 4 oz (110 g) of the rye meal and the salt. Knead the mixture in the bowl to make a smooth dough (see page 13). Cover it with a clean dry cloth and leave it in a warm place for 10 minutes.

Ruisreikaleivat

To make three rings and three small buns:

First Day:

1¾ pints (1 litre) water
1 oz (25 g) fresh yeast or 1 tablespoon dried
3 rye crispbreads (such as Ryvita)
18 oz (500 g) rye meal

Second Day:

2 oz (50 g) fresh yeast or 2 tablespoons dried
2 tablespoons salt
1 lb (450 g) rye meal

● *Ruisreikaleivat*

On the first day, dissolve the yeast in the water, crumble in the Crispbreads and stir in the 18 oz (500 g) rye meal. Cover and leave in a warm place overnight.

On the second day, with the dough still in the bowl, knead in the yeast, salt and further rye meal. Turn the dough on to a floured work surface and knead it. It will be soft and sticky, but keep going. You will have to use quite a bit of extra flour for your hands and the work surface. Return the dough to the bowl, cover it and leave it in a warm place to rise for 1 hour or until it has doubled in size.

Preheat the oven to 450°F/225°C/gas 7. Knead the dough again. It will still be very moist. Divide it in three and make each piece into a round, flat loaf. Using a pastry cutter dipped in flour, stamp out a 2½ inch (6 cm) round from the centre of each one. Put the loaves and the middles on to floured baking sheets and leave them to prove for 30 minutes.

Bake the loaves for 25 minutes and the middles for 10 minutes. Cool them on wire racks.

Wheat and barley flours are also used in Finland, but in much smaller quantities. The Rieska, made in the north of the country, is a flat, unleavened barley loaf and the Ohraleipa is a leavened loaf made from a mixture of wheat and barley flour, and milk. The American, whole-wheat, Graham flour is also used, in conjunction with either white wheat or rye flour. Potato bread became popular after the rather late introduction of the potato in the eighteenth century and there are also many varieties of Crispbreads and Rusks.

A definite Finnish speciality is the filled loaf, made with a leavened or unleavened dough and filled with either savoury or sweet mixtures. The most traditional fillings are fish, a mixture of pork and fish, or pork and rutabagas (swedes) or turnips, or local berries such as lingonberries and blackberries. The filling is sealed inside the dough which is frequently basted with melted lard during a long baking. When the loaf is served, the crust is separated from the filling, broken into pieces and buttered, and the filling is served alongside it. The Kalakukko, below, is a typical example. The filling is very rich and so a little will go a long way. As an alternative, replace the fish with 1 lb (450 g) of rutabaga (swede), cut into small, thin pieces. Some doughs for this type of dish are made simply of rye meal and water.

Kalakukko

To make one large filled loaf:

1 oz (25 g) fresh yeast or 1 tablespoon dried

10 fl oz (275 ml) warm water

1 lb (450 g) rye meal

2 teaspoons salt

8 oz (225 g) belly of pork rashers

1 lb (450 g) small oily fish such as sprats or sardines

2 tablespoons salt

3 oz (75 g) lard, melted

● *Rich arable land, Finland*

In a large mixing bowl, sprinkle the yeast into half the water and leave it – five minutes for fresh and 15 for dried. Add the rest of the water and then the flour and salt. Turn the dough on to a floured work surface and knead it until it is smooth. Return it to the bowl, cover it and leave it in a warm place for 1 hour or until it has doubled in size.

Remove the rind from the pork rashers and cut into 2 inch (5 cm) pieces. Head and gut the fish and remove the backbones.

Preheat the oven to 400°F/200°C/gas 6. Roll out the dough into a large round, reserving about one sixteenth. Layer the fish and pieces of pork in the centre of the dough, sprinkling them liberally with the salt. Fold over the edges of the dough and seal them. Turn the dough packet over, place it on a baking sheet and form it into an oval shape. Leave it in a warm place to prove for 30 minutes.

Place the loaf in the oven for 10 minutes. Turn the heat to 300°F/150°C/gas 3 and bake the loaf for a further 4 to 5 hours, basting it frequently with the melted lard.

Should the loaf leak, plug up the holes with the reserved dough to keep the juices inside.

Much bread in Finland is now commercially made, but the local specialities still survive. Verileipa (blood bread or black bread) was once made all over western Finland at the time of the autumn slaughters, using animal blood to enrich and colour; and there is a barley bread in Lapland, made by steeping barley in buttermilk, mixing in egg and baking the mixture to make a rich, chewy flat bread.

NORWAY

Flat breads, called Lefse, are the speciality of Norway, particularly in the rural areas. They are baked on a griddle and served with fish, mutton, cheese and pickles. Sometimes they are baked as crumbles served with soured cream, as a dessert. They are made from flour or flour mixed with mashed potato, and should be soft and pliable. Often they are made in batches to be stored and dipped in hot water to soften them before serving. Many Norwegian housewives have a special Lefse rolling pin which is ridged to make a crinkled pattern on the thin round of dough.

Lefse

To make sixteen round flat breads:

16 fl oz (450 ml) milk
2 oz (50 g) butter
1 teaspoon salt
8 oz (225 g) ordinary plain flour

Place the milk, butter and salt in a saucepan (make sure that the saucepan is large enough to take the flour later). Set them on a low heat and stir until the butter has dissolved. Bring them to the boil and stir in the flour all at once. Stir on the heat until the mixture is very thick. Take it from the heat and cool it completely.

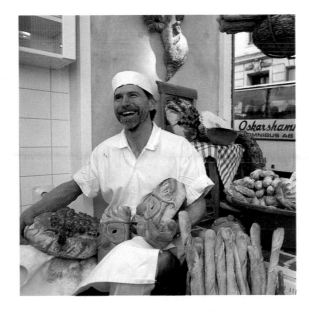

● *Special-shaped loaves, Sweden*

Divide the dough into 16 pieces and, using plenty of flour on your work surface and rolling pin, roll each piece into a flat round. Bake the rounds on an ungreased griddle, pre-heated on a medium heat, until they are speckled brown and dry looking. Stack them up as they are done.

If you are making them in advance, stack them and wrap them in greaseproof paper and store them in a cool, dry place. They will become dry and crisp. Just before serving, dip them quickly in hot water and stack them with a layer of clingfilm or a clean dry cloth between each one.

The Lefse can be served with savoury dishes or they can be covered with a mixture of melted butter, ground cinnamon and sugar, or raisins, and served rolled up like a pancake.

At country weddings in the Voss area, the local wedding cake, called Brudlaupskling, is traditionally made from huge flat white breads, layered with a mixture of butter, cheese, double cream and syrup, and served cut into squares. The tradition goes back to the days when white bread was a luxury that could only be enjoyed on special occasions.

For sandwiches, the Norwegians prefer bread made with whole-wheat flour or rye meal, often slightly sweetened with molasses, syrup or brown sugar. The following bread has a light, soft texture and slightly sweet flavour.

Hvetekake

To make two 1 lb (450 g) loaves:

1 oz (25 g) fresh yeast or 1 tablespoon dried
1 pint (570 ml) warm water
2 oz (50 g) dark Muscovado sugar
12 oz (350 g) strong plain flour
1½ oz (40 g) butter, softened
2 teaspoons salt
12 oz (350 g) whole-wheat flour

In a large bowl, stir the yeast into 16 fl oz (450 ml) of the water. Leave it five minutes for fresh yeast and 15 for dried. Stir in 1 tablespoon of the sugar and all the strong plain flour. Cover the mixture and leave it in a warm place for 30 minutes to form a sponge. In a small bowl, dissolve the rest of the sugar in the remaining water. Stir in the butter and salt. Beat the mixture into the sponge and gradually knead in the whole-wheat flour. Turn the dough on to a floured work surface and knead it until it is smooth. Return it to the bowl, cover it and leave it in a warm place for 1 hour or until it has doubled in size.

Preheat the oven to 350°F/180°C/gas 4. Cut the dough into two equal pieces and form them into loaf shapes. They can be made into round or long loaves to be baked on sheets or put into loaf tins. Leave the shaped loaves in a warm place for 20 minutes to prove.

Brush the tops of the loaves with water. Bake them for 40 minutes or until they sound hollow when tapped. Cool them on wire racks.

Like all Scandinavians, the Norwegians are fond of Crispbreads and Rusks. This recipe, although specifically from Norway, is typical of those from all the countries in the region. You can serve these crisp Kavring rolls with butter and cheese, but they also make a wonderful accompaniment to a light snack, such as a salad.

Kavring

To make twenty-four rolls:

1 oz (25 g) fresh yeast or 1 tablespoon dried
10 fl oz (275 ml) warm water
2 teaspoons sugar
1 teaspoon salt
1 oz (25 g) butter, softened
8 oz (225 g) wholemeal flour
8 oz (225 g) strong plain flour

In a large bowl, sprinkle the yeast into half the water and leave it – five minutes for fresh yeast and 15 for dried. Add the rest of the water, the sugar, salt, butter and flours. Mix them to a dough. Turn it on to a floured work surface and knead it. Return it to the bowl, cover it and leave it in a warm place for 1 hour or until it has doubled in size.

Preheat the oven to 425°F/220°C/gas 7.

Knead the dough again, divide it into 12 pieces and form each piece into a round bun. Lay the buns on floured baking sheets, without pressing them down. Leave them in a warm place for 20 minutes to prove. Bake the buns for 12 minutes, or until they are golden brown.

Cool them on wire racks.

Turn the oven down to 250°F/120°C/gas 2. Put the buns back on to the floured baking sheets and, using two forks to avoid burning yourself, tear them apart. Leave the halves split side up and put them into the oven for 1 hour so they dry out and become very crisp. They should only colour very lightly. Once again, cool them on wire racks.

These rolls stay crisp if they are stored in an airtight tin. Do not freeze them.

● *A natural bread oven in the volcanic terrain*
of north-east Iceland

ICELAND

Bread in Iceland is a mixture of the old and the new. The indigenous breads are the various kinds of flat bread that were once baked on hot stones but are now made on a griddle, and the dark, Pumper-nickel types that have a sweet-sour flavour. The newer types have been introduced only within the last twenty years, mainly from Germany.

Very little grain has ever been grown in Iceland, so most is imported, a fact which for many centuries determined the diet of the Icelandic peoples. In the thirteenth century, Iceland had an agreement with Norway by which Norway sent in six loaded food ships each year. At the beginning of the fifteenth century, however, this ceased, and for a long time no food was imported. Apparently the poor then ate dried fish instead of bread and this continued until around 1800. Even then, bread was made almost exclusively only by the better-off town dwellers. Consequently, there are only a few Icelandic bread recipes to be found.

The first recipe here is an example of a flat bread, the simplest of which are made with rye meal and water only. When mixed with milk, the breads become soft-textured. They can be served with all kinds of savoury dishes, with cheese and with paté. They are also good topped with jam.

Flatbread with Milk

To make thirty-two round, flat breads:
7 oz (200 g) rye meal
7 oz (200 g) whole-wheat flour
7 oz (200 g) ordinary plain flour
4 teaspoons baking powder
1 teaspoon salt
15 fl oz (425 ml) hot milk

Place all the flours in a bowl with the baking powder and salt. Make a well in the centre and pour in the hot milk. Mix everything to a dough and knead it until it is smooth. Divide the dough into 32 pieces and roll each one into a thin, 7 inch (18 cm) round.

Cook the rounds on a preheated, ungreased griddle, over a medium heat, until they are cooked through and speckled brown but still soft. Serve them hot, spread with butter.

Laufabread

To make eighteen flat cakes:
1 lb (450 g) ordinary plain flour
1 teaspoon baking powder
1 tablespoon sugar
1 oz (25 g) butter
8 oz (225 g) hot milk

Place the flour, baking powder and sugar in a bowl and rub in the butter. Make a well in the centre and pour in the hot milk. Mix everything to a dough and knead it until it is smooth. Divide the dough into eighteen pieces and roll each piece into a flat round. Using a sharp knife, cut a circle of eight pointed, radiating petals in each flat cake. Use the cut-out pieces to make extra cakes.

Deep fry the cakes in hot oil until they are golden brown, crisp and puffy. Drain them on paper towels and serve them hot.

Laufabread (leaf bread) are deep-fried flat, slightly sweet breads, traditionally served at Christmas to accompany the seasonal dish of salted lamb.

The Scandinavians, Germans and eastern Europeans who came to Canada and America, brought with them a preference for rye bread, which is still popular today. The following recipe, made with yeast, is based on one which appeared in *The Original Boston Cooking School Book* by Fannie Farmer, which was first published in 1896.

Fannie Farmer's Rye Bread

To make one 2 lb (1 kg) loaf:

4 tablespoons warm water
4 fl oz (120 ml) scalded milk
6 fl oz (175 ml) boiling water
1½ oz (40 g) butter
1 oz (25 g) dark Muscovado sugar
2 teaspoons salt
1 oz (25 g) fresh yeast or 1 tablespoon dried
6 oz (175 g) strong plain flour
12 oz (350 g) rye meal

In a large mixing bowl, sprinkle the yeast over the 4 tablespoons of water. Leave this to stand – five minutes for fresh yeast and 15 for dried. In another bowl, mix together the scalded milk and boiling water, and stir in the butter, sugar and salt. Cool the mixture to lukewarm and then stir it into the yeast. Stir in the flour and leave the mixture in a warm place for 30 minutes until it begins to bubble up the sides of the bowl. Add the rye meal and knead it in. Then knead the dough on a floured work surface. Return it to the bowl, cover it and leave it in a warm place for 1 hour or until it has doubled in size.

Preheat the oven to 400°F/200°C/gas 6. Knead the dough again and form it into a rectangular loaf. Place it in a 2 lb (1 kg) loaf tin and leave it for 20 minutes in a warm place to prove. Bake the loaf for 45 minutes, or until it is golden brown and sounds hollow when tapped. Cool it on a wire rack.

In eastern America, there were unlimited supplies of white flour, and yeast was used in preference to sourdough starters. The result of this was the development of more sophisticated bread recipes. The following buns were a favourite in Philadelphia. They are soft, sweet and spicy, with a sweet, dark-brown shiny top.

Philadelphia Sticky Buns

To make about eight buns:

1 oz (25 g) fresh yeast or 1 tablespoon dried
4 tablespoons warm water
8 fl oz (225 ml) warm milk
4 oz (110 g) butter, softened
4 oz (110 g) sugar
2 egg yolks
1 lb 2 oz (500 g) strong plain flour
1 teaspoon ground cinnamon
1 teaspoon salt

Filling and Glaze:

4 fl oz (120 ml) water
6 oz (175 g) dark Muscovado sugar
1 oz (25 g) butter
3 oz (75 g) chopped walnuts or currants

In a large mixing bowl, sprinkle the fresh yeast over the water. Leave it to stand – five minutes for fresh yeast and 15 for dried. Stir in the milk, butter, sugar and egg yolks and then the flour, cinnamon and salt. Knead the mixture in the bowl (see page 13) until it is smooth. Cover it and leave it in a warm place for 1 hour to double in size.

To make the glaze, put the water, sugar and butter into a saucepan and stir them over a low heat until the sugar and butter have dissolved.

Preheat the oven to 350°F/180°C/gas 4. Butter a 10 inch (25.5 cm) diameter cake tin. Knead the dough on a floured work surface and roll it into a rectangle 12 inches (30 cms) long and ½ inch (1 cm) thick. Gradually pour about half the sugar glaze over the surface. If you are using currants, sprinkle them all over the top; if chopped walnuts, then only sprinkle on two thirds of them. Quickly roll up the dough and cut it into 1 inch (2.5 cm) thick slices. Pour the remaining glaze into the buttered tin and scatter in the remaining walnuts. Place the rolled slices of bun on top. Leave them in a warm place for 20 minutes to prove.

Bake the buns for 30 minutes, or until they are well browned on top. Turn the whole lot together on to a wire rack and leave them, sticky side up, to cool. To serve, gently ease the buns apart with a knife.

● *Parker House Rolls (see page 132)*

• *Harvesting in Minnesota, USA*

Small white rolls in many shapes and sizes became popular in America's fashionable restaurants. The Parker House Restaurant opened in Boston in 1855 and its Parker House Rolls became essential fare at smart dinners all over the country. They are basically a light roll, enriched with milk, eggs and a little butter. Their chief distinction from any other type of roll is their folded shape.

Parker House Rolls

To make about twenty rolls:

1 oz (25 g) fresh yeast or 1 tablespoon dried
4 tablespoons warm water
8 fl oz (225 ml) warm milk
1 egg, beaten
1 lb (450 g) strong plain flour
1 teaspoon salt
1 oz (25 g) butter, melted

In a large mixing bowl, sprinkle the yeast over the warm water. Leave it to stand – five minutes for fresh yeast and 15 for dried. Stir in the milk and egg and then the flour and salt. Mix everything to a dough. Turn it on to a floured board and knead it. Return it to the bowl, cover it and leave it in a warm place for 1 hour or until it has doubled in size.

Preheat the oven to 400°F/200°C/gas 6. Knead the dough again and roll it out to a thickness of about ½ inch (1 cm). Stamp it into 3 inch (7.5 cm) rounds with a pastry cutter. Brush each with the butter. Using the back of a knife, make a deep groove across each round, then fold the round in half and press the edges together.

Place the rolls on floured baking sheets and leave them in a warm place for 20 minutes to prove. Bake them for 20 minutes, or until they are golden brown. Cool them on wire racks.

Both the Canadians and the Americans are fond of sweet breads and it is very often difficult to distinguish what is bread and what is cake. There are many different recipes, both old and modern for what the British would call tea breads – sweetened breads, raised with soda and baking powder and containing dried fruits and nuts. One from Quebec, Canada, is mixed with beer and contains walnuts and dates; another, called Paradise Lemon Bread, can be found in households in Paradise Valley, Alberta, Moncton, New Brunswick and Montreal.

Muffins and Doughnuts also fall in the middle ground between being cakes and being breads. The Doughnut recipe below comes from a descendant of one of the Scottish communities who settled in Compton County in eastern Quebec in about 1840. Doughnuts were a favourite breakfast on both sides of the border. Eat these warm, either plain, or sprinkled with sugar or drizzled with warm maple syrup.

Old-fashioned Doughnuts

To make about thirty-six doughnuts:

8 oz (225 g) sugar
1 oz (25 g) shortening or lard, melted
2 eggs, beaten
½ teaspoon vanilla essence
1 lb 2 oz (500) ordinary plain flour
2 teaspoons baking powder
1 teaspoon bicarbonate of soda
1 teaspoon salt
1 teaspoon ground nutmeg
12 fl oz (300 ml) cultured buttermilk or sour milk
oil for deep frying

Place the sugar in a large mixing bowl and beat in the shortening or lard, eggs and vanilla essence. Mix the flour with the baking powder, bicarbonate of soda, salt and nutmeg. Beat it into the sugar mixture, a little at a time, alternately with the buttermilk or sour milk. You should have a very moist dough. Place this dough, still in the bowl, in the refrigerator for 1 hour to chill and firm.

Turn the dough on to a floured work surface and coat it well with flour. Roll it out to a thickness of about ½ inch (1 cm). Stamp it into 2½ inch (6 cm) rounds and stamp a ½ inch (1 cm) hole in the centre of each one. You can use a Doughnut cutter for this or a large and a small pastry cutter or, if you do not have a small enough pastry cutter, use an apple corer for the centre hole. The dough will still be quite sticky, so flour the cutters well by dipping them into the flour bag and handle the cut Doughnuts gently, lifting them with a palette knife. Keep your fingers well floured as well.

Heat a pan of oil over a high heat. Place the Doughnut rounds in the pan about three at a time. Cook them for about a minute, until they are golden brown on one side. Turn them over and brown the other side. Lift them out with a slotted spoon and drain off the excess oil by placing them on paper towels.

Another sweet speciality is Muffins. The Muffins in Fannie Farmer's cook book are very similar to English Muffins, made with a moist dough and cooked on a griddle. However, over the years, traditional American Muffins have developed.

In a book called *Breads and More Breads*, compiled in 1941 from recipes submitted by cooks all over America, there are no fewer than thirty variations in flavourings, some of which, for example ketchup, pickle, or pepper relish, sound rather odd. Others, such as banana, sweet corn or spice, sound delicious. Here is the basic Muffin recipe, plus a few suggestions.

Muffins

To make ten Muffins:

4 oz (110 g) ordinary plain flour
4 oz (110 g) whole-wheat or Graham flour
1 teaspoon salt
2 teaspoons baking powder
2 tablespoons dark Muscovado sugar
8 fl oz (225 ml) milk
1 egg, beaten
1½ oz (40 g) shortening, melted

Preheat the oven to 400°F/200°C/gas 6. Place the flours in a bowl with the salt, baking powder and sugar. Make a well in the centre and beat in the milk, egg and shortening. Beat to make a thick batter. Half fill 10 muffin pans or muffin cases with the mixture. Place on baking sheets. Bake the Muffins for 20 minutes or until they are risen and cooked through.

Variations and Flavourings:

- use all plain flour or all whole-wheat or Graham flour.
- add 4 oz (110 g) raw blueberries.
- add 4 oz (110 g) raw cranberries, halved and mixed with 2 oz (50 g) icing sugar.
- gently stew 1 large, chopped cooking apple to a purée with 2 oz (50 g) sugar and add this to the mixture.
- add 4 oz (110 g) raisins, sultanas or chopped dates.
- add 3 oz (75 g) chopped nuts.
- add 3 oz (75 g) chocolate chips.
- add 4 oz (110 g) grated cheese.
- add 4 oz (110 g) fried bacon.

● *Old-fashioned Doughnuts*

CENTRAL AND SOUTH AMERICA

The Spanish conquered Mexico some five hundred years ago, and were amazed at many of the things they found – including the food. There were previously unknown vegetables and fruits, chocolate that was used to flavour not just drinks but rich meat dishes as well, and the most important energy provider in the diet of the native South American Indians – corn.

Corn was so essential to the lives of the Mayans that they even believed that man had been created from corn dough. Later, explorers found corn in Cuba, where it was grown in small fields and called something which sounded like 'may-ees' by the local population. To the Europeans, it therefore became 'maize'.

Maize had been developed by the native Indians of Central and South America from a variety of coarse grass which is now extinct. It bore small, inch-long ears, each wrapped in a separate husk, and had edible kernels similar to very small peas. By the time the Spaniards arrived, the Indians had developed hundreds of different varieties to suit all climates and altitudes – among them white, yellow, red and black corn, sweet corn and popcorn. There are even more varieties known today: some are best for drying and grinding into flour and others for eating.

Corn or maize meal differs from flour made with wheat in that it contains only very small amounts of gluten and other protein. However, the Indians overcame this by adding accompanying foods. Freshly-prepared maize meal was made into flat, unleavened breads, similar to the early European Hearth Cakes. Once cooked, these cakes were typically wrapped around nutritious foods such as beans, meat or fish, so providing the constituents of a healthy diet. These cakes are called Tortillas, and they are the same today as they were five hundred years ago.

Tortillas are Mexico's national bread. The name comes from the Spanish, meaning 'little cakes'. The Indians originally called them long, complicated names, according to the type of corn used in them. White corn Tortillas were Iztactlaolli, and those made from black corn were Yauhtlaolli. It was much easier to call them all Tortillas and, as the languages and races blended, the name became universal.

The Indians developed the technique for making Tortillas centuries ago. The first process involves soaking the corn kernels in a solution of lime. The kernels swell considerably and the husks loosen, to form a mixture known as *nixtamal*. This is then pounded and ground to a paste or moist dough, called *masa*.

Every Mexican woman once knew how to shape and fashion a Tortilla. She would take a small ball of masa dough, about the size of a golf ball, and pat it between her hands until it was thin and flat, before transferring it to a hot griddle. It is said that the early morning sound of Mexico was the patting of Tortillas for breakfast.

Nowadays, Tortillas are still prepared by hand, but there are also Tortilla factories and Tortilla shops which provide them in various stages of making. The masa is rarely prepared at home, but can be bought, moist and freshly prepared. For those without the time or experience to fashion the dough, a Tortilla press can be used, or Tortillas can be bought already shaped but uncooked, or completely cooked and ready to eat.

It is impossible to buy fresh masa in most countries outside of Latin America, but masa harina, dried masa, is available in specialist food shops and those selling Mexican goods. The best brand is the white masa harina, produced and packaged by the Quaker Oats company.

In the recipe below, the amount of water you need may vary with the type of masa you are able to get.

Tortillas de Maiz

To make twelve 6 inch (15 cm) Corn Tortillas:

8 oz (225 g) masa harina
10 fl oz (275 ml) warm water

Place the masa harina in a bowl and make a well in the centre. Add the water a little at a time and check the consistency of the dough. It should hold together and be moist enough to handle and roll without pieces crumbling away. Leave the dough in the bowl, cover it with a clean, dry cloth and let it rest for 15 minutes. This makes it more workable.

Form the dough into twelve pieces about the size of golf balls. Place one piece in the palm of your left hand and begin to pat it with your right (or the other way round if you are left handed). As the Tortilla begins to get larger, turn it round a little and pat it from hand to hand, gently pushing the edges round the bottom of your palm. (Apparently Mexican women used to make very thin, large Tortillas by stretching them over their knee!) Continue doing this until you have a 6 inch (15 cm) round. After several Tortillas you will begin to get the knack but, if it still proves impossible, put the ball of dough between two pieces of clingfilm and roll it with a rolling pin.

Heat an ungreased griddle over a low heat. Place one Tortilla at a time on the griddle and cook it for about one minute on each side or until it is cooked through and the sides look dry and speckled brown. Lay a clean, dry cloth over a large plate. Lay the Tortilla on it and cover it up while you cook the next. Build up a pile of Tortillas on the plate, covering them up each time.

Serve the Tortillas warm. If you want to make them in advance you can wrap them in clingfilm and store them in the refrigerator. To reheat them, sprinkle them lightly with a few drops of water and place them on the griddle again.

● *Lime-soaked maize for Tortillas*

● *Market at Port au Prince, Haiti*

Pan Dulce de Harina de Maiz

To make one 2 lb (1 kg) loaf:

1 small coconut
6 oz (175 g) cornmeal
2 oz (50 g) ordinary plain flour
1 tablespoon baking powder
½ teaspoon ground cinnamon
½ teaspoon ground nutmeg
½ teaspoon ground cloves
2 oz (50 g) sugar
½ teaspoon salt
grated rind 1 lime or lemon
1½ oz (40 g) butter
1½ oz (40 g) lard
2 eggs, beaten
4 oz (110 g) mixed raisins, sultanas and chopped mixed peel

Skewer the 'eyes' of the coconut and drain out the water. Break the coconut. Peel it, using a potato peeler, extract all the white flesh, and grate it. Reserve 4 oz (110 g) of the grated coconut. To make what is known as coconut milk, place the rest of the coconut in a blender, pour on an equal volume of hot, but not boiling, water and blend until you have a smooth, white liquid. Strain it through a sieve, pressing down hard. This is far more than you will need for the recipe, but you can keep the remainder in the refrigerator for up to two days and use it for making curries.

Preheat the oven to 350°F/180°C/gas 4. Mix together all the dry ingredients, including the sugar and the lime rind. In a large mixing bowl, cream together the butter and lard and gradually beat in the dry mixture. Beat in 3 fl oz (90 ml) of the coconut milk and the two eggs. Mix in the grated coconut and the fruits and peels. Place the mixture into a greased, 2 lb (1 kg) loaf tin. It will come half to three-quarters of the way up the sides. Bake the loaf for 35 minutes, or until it is golden brown and a skewer inserted into the centre comes out clean.

When the Europeans first sent for flour, they used it to make the breads to which they were accustomed, raised with yeast and with as much white flour as possible. These dinner rolls sound very English. You can imagine a planter's family sitting down to dinner with a roll beside each plate.

Dinner Rolls

To make twelve rolls:

1 oz (25 g) fresh yeast or 1 tablespoon dried
4 tablespoons warm water
8 fl oz (225 ml) warm milk
2 teaspoons sugar
1 teaspoon salt
1 oz (25 g) shortening
1 lb (450 g) strong plain flour

● *Pan Dulce de Harina de Maiz*

In a large mixing bowl, sprinkle the yeast into the warm water and leave it to stand – five minutes for fresh yeast and 15 for dried. Stir in the milk, sugar, salt and shortening. Add the flour and mix everything to a dough. Turn it on to a floured work surface and knead it until it is smooth. Return it to the bowl, cover it and leave it for about 1 hour or until it has doubled in size.

Preheat the oven to 400°F/200°C/gas 6. Knead the dough again. Divide it into twelve pieces and form each one into a round or oval roll. Lay the rolls on floured baking sheets and leave them in a warm place for 20 minutes to prove.

Bake the rolls for 20 minutes or until they are golden brown. Cool them on wire racks.

● *Floats*

Another very European bread which arrived in the nineteenth century is the Pan de Majorca. In 1848, an immigrant from Majorca opened up La Mallorquina restaurant in San Juan, Puerto Rico, and started to make the rolls that in his native country were called Enseimadas – sweet rolls enriched with lard and dusted with sugar. Every morning, a plate of freshly-baked Enseimadas were placed on the breakfast table. They came to be known as Pan de Majorca and can now be bought from bakers' shops in San Juan.

Pan Serra, a very close-textured loaf, is the speciality of Curaçao where it is served with the rich fish stew called Sopito. It is apparently ideal for soaking up the last remnants in the bowl.

Modern breads of the Western world have spread to all countries and the standard brown and white yeasted breads are commercially baked in most of the Islands. Baking bread dough is not, however, the only thing that you can do with it. You can also deep fry it. Floats are deep-fried circles of rich dough that puff up and become crisp and golden. In Trinidad they are the accompaniment to Accra, cakes made with salt-fish and batter. Accra and Floats, you could say, is the Trinidadian equivalent of the British fish and chips.

The Indians brought with them their own flat breads. The Chapati changed over the years to become what are now called Roti (which simply means bread), 10 inch (25.5 cm) diameter flat cakes which are cooked on a griddle. Traditionally, they are served with curries. The Indian population provides the food for the local carnival in Port of Spain. They prepare Roti literally by the stack, and fill them with spoonfuls of savoury mixtures such as beef stewed in tomatoes, potato curry and split-pea purée.

Roti are soft with a buttery outside. In Jamaica, the Indians would use their authentic ghee, a butter that has been clarified. You can clarify butter by melting and skimming it, but you can simply use plain melted butter.

Floats

To make twenty Floats:

½ oz (10 g) fresh yeast or 2 teaspoons dried
12 fl oz (300 ml) warm water
1 lb (450 g) ordinary plain flour
1 teaspoon salt
4 oz (110 g) lard
oil for deep frying

In a small bowl, sprinkle the yeast on to about 3 fl oz (90 ml) of the water. Place the flour and salt in a large mixing bowl and rub in the lard. Make a well in the centre and pour in the yeast mixture and the remaining water. Mix everything to a dough. Turn it on to a floured work surface and knead it until it is smooth. Return it to the bowl, cover it and leave it in a warm place for 45 minutes, or until it has doubled in size.

Knead the dough again and divide it into 20 small balls about 1½ inches (4 cm) in diameter. Place them on a floured board or baking sheet, cover them and leave them in a warm place for 45 minutes, or until they have doubled in size. Without any further kneading, roll each ball into a flat round about 3 inches (7.5 cm) in diameter. Heat a pan of deep oil on a high heat. Put in the Floats, one at a time, and fry them for about 1 minute on each side until they are golden brown and puffy. Drain them on paper towels and serve them warm.

Roti

To make about four Roti:

8 oz (225 g) ordinary plain flour
1 teaspoon baking powder
1 teaspoon salt
1½ oz (40 g) butter or shortening
5 fl oz (150 ml) cold water
3 oz (75 g) ghee or butter, melted

Place the flour, baking powder and salt in a bowl and rub in the butter or shortening. Make a well in the centre and add the water, a little at a time, to make a stiff dough. Place the dough on a floured work surface and knead it until it is smooth. Return it to the bowl, cover it and let it rest in a warm place for 30 minutes.

Knead the dough again and divide it into four pieces. Form each one into a ball and then roll it into a 10 inch (25.5 cm) round. Fold the round in half and then in half again. Leave the folded rounds for 15 minutes. This makes the Roti firm and easy to handle. Using your hands and a rolling pin, roll the folded pieces once more into circles.

Heat a griddle on a medium heat. Place one Roti on the griddle and cook it for 1 minute so that it is dry, but not at all coloured on the underside. Turn it over and brush it with the ghee or butter. Cook it for about three minutes longer, brushing on more ghee after the first 2 minutes. The top will bubble and sizzle. Turn the Roti over and finish cooking the first side for about 2 minutes, or until it just begins to brown. The Roti should be firm and pliable. Should the outside be too crisp, lay the Roti on a work surface and bang it with a wooden spoon or wooden mallet to make the outside flaky.

Place the Roti on a clean, dry cloth and fold the sides of the cloth over it. Cook the other Roti in the same way, adding them to the first one inside the cloth as they are done.

THE MIDDLE EAST
(INCLUDING GREECE AND TURKEY; EGYPT, TUNISIA AND MOROCCO)

There are many different peoples and cultures, three different religions and a wide variety of foods in the area that we now call the Middle East.

There has never been an official agreement as to where the Middle East begins and ends, but when, for the purposes of the Second World War, the British moved their Middle East Command to Egypt, the term came to include the countries that are at the eastern end of the Mediterranean, including Greece, Turkey and Cyprus.

The northern North African countries: Morocco, Algeria, Tunisia, Libya and Egypt, share many of the same cooking styles and they too have been included in this section.

The foods common to most of these countries are olives and their oil, beans, lentils, and lamb. There is a preference for yoghurt rather than for fresh milk, and the main source of carbohydrates is bread made from wheat flour. Rice comes a close second, but bread, or khobz, as it is called in so many of the countries, is eaten more than meat, vegetables or fruit, and its consumption is rising even now. In the Middle East, bread has kept its traditional characteristics – and in many of the countries the white sliced loaf, so common throughout the Western world, has never been popular.

Bread is seen in many Middle Eastern countries as a gift from God, and if any piece is found on the floor it is picked up with reverence and put into a place where it will not be trodden on. Indeed, housewives baking bread say a prayer before kneading and again before putting their bread into the oven, to make sure that it will be successful.

Bread is eaten with every meal. Flat breads are folded over ingredients, to become both eating utensil and food. Thicker breads are dipped into the communal pot to soak up the gravy and rich juices, and pockets of bread are filled with a variety of meats, beans and fresh salad vegetables. Left over breads are diced, crumbled or toasted to make a base for a variety of dishes.

There are hundreds of different breads in the Middle East and North Africa, but the most common, and also the oldest, is Lavash, a thin, slightly crispy bread which is baked in ovals and rounds of varying sizes, even up to 24 inches (60 cm) wide.

Because Lavash is crisp, it lasts for a long time; and in many households enough is made to last a family for up to four months, wrapped in linen for storage. Lavash is normally baked in a clay oven called a *tonir*, which is similar to the Indian tandoor, but when made out in the open, it is cooked on a *saj*, a cast-iron dome that is heated from underneath with a fire of wood chippings and camel dung.

Lavash can be baked with white flour, whole-wheat flour or a mixture. Serve it plain with curries or other hot dishes, with dips, or buttered with a salad.

● *Flat breads made for a wedding, Turkey*

149

● *Lavash*

Lavash

To make ten Lavash:

1 oz (25 g) fresh yeast or 1 tablespoon dried
10 fl oz (275 ml) warm water
1 lb (450 g) ordinary plain flour
1½ teaspoons salt

In a small bowl, sprinkle the yeast over half the water. Place the flour and salt in a mixing bowl and make a well in the centre. Pour in the yeast mixture and remaining water. Mix everything to a dough, turn it on to a floured work surface and knead it well. Return it to the bowl, cover it with a cloth and leave it in a warm place for 1 to 1½ hours or until it has doubled in size.

Preheat the oven to 400°F/200°C/gas 6. Knead the dough again, divide it into ten equal pieces and form them into balls. Roll each ball into a flat round, 8 to 10 inches (20-25.5 cms) in diameter. Prick each one all over with a fork. Line a baking sheet with aluminium foil and put it in the very bottom of the oven to heat. Lay one of the dough rounds on the foil and put it in the oven for 3 minutes or until it is cooked through and bubbly. Wrap the bread in a clean, dry cloth and cook the others in the same way, adding them to the first one as they are done. Serve the Lavash warm.

The second most popular bread is Khobz Arabi, literally Arab bread, and this has become well-known in the West in recent years as Pitta bread, from the Armenian variation of Khobz Arabi known as Pideh. Khobz Arabi can be made with white flour, whole-wheat flour or a mixture. This is the recipe that I have been using for many years.

Khobz Arabi

To make eight Pitta Breads:

basic bread dough (see page 12) made with 1 lb (450 g) strong plain or whole-wheat flour or half and half

Mix and knead the dough and leave it to rise for 1 hour. Preheat the oven to 450°F/230°C/gas 8. Knead the dough again and divide it into eight pieces. Roll each piece into an oval of 5 × 8 inches (13 × 20 cms). Leave the pieces covered with a cloth and let them prove for 20 minutes.

Flour enough baking sheets to take all the breads and place them in the oven for 5 minutes so they become really hot. Lay the breads on the baking sheets and put them in the oven for 15 minutes, or until they are only just beginning to brown.

If the breads are to be served immediately, wrap them in a clean cloth to keep them warm. You can also cool them on wire racks and warm them under the grill when needed.

● *Sieving grain (left) and baking (centre) in Cyprus. Stall in Istanbul, Turkey (right)*

GREECE

Many people regard Greece as being a Western country, but most of its influences, including culinary ones, have come from the East. Pitta bread has become almost synonymous with Greek food in recent years. The other Greek everyday bread is a crusty plain loaf, sometimes round and sometimes oval, golden brown and often sprinkled with sesame seeds.

The main religion in Greece is Orthodox Christianity and the highlight of the Orthodox year is Easter. During the seven weeks of Lent, devout Christians in Greece abstain from meat and fish and sometimes also eggs, butter, milk and cheese. Easter, then, is a time of great feasting as well as religious celebration. To accompany the Eastern lamb there are salads, yoghurt, feta cheese, hard-boiled eggs dyed red, and the special, rich bread called Tsoureki. Tsoureki is baked in many different shapes, the most common of which is the spiral with a red egg in the centre.

I must admit that I wondered about baking a hard-boiled egg, but I needn't have worried. The egg nestled comfortably in the dough and didn't explode, but made the loaf look rather turban-like when it came from the oven. The bread itself is soft, rich and sweet and, personally, I prefer the lemon flavouring to the caraway. We divided the egg up. It tasted just like a hard-boiled egg, except that the part that stood up from the dough was slightly browned on top and tougher than ordinary boiled white. Tsoureki makes an unusual Easter treat in any country.

Tsoureki

To make one 8 inch (20 cm) diameter loaf:
1 oz (25 g) fresh yeast or 1 tablespoon dried
4 tablespoons warm milk
10 oz (275 g) strong plain flour
2 eggs, beaten
½ teaspoon salt
2 oz (50 g) sugar
½ teaspoon caraway seeds, or grated rind ½ lemon
3 oz (75 g) butter, preferably unsalted, softened
1 egg, hard boiled with red food colouring in the water
1 egg yolk

Sprinkle the yeast into a large mixing bowl. Add the milk and 1 oz (25 g) of the flour. Cover the mixture and leave it in a warm place for 20 minutes to form a sponge. Mix in the eggs, the remaining flour, salt, sugar and caraway seeds or lemon rind. Knead in the butter. Turn the dough on to a floured work surface and knead it until it is smooth. Return it to the bowl, cover it and leave it in a warm place for 1 hour to double in size.

Preheat the oven to 350°F/180°C/gas 4. Knead the dough again. Roll

151

it into a long sausage shape about 1½ inches (4 cm) in diameter. On a baking sheet, coil it round into a tight spiral about 6 inches (15 cm) in diameter. Press the dyed hard-boiled egg into the centre and brush the loaf with the egg yolk.

Bake the loaf for about 45 minutes, or until it is golden brown.

The Greeks also bake a special bread on New Year's Eve. Called Vassilopitta, it is sometimes made by the same recipe used for Tsoureki, but sometimes with different proportions of milk, butter and eggs. It is baked in a round tin called a *tapsi*, brushed with egg white and sprinkled with sesame seeds. All the family assemble to eat this special bread, which is cut by the head of the household. The first piece for Christ, and the second, for the house, are put aside. The third piece, is for the head of the house and the fourth for his wife, and so on according to age, and boys before girls, until every member has a slice.

TURKEY

One of the everyday breads of Turkey is a sourdough bread made with white wheat flour which was once baked in outdoor brick or clay ovens.

The following recipe comes from Arto der Haroutounian's book, *Middle Eastern Cookery*, published in 1982. It is, he says, a speciality of Antakya (the once famous Antioch). It is also popular in Greece where it is eaten during Lent to relieve a monotonous diet. In Cyprus it is called Elioti and in Armenia, Tsit-hats, and it can also be found in northern Syria where it is called Khubz-el-zeytoun.

Essentially, this is a white bread dough, rolled around a filling of olives and onions. It is excellent with salads and soups

Zeytin Ekmegi

To make two 16 inch (40 cm) long Olive Breads:

basic bread dough (see page 12) made with 1 lb (450 g) strong plain flour
3 tablespoons olive oil
1 medium onion, finely chopped
20 black olives, half and stoned

Mix and knead the dough, let it rise and knead it again. Preheat the oven to 375°F/190°C/gas 4.

Divide the dough in two and roll each piece into a rectangle about 8 × 16 inches (20 × 40 cm). In a small frying pan, soften the onion in the oil. Stir in the olives and take the pan from the heat. Divide the olive mixture between the two

rectangles of dough, spreading it evenly over the surface, but leaving a gap of about ¾ inch (2 cm) all round the edge. Roll up each piece of dough from one long side and seal the ends to make a long loaf with pointed ends. Cut two crosses on each loaf and leave the loaves in a warm place to prove for 20 minutes.

Bake the loaves for 30 minutes, or until they are golden brown and sound hollow when tapped.

SYRIA

Syria borders on southern Turkey, so it is no wonder that the countries share similar tastes and recipes. This onion bread from Syria has similar flavourings to the Turkish olive bread, and is actually made on both sides of the border. The differences are that the dough is made with baking powder and bicarbonate of soda instead of with yeast, and chopped olives and raw onions are actually incorporated into the mixture. It is a good savoury loaf for lunches and picnics, and is easily and quickly made.

Khobz Basali

To make one 1 lb (450 g) Onion Loaf:

8 oz (225 g) ordinary plain flour
½ teaspoon salt
1 teaspoon baking powder
1 teaspoon bicarbonate of soda
½ teaspoon ground cumin
¼ teaspoon chilli powder
1 teaspoon chopped thyme (or ½ teaspoon dried)
10 black olives, stoned and chopped
1 small onion, finely chopped
5 fl oz (150 ml) water
5 tablespoons olive oil

Place the flour in a mixing bowl and add the salt, baking powder, bicarbonate of soda, cumin, chilli powder, thyme, olives and onion. Mix them together. Make a well in the centre and add the water. Mix everything to a dough. Turn the dough on to a floured work surface and knead it until it is smooth. Knead in the oil, a tablespoon at a time. Place the dough in an oiled mixing bowl, cover it and leave it for 30 minutes.

Preheat the oven to 350°F/180°F/gas 4. Place the dough in a greased, 1 lb loaf tin and bake it for 40 minutes, or until it is golden brown. Turn it on to a wire rack to cool.

● *Zeytin Ekmegi*

THE LEBANON

From the Lebanon, comes Mannaeesh – small circles of white bread dough topped with a mixture of thyme and marjoram. These are definitely an acquired taste, as the larger quantities of dried thyme give a rather bitter flavour. For western tastes you could use one quarter the amount.

Mannaeesh

To make ten 5 inch (13 cm) rounds:

basic bread dough (see page 12) made with 1 lb (450 g) strong plain flour and ¹/₂ oz (15 g) fresh yeast or 2 teaspoons dried

Topping:

3 fl oz (90 ml) olive oil

¹/₂ oz (15 g) dried thyme

¹/₄ oz (5 g) dried marjoram

3 tablespoons sesame seeds

Knead the dough for the first time and let it rise. Preheat the oven to 450°F/230°C/gas 8.
Knead the dough for a second time. Divide it in ten pieces, make them into balls and roll them flat into 5 inch (13 cm) diameter circles. Leave them in a warm place for 20 minutes to prove.

Brush the circles with some of the oil. Mix the remaining oil with the thyme, marjoram and sesame seeds and spread the mixture evenly over the dough circles.

Preheat two floured baking sheets in the oven. Place the Mannaeesh on the hot sheets and cook them for about 8 minutes or until they are cooked through and only lightly coloured.

ISRAEL

Israel is a relatively new country, made up of peoples of eighty or more nations, all of whom have contributed to the country's cuisine. Their religion and religious customs and festivals bind them together. Cholla is made to welcome the Jewish Sabbath. It is a light, soft bread with a thin, golden, crisp crust.

Cholla

To make one plaited loaf:

1¹/₂ oz (40 g) fresh yeast or 1¹/₂ tablespoons dried

5 fl oz (150 ml) warm water

1 lb 4 oz (560 g) strong plain flour

1 tablespoon sugar

2 teaspoons salt

3 eggs, beaten

1¹/₂ oz (40 g) shortening

1 egg yolk, beaten with 1 tablespoon water

poppy seeds, optional

In a small bowl, sprinkle the yeast into the warm water and leave it to stand – five minutes for fresh yeast and 15 for dried. Place the flour, sugar and salt in a mixing bowl and make a well in the centre. Add the yeast mixture, eggs and shortening. Mix everything to a dough. Turn it on to a floured work surface and knead it until it is smooth. Return it to the bowl, cover it and leave it in a warm place for 1 hour or until it has doubled in size.

Preheat the oven to 400°F/200°C/gas 6. Knead the dough again and divide it into four equal pieces. Shape each piece into a rope about 22 inches (60 cm) long. Form these pieces into the arms of a cross,

● *Cholla*

joining the ends in the centre. Then make a four-part plait. Lift the ends of two opposite pieces and fold them over so that they change places. Do the same with the other two pieces. Continue doing this, angling the lengths of the vertical strip slightly to the right as you cross them over each other, until all the lengths are used up. Tuck the loose ends underneath and place the loaf on to a floured baking sheet. Leave it in a warm place for 20 minutes to prove.

Brush the loaf with the egg and water mixture and scatter it with the poppy seeds, if you are using them. Bake the loaf for 15 minutes. Then turn the heat to 375°F/190°C/gas 5 and bake for a further 30 minutes, or until the Cholla is golden brown and cooked through. Cool it on a wire rack.

THE YEMEN, MUSCAT AND OMAN

Flat, round breads are popular throughout the Middle East, and the speciality in these countries is to top them with a pounded mixture of fresh coriander and soaked fenugreek seeds. The result of this is a curry-like aroma and flavour, and breads that go well with dishes that have rich, spicy sauces.

Khobz-el-Saluf

To make ten 7 inch (18 cm) rounds:

basic bread dough (see page 12) made with 8 oz (225 g) whole-wheat flour and 8 oz (225 g) strong plain flour, kneaded and risen

Topping:

2 teaspoons fenugreek seeds, soaked in 4 fl oz (125 ml) water overnight
1 clove garlic
2 oz (50 g) chopped fresh coriander leaves
½ teaspoon salt
1 tablespoon lemon juice
2 tablespoons water
2 oz (50 g) ghee or butter, melted

While the bread dough is rising, drain the fenugreek and place it in a blender with the garlic, coriander, salt, lemon juice and water. Blend the mixture to a paste, place it in a bowl and refrigerate it until it is needed.

Preheat the oven to 500°F/250°C/gas 10. Heat two floured baking sheets. Knead the dough and divide it in 10 pieces. Form the pieces into balls and then roll each one flat, into a 7 inch (18 cm) circle. Prick the circles four times with a fork and brush them with the melted ghee or butter. Divide the fenugreek and coriander paste between the circles and spread it evenly. Place the circles on the heated baking sheets and bake them for 5 minutes. Khobz-el-Saluf are at their best when served warm.

IRAN

The Iranian version of the flat Lavash bread is called Nane Lavash. The proportion of flour in the basic dough is the same as for Lavash (see page 150), but a large amount of whole-wheat flour is used. Nane Lavash is only made commercially, as the dough is rolled into rounds that are too large and unwieldy to bake in a domestic oven. In the commercial bakeries, the worktops are made of a stone compound and have up to thirty large, round rubs built into them. The dough is left to rise in these until it comes above the level of the bench. Pieces are then cut off by apprentice workers who roll them out into round or oval shapes. The rolled dough is then taken to a more experienced baker who throws it from hand to hand, making it even bigger and flatter. He lays it on a table and rolls a spiked wheel, called a *jella*, across it three times before throwing it on to a *manjak* – a slightly domed, oval cushion that measures about 12 × 24 inches (30 × 60 cms). The cushion is used to carry the bread to the oven without it splitting apart or stretching even further. The oven is a large, domed, clay construction called a *tannour* or *tonir*. The baker holds the cushion by a pocket at the back and presses it on to the hot wall of the oven. In just over half a minute, when the bread is bubbling, golden brown and crisp, another baker with a metal hook on a long rod, called a *mengash*, pulls off the cooked bread and flicks it through an opening into the shop – where it is sold, still hot and crisp.

The same bread is made at home in smaller rounds which are called Taftoon.

Taftoon

To make ten Taftoons:

1 oz (25 g) fresh yeast or 1 tablespoon dried
10 fl oz (275 ml) warm water
12 oz (350 g) wholemeal flour
4 oz (110 g) ordinary plain flour

In a small bowl, sprinkle the yeast into half the water. Leave this to stand – five minutes for fresh yeast and 15 for dried. Put the flours into a mixing bowl and make a well in the centre. Pour in the yeast mixture and remaining water. Mix everything to a dough, turn it on to a floured work surface and knead it well. Return it to the bowl, cover it with a cloth and leave it in a warm place for 1 to 1½ hours or until it has doubled in size.

Heat the oven to 400°F/200°C/gas 6. Knead the dough again, divide it into ten equal pieces and form them into balls. Roll each ball into

● *Selling Bagels in the streets of Jerusalem, Israel*

a flat round, 8 to 10 inches (20-25.5 cms) in diameter. Prick each one all over with a fork. Line a baking sheet with foil and put it into the very bottom of the oven to heat. Lay one of the dough rounds on the foil and put it into the oven for 3 minutes or until it is cooked through and bubbly. Wrap the bread in a clean dry cloth and add the others as they are done. Serve the Taftoon warm.

Sangyak is another bread made using these ingredients (usually with a large proportion of whole-wheat flour), and it is shaped in the same way. The rolled, flat loaves are brushed with oil and patterned with fingertip indentations before being baked on a bed of hot pebbles so that they become bubbly and crisp.
Barbari are long, flat, plain loaves with four deep slits along their length.

Barbari

To make four 5 × 12 inch (13 × 30 cm) loaves:

1 oz (25 g) fresh yeast or 1 tablespoon dried
13 fl oz (350 ml) warm water
1 lb 4 oz (600 g) strong plain flour
2 teaspoons salt
1 tablespoon olive oil, plus extra for shaping

In a small bowl, sprinkle the yeast into 4 tablespoons of the water. Leave this to stand – five minutes for fresh yeast and 15 for dried. Place the flour and salt in a mixing bowl and make a well in the centre. Pour in the yeast mixture and about half the remaining water. Mix in a small portion of flour from the sides of the well. Leave the bowl in a warm place for 20 minutes until the liquid in the centre is frothing. Add the remaining water and the oil. Mix everything to a dough. Turn it on to a floured work surface and knead it until it is smooth. Return it to the bowl, cover it and leave it in a warm place for 1 hour or until it has doubled in size.

Preheat the oven to 425°F/220°C/gas 7. Turn the dough on to an oiled work surface and divide it into four equal pieces. With oiled hands and an oiled rolling pin, roll each piece into a rectangle about 5 × 12 inches (13 × 30 cms) and ½ inch (1 cm) thick. Lay the loaves on floured baking sheets. Brush the tops with oil and make four parallel cuts down each loaf, stopping ¾ inch (2 cm) from the ends. Make the cuts wider by running a finger down them. Leave the loaves for 5 minutes and then bake them for 15 minutes, or until they are golden brown. Cool them on wire racks.

EGYPT

The first leavened bread was made in ancient Egypt, where the basic loaf was made of wheat or barley flour with the additions for the wealthier of mashed dates or honey. Egypt's consumption of bread is still large. Semit, bread rings coated with sesame seeds, are sold in the streets of Cairo today, by vendors who carry them strung on poles. The following recipe is described in Claudia Roden's *Middle Eastern Food*.

Semit

To make ten 7 inch (18 cm) diameter rings:

1 oz (25 g) fresh yeast or 1 tablespoon dried
5 fl oz (150 ml) warm water
1 lb (450 g) strong plain flour
2 teaspoons salt
½ oz (15 g) butter
½ oz (15 g) lard
5 fl oz (150 ml) warm milk
1 egg, beaten
3 oz (75 g) sesame seeds

In a small bowl, sprinkle the yeast into the water and leave it to stand – five minutes for fresh yeast and 15 for dried. Place the flour and salt in a mixing bowl and rub in the butter and lard. Make a well in the centre and pour in the yeast mixture and the milk. Mix everything to a dough. Turn it on to a floured work surface and knead it. Return it to the bowl, cover it and leave it in a warm place for 1 hour or until it has doubled in size.

Preheat the oven to 450°F/250°C/gas 8.

Cover baking sheets with oiled foil. Knead the dough again and divide it into ten pieces. Form each piece into a ring about 7 inches (18 cm) in diameter and ¾ inch (2 cm) thick.

Brush them on both sides with beaten egg and dip them in sesame seeds. Place the rings on the prepared baking sheets and leave them in a warm place for 20 minutes to prove. Bake them for 10 minutes. Turn the heat to 350°F/180°C/gas 4 and continue baking for 15 minutes or until the rings are golden brown.

Cool them on wire racks.

TUNISIA

Khobz Arabi is the most popular everyday bread in Tunisia, but a speciality is a bread made entirely of semolina. It is really golden, with a soft, creamy-coloured crumb, gently flavoured with sesame and anise.

Semolina Bread

To make one round 2 lb (1 kg) loaf:
1½ oz (40 g) fresh yeast or 1½ tablespoons dried
7½ fl oz (225 ml) warm water
1 lb (450 g) fine semolina
1 teaspoon salt
2 tablespoons olive oil
½ oz (15 g) lard, softened
1½ tablespoons sesame seeds, toasted in a dry frying pan on a medium heat for 2 minutes and cooled
½ teaspoon anise seed
1 egg, beaten

In a small bowl, sprinkle the yeast in the water and leave it to stand – five minutes for fresh yeast and 15 for dried. Place the semolina in a mixing bowl and add the salt. Rub in the oil and lard. Make a well in the centre and pour in the yeast mixture. Mix everything to a dough. Turn it on to a board sprinkled with semolina and knead it. When you first start to knead the loaf it will feel very grainy, almost as though your dough is made from a mixture of sand and flour. Keep kneading for about ten minutes and it will become as smooth as ordinary bread dough. Return it to the bowl, cover it and leave it in a warm place for 1 hour or until it has doubled in size.

Preheat the oven to 450°F/250°C/gas 8. Knead the dough again and knead in the sesame and anise seeds. Form the dough into a round loaf. Place it on a baking sheet that has been scattered with a little semolina and leave it in a warm place for 20 minutes to prove.

Brush the loaf with the beaten egg. Bake it for 15 minutes. Lower the heat to 350°F/180°C/gas 4 and bake it for a further 15 minutes, or until it is golden brown. Cool on a wire rack.

MOROCCO

Morocco is in the far north-west corner of Africa, and its culinary influences come, in the north, from Spain, and, in the south, from Africa.

The everyday bread of Morocco is called Kisra or Khboz. It is round or conical shaped, often spicy and with a slightly heavy texture. For home use, it is made with whole-wheat or barley flour. White flour bread is reserved for visitors and for special occasions.

The great character of Moroccan bread is that it is used to soak up the juices from richly-spiced dishes such as *tangines*. These dishes are often served in a communal pot and meals are eaten with the fingers. Bread is always on the side for scooping and dipping and also for wiping fingers on.

Bread is made at home in most Moroccan households and then taken to the communal bakery for cooking. Every morning, housewives knead their dough in a large, unglazed earthenware pan called

• *Bedouin in the Sinai desert, Egypt*

158

● *Barbari (see page 157)*

a *qas'a*. The loaves are shaped and stamped with the family's special mark and then arranged on linen-covered trays. These are carried to the bakery on the heads of the children of the house who wear padded caps to help to balance them.

Kisra

To make two small conical loaves:
1 oz (25 g) fresh yeast or 1 tablespoon dried
7½ fl oz (225 ml) warm water
1 lb (450 g) strong plain flour
4 oz (120 g) whole-wheat flour
2 teaspoons salt
1 teaspoon sesame seeds
1 tablespoon anise seeds
4 fl oz (125 ml) warm milk
oil for greasing
cornmeal for dusting

In a small bowl, sprinkle the yeast in the warm water. Leave this to stand – five minutes for fresh yeast and 15 for dried. Place the two types of flour in a mixing bowl, add the salt, sesame seeds and anise seeds and toss them together. Make a well in the centre. Pour in the yeast and milk. Mix everything to a dough. Turn it on to a floured work surface and knead it until it is smooth. Divide the dough into two pieces and leave them on the board for 5 minutes.

Oil a clean mixing bowl. Roll one of the balls of dough around in the bowl so that it becomes covered with oil. Partly by rolling it around the sides of the bowl and partly by manipulation with your hands, form the dough into a cone shape. Place the cone on a baking sheet that has been sprinkled with cornmeal. Shape the other piece of dough in the same way. Cover the loaves with a clean, dry cloth and leave them in a warm place for 1 hour or until they have doubled in size.

Preheat the oven to 400°F/200°C/gas 6. Using a fork, prick each quarter of each loaf, holding the fork so that the holes made by the tines are in vertical lines up the side of the loaf. Bake the loaves for 10 minutes. Reduce the heat to 300°F/150°C/gas 3 and continue baking for a further 30 minutes or until they are golden brown and sound hollow when tapped. Cool the loaves on wire racks.

AFRICA AND SOUTH AFRICA

In many parts of Africa, bread is a luxury, and, even in the relatively well-off African countries such as Nigeria, it takes second place to other carbohydrate foods such as cassava, millet, rice, maize and sorghum.
There are troubles enough in South Africa, but at least most people there have adequate supplies of food. Athough it has a greater African than European population, South Africa is probably the most 'Europeanized' of all African countries and its traditional recipes reflect this.

To find out about African bread I looked at Laurens van der Post's *African Cooking*, one of Time-Life Books' 'Foods of the World' series. It was published in 1970, when Ethiopia was at peace and food supplies were sufficient to ensure that no one starved. At the time there were many different sorts of bread in Ethiopia because the soil was fertile and the climate kind – making it possible to grow wheat and barley alongside millet. Flours produced from these grains were made into leavened and unleavened breads of many different types, shapes and sizes – all specific to local areas.

The most popular kind of bread throughout Ethiopa was the round, flat Injera, made from *teff*, a very high grade of refined millet flour. The Injera was made both in bush homes and city restaurants. To make it, the flour was mixed with water to make a batter, and then left in a warm place to ferment for three or four days. When ready, the batter was poured, in a spiral fashion into a large, heated ceramic griddle. When a thin layer had covered the bottom, a lid was put on and sealed all round with a damp cloth. In just a few minutes the Injera was ready, pale-yellow coloured, soft enough to fold, and with a bubbled surface. Apparently Injera have a faintly sour flavour and are made to be eaten with a variety of cooked dishes and at the same time used as an eating utensil.

Another bread in Ethiopia was Dabo Kolo. Wheat flour was made into a thick dough by gradually stirring water into it, and the mixture was sometimes flavoured with *berbere*, a hot spice paste. Cooking oil was kneaded into it and the dough was rolled and cut into small rounds which were baked until brown.

For a quickly-made snack to eat with the local *talla* beer, barley flour was roasted, mixed with salt and rolled between the fingers into large, round pellets.

SOUTH AFRICA

The original South African inhabitants grew millet. This was pounded into a type of thick porridge which is still eaten today. The European influence came from the Dutch, French Huguenots, Scots, English and Germans, while the Malays, who were brought in as slaves, later added their style to South African cooking.

The first European settlers in South Africa were Dutch. They arrived in 1652, with Jan van Riebeek, to establish a supply port for Dutch ships which regularly called at the Cape. The settlers grew wheat, barley, oats and rye, and also maize, which came to be known locally as mealie. This was as successful with the Africans as it was with the settlers, and mealie meal porridge soon rivalled millet porridge in popularity.

In their first homes around the Cape, Dutch housewives had to bake enough bread each week to cater for large families, employees and servants. Ovens had to be big and were constructed outside the house. They were made of red brick, about eight feet (2.5 metres) long, with a high-domed roof, and soon became known as 'Dutch ovens'.

Yeast and raising agents were hard to come by, so breadmakers devised ways of making their own. There were various ways of making sourdough bread and there was also Salt Rising bread, different from the American version in that no milk was needed for the initial mixing and wheat flour or maize meal was used as a starter. This is a modern recipe for Salt Rising Bread. Whole-wheat and mixed-grain breads are popular in South Africa today and so a choice of flours is given. Salt Rising Bread is close-textured with a rich, nutty flavour.

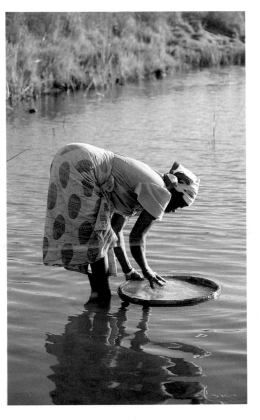

● *Washing maize, Zambia*

161

Salt Rising Bread

To make two 2 lb (1 kg) loaves:

First Day:

2 teaspoons salt
1 tablespoon sugar
10 fl oz (275 ml) boiling water
5 fl oz (150 ml) cold water
4 oz (110 g) whole-wheat flour or mealie meal (cornmeal)

Second Day:

10 fl oz (275 ml) hot water
2 lb (1 kg) whole-wheat flour or strong plain flour or a half and half mixture

In a large mixing bowl, mix together the salt, sugar, boiling water and cold water. Sprinkle the whole-wheat flour or cornmeal over the top and cover with clingfilm. Leave the mixture in a warm place for 24 hours.

The next day, stir in the hot, but not boiling, water and then beat in the flour to make a very moist dough, almost like a thick batter. Leave the dough in the bowl and sprinkle a little more flour over the top. Cover the bowl and leave it in a warm place for 1 hour for the dough to double in size.

Preheat the oven to 400°F/200°C/gas 6. Divide the dough between two 2 lb (1 kg) bread tins and leave it in a warm place for about an hour, or until it rises almost to the top of the tins. Bake the loaves for 40 minutes or until they are browned on top and sound hollow when tapped. Cool them on wire racks.

Rusks, both sweetened and unsweetened have always been popular in South Africa. Boerbeskuit (Farmers' Rusks) are savoury, and are made with a salt-rising starter. They keep for a long time and are good with butter and cheese. They are also particularly good when they first come out of the oven, have just been separated from each other and are still quite warm.

Boerbeskuit

To make about 32 Rusks:

1 lb (450 g) strong plain flour
1 teaspoon salt
3½ fl oz (100 ml) salt-rising starter (see above)
3½ fl oz (100 ml) warm milk
4 oz (110 g) butter, softened
1 oz (25 g) butter, melted

Place the flour and salt in the bowl. Make a well in the centre and add the starter, the milk and the butter. Mix everything to a dough. Turn it on to a floured board and knead it until it is smooth. Return it to the bowl, cover it and leave it in a warm place for 1 hour or until it has doubled in size.

Preheat the oven to 350°F/180°C/gas 4. Knead the dough again and roll it into a long rope about 1½ inches (4 cm) in diameter. Cut it into pieces about 1½ inches (4 cm) long. Lay half the pieces on a floured baking sheet, packed closely together, with the cut sides top and bottom. Brush them with melted butter and put a second layer on top. Brush the top layer with the butter. Leave the rusks in a warm place for 20 minutes to prove.

● *Tuareg, baking in the Sahara, North Africa*

● *Boerbeskuit*

● *Mosbolletjies*

164

Bake them for 40 minutes or until they are golden brown and crisp on the outside. Separate the rusks and cool them on wire racks. Place them on the baking sheets again, this time well apart from each other. Place them in a preheated 200°F/100°C/gas 2 oven for 30 minutes or until they are golden brown and completely dry. Cool them on wire racks again.

The Mosbolletjie is unique to South Africa and it was first introduced by the Protestant Huguenots from France. Mos is the word for grape juice which is in its first stage of fermentation. A bolletjie is a small bun. Mos contains natural yeasts and makes a good raising agent. Where no fresh grapes were available, settlers used raisins soaked in warm water. The process is a surprisingly easy one, involving only long waiting periods. The buns are soft and sweet with a light texture that is slightly more substantial than that of buns made with yeast. Baking them close together ensures that they stay soft all through.

Mosbolletjies

To make sixteen buns:

Mos Starter:

1 oz (25 g) raisins
16 fl oz (450 ml) warm water

Buns:

1 lb (450 g) strong plain flour
5 fl oz (150 ml) mos
5 fl oz (150 ml) warm milk
2 oz (50 g) butter, softened
4 oz (110 g) sugar
½ teaspoon anise seeds
1 egg, beaten with 2 tablespoons milk

To make the mos, place the raisins in a jar and pour in the water. Cover the jar and leave it in a warm place for 3 to 4 days to ferment. When it is ready, the raisins will have floated to the top.

Place 6 oz (175 g) of the flour in a mixing bowl. Make a well in the centre and mix in the mos. Cover the bowl tightly and leave it for 8 hours so the mixture forms a sponge. Mix in the milk and the remaining flour and the butter, in small pieces. Knead everything together to make a dough. Turn it on to a floured work surface and knead it until it is smooth. Return it to the bowl, cover it and leave it in a warm place to rise for a further 8 hours.

Preheat the oven to 400°F/200°C/gas 6. Knead the dough again and knead in all but 1 tablespoon of the sugar and the anise seed. Divide the dough into sixteen even-sized pieces and form them into long roll shapes. Place the rolls next to each other on a floured baking sheet, setting them on their shortest ends (they will sink to form a tray of joined round buns) to prove. Brush them with the egg and milk and sprinkle them with the remaining sugar.

Bake the rolls for 20 minutes or until they are golden brown. Slide them on to a wire rack, and leave them, still stuck together, to cool. Separate the buns only as you want to eat them.

As early as 1657, land outside the immediate Cape area was granted to officials, who were known as free burghers, on the understanding that they would grow wheat and other cereal crops. To get to these areas, whole families had to trek many miles through the open country, taking with them only the minimum of survival equipment. On the trek there were no ovens and cooking utensils had to be improvised. They took with them supplies of long-keeping Boerbeskuit, but when this ran out more bread had to be cooked. The trekkers occasionally found and excavated an anthill which could be used in a similar way to a Dutch oven, but usually they relied on their camp cooking pot, which was three-legged and made of cast iron. All their cooking, including the baking of bread, was done in this pot over an open fire. Potbrood (Pot Bread) is still popular today and is cooked at *braais*, which can only be described as barbecue parties.

Three-legged pots, together with fitting lids, can be bought from hardware stores and agricultural suppliers in South Africa. Before use they must be seasoned by gently melting meat fat in the bottom of the pot and then smearing the fat all round the sides. The pot is wiped clean with paper towels and after this should only be washed lightly, without detergent, and never scoured. If you are unable to get hold of such a pot, a cast-iron casserole dish, with a lid, is a good substitute.

Pot Bread is made from basic bread dough (see page 12), often with a mixture of whole-wheat and white flours. After the dough has risen, it is kneaded and placed in the pot, covered, left to prove, and given a brushing of melted butter. The lid is replaced and the pot set in a hole on top of the hot coals. A few coals are heaped on top and the bread left to bake for 45 minutes to 1 hour, depending on the heat of the fire.

If you have no open fire, you can still make Potbrood.

Potbrood

Use a cast-iron casserole with a good fitting lid. Grease it and put in the dough. After proving and brushing with butter, cook the loaf in a preheated 400°F/200°C/gas 6 oven for 45 minutes. When you take off the lid, a rich yeasty flavour wafts out. The loaf is well-risen and rounded, with a soft bouncy texture and a thin crisp crust.

Another way of cooking bread dough on a trek was to roll it round a stick which was then held over an open fire. This method is still a great favourite with children at braais.

Griddle cookery was also possible over camp fires, and the Scots introduced their Bannock (see page 81) which quickly became popular. Another griddle-cooked bread was Roosterkoek, made by cutting a long rope of bread into slices. The secret of well-cooked Roosterkoek is not to let the rolls brown too much before they are cooked through. They are delicious split and buttered straight off the griddle.

Roosterkoek

To make about 20 rolls:

basic bread dough (see page 12) made with 1 lb (450 g) whole-wheat or strong plain flour, or a mixture

1 oz (25 g) lamb tail fat, melted; or butter, softened

When the dough is made, knead in the fat or butter. Leave the dough to rise. Knead the dough again and roll it into a long rope about 1½ inches (4 cm) in diameter. Cut it into diagonal slices of the same thickness. Lay the pieces on a floured surface and leave them for 20 minutes to prove. Heat an ungreased griddle over a medium heat. Cook the Roosterkoek for about 6 minutes on each side, or until they are cooked through and lightly browned. Serve them hot and buttered.

Rusks, Potbrood and griddle-cooked breads accompanied the trekkers into the bush, and all are popular even now.

The South Africans are fond of whole-wheat and sifted meal breads. Many different types are made alongside the more standard white loaves, including health breads which contain a mixture of flours plus sesame and sunflower seeds.

The following brown bread has a rich, heavy texture and unusual sweet-sour flavour brought about by the vinegar, which also appears in older South African recipes. It is good buttered as a semi-sweet bread and is also excellent toasted as a base for baked beans. In many ways it is similar to the steamed brown breads of America and Canada.

Brown Batter Bread

To make one 2 lb (1 kg) loaf:

1 oz (25 g) fresh yeast or 1 tablespoon dried

7 fl oz (200 ml) warm water

14 oz (400 g) whole-wheat flour

1 teaspoon salt

3 oz (75 g) dark Muscovado sugar

7 fl oz (200 ml) warm milk

2½ fl oz (70 ml) vinegar

1 tablespoon oil

● *Potbrood (see page 165)*

In a small bowl, sprinkle the yeast into the water and leave it – five minutes for fresh yeast and 15 for dried. Place the flour, salt and sugar in a mixing bowl. Beat in the yeast mixture, milk, vinegar and oil. Pour the batter into a greased 2 lb (1 kg) loaf tin and leave it in a warm place for 1 to 1½ hours to rise to the top of the tin.

Preheat the oven to 400°F/200°C/gas 6. Bake the loaf for 50 minutes or until a skewer inserted in the centre comes out clean.

Vetkoek is a popular snack in South Africa and it can be eaten hot or cold. It is deep fried bread, crisp and flaky on the outside and rich and soft in the middle.

Vetkoek

To make twenty-four Vetkoek:

basic bread dough (see page 12) made with 1 lb (450 g) strong plain flour or wholemeal flour, risen

oil for deep frying

Knead the dough and divide it into twenty-four small pieces. Roll the pieces into balls and gently flatten them. Leave them for 10 minutes to rise. Deep fry them in hot oil for about 1 minute on each side or until they are golden brown, puffy and crisp. Drain them on kitchen paper and eat them hot.

When you are in a hurry you can make Vetkoek with baking powder instead. Vetkoek made in this way are uneven-shaped golden balls and they can be eaten hot or cold.

The old-fashioned recipe for Vetkoek was to make them with ordinary plain flour and baking powder, a little sugar, eggs and milk, mixed to a thick batter.

The Vetkoek were eaten either with jam for breakfast or as a substitute for bread.

Quick Vetkoek

To make about twelve Vetkoek:

9 oz (250 g) whole-wheat or strong plain flour

½ teaspoon salt

1 tablespoon baking powder

11 fl oz (290 ml) milk for plain flour, 13 fl oz (350 ml) for whole-wheat flour

oil for deep frying

Mix all the dry ingredients together and add in the milk to make a soft batter. Ladle individual spoonfuls of the mixture into hot oil and deep fry them for about 1 minute on each side, or until they are golden brown and risen. Drain them on kitchen paper and eat them hot.

● *Quick Vetkoek*

INDIA

India is a land of many peoples, languages, cultures and religions. It is vibrant with colour and spice. Its food is the same, varying from region to region and from religion to religion. The staple foods of India are bread and rice and although both can be found all over the country, there is more bread in the wheat-growing north and more rice in the south. There is rarely a meal served without one or both, and, typically, they appear in succession, usually with the rice first.

The traditional bread of India is flat, unleavened, and cooked on a form of cast-iron griddle called a *tava*. The Moslems in the north introduced the domed clay ovens called tandoors in which similar or slightly thicker breads could be baked. Later, the Europeans (British, Dutch, Portuguese and French) introduced their own yeasted breads. The Indians called them Dubble Roti, which means double bread, and served them with spiced dishes that had rich sauces in need of mopping up. Sometimes they used the crusted ends of such bread with the crumb removed for use as a filling for other foods.

Wheat is the most used bread flour in India, but there are also breads made from barley, millet, buckwheat and gram (chick-pea) flours. Most of the flour is unrefined and much of it is ground at home. Although whole-wheat, it is more finely ground than Western whole-wheat flours – and its use is essential for the successful cooking of many of the breads. Indian flour can be bought in the West in health and Indian food stores. It is generally sold under the name of Chapati flour. If you cannot find any, use a half and half mixture of whole-wheat and ordinary plain flour.

The Chapati was the first Indian bread to be made popular in the West by Indian restaurants. It is a flat, soft bread, unleavened and griddle cooked, thin and between 6 and 8 inches (15 and 20 cms) in diameter.

Chapati dough is easy to mix, but it improves if it is allowed to stand for a long time, a process which makes the final bread pleasantly soft and pliable.

● *Chapatis*

Chapati dough is also made into Phulkas, which are almost exactly the same only smaller. There is also a Chapati made entirely of corn flour (the refined flour, not cornmeal) which is crisp and biscuit-like in texture.

Chapatis

To make 8 Chapatis:

8 oz (225 g) Chapati flour
1 teaspoon salt
7 fl oz (200 ml) water

Place the flour in a bowl. Make a well in the centre and gradually mix in the water. Check the consistency when you have added about 5 fl oz (150 ml) and add the remainder, as needed, by the tablespoon. The flour should absorb all the water and it should be possible to knead it to a smooth and elastic dough without the addition of any further flour. Knead the dough on a floured work surface for 5 to 10 minutes. Cover it with wet muslin or with a wet cloth and leave it for at least 30 minutes, or refrigerate it for up to seven hours.

Divide the dough into 8 small balls. Dust each one with flour and roll them out very thinly into rounds about 10 inches (25 cm) in diameter. Leave them separate and don't stack them whilst you are waiting to cook them, or they will all stick together and you will have to begin again.

Heat an ungreased griddle on a medium heat. Warm a dish and a clean dry cloth. Place one of the Chapatis on the griddle and cook it until it begins to bubble in places. Turn it over and leave it until it is cooked through, turning it frequently so that it cooks evenly. Lay the cloth over the heated dish and place the Chapati on it. Cover the Chapati with the edges of the napkin. Cook the rest, adding them to the first one as you do so.

Chapatis can also be made from gram flour, a chick-pea flour also available from specialist shops. Gram Flour Chapatis are often flavoured with fresh coriander, green pepper or chillies and chopped raw onion. They have a savoury flavour with a touch of freshness and are really good with hot, spicy curries.

Gram flour dough is very soft and, because of the pieces of pepper and onion in it, quite difficult to roll out without getting holes in it. You will be more successful if you make Gram flour Chapatis smaller and thicker than those made with ordinary Chapati flour.

Gram flour Chapatis

To make ten Chapatis:
4 oz (110 g) gram flour
6 oz (175 g) ordinary plain flour
1 teaspoon salt
1 small onion
1 tablespoon fresh coriander leaves, chopped
1 small green chilli, or ¼ green pepper
7 fl oz (200 ml) ice-cold water
1 oz (25 g) ghee or shortening, melted

In a bowl, mix together the flours and the salt. Very finely chop the onion, coriander and chilli or pepper, and add them to the flours. Make a well in the centre and gradually mix in the water to make a soft dough. Divide the dough into 10 round balls and roll them out into circles, 6 to 7 inches (15 to 18 cm) in diameter.

Heat a griddle on a medium heat and brush it with the melted ghee or shortening. Cook as for the plain Chapatis above.

● *Making Chapatis*

● *Gram flour Chapatis*

Roti is another plain, flat bread that is served in similar ways to the Chapati. The dough mixture is the same as for Chapatis but the cooking method is slightly different. The recipe below is from Madhur Jaffrey's book, *Eastern Vegetarian Cooking.*

For Tandoori-style Roti, first make the Roti, following the recipe below. Instead of using a griddle, heat baking sheets covered with foil in a preheated 400°F/200°C/ gas 6 oven. Put the Roti on the baking sheets, cover them with the hot foil and cook them for 5 minutes. Wrap them in a warmed cloth as soon as they come out of the oven and keep them warm. Dot them with butter and serve hot.

Roti

To make twelve Roti:

dough as for plain Chapatis, left to rest in the same way

Divide the dough into twelve equal pieces, form the pieces into balls and roll them into 5 inch (13 cm) circles.

Heat a griddle on a low to medium heat. Place one Roti on the griddle and cook it for 1 minute, or until bubbles form inside it. Turn it over and cook the second side for 30 seconds. If you have a gas stove, light a second burner on a medium flame and place the Roti directly on it. Using cooking tongs, turn the Roti round so that the whole surface has been exposed to the flame. Do this for about 5 seconds. Turn the Roti over and repeat for about 3 seconds. The Roti should puff up.

Wrap the Roti in a warm cloth and cook the rest in the same way.

If you have an electric stove, place the griddle under the grill for a few seconds with the Roti on it.

If your griddle is a large cast-iron one you will probably find that it is either too large or too heavy to be put safely under a grill, so instead you can use a frying pan which fits underneath much better.

● *Rajasthani women sifting*

Chapatis and Roti are very thin breads. When something more substantial is wanted there is the Paratha, which was brought to Delhi and other parts of India by Punjabi refugees. Parathas are made with the same flour as Chapatis, but they are made richer by the addition of milk to the mixture plus a brushing of ghee. Ghee is a special clarified butter from which all milk solids have been removed. It can be bought from the same sort of shops as the Chapati flour. You can make a substitute by gently melting butter and skimming off all the foam, or you can use a good-quality vegetable oil. Parathas can be left plain, or they can be gently spiced with the addition of a few bruised lovage seeds. If these are unavailable, try fennel or cumin seeds.

Parathas

To make six Parathas:

8 oz (225 g) Chapati flour

½ teaspoon salt

12 lovage seeds, bruised, optional

7 fl oz (200 ml) water, or milk and water mixed

4 oz (110 g) ghee or clarified butter, melted, or 4 fl oz (125 ml) vegetable oil

Place the flour, salt and lovage seeds, if using any, in a mixing bowl and make a well in the centre. Mix in the water, or water and milk mixture, a little at a time to make a soft dough. Knead the dough on a floured work surface for 5 minutes. Cover it with wet muslin or a wet cloth and leave it in a cool place for 1 hour or in the refrigerator for up to 7 hours.

Divide the dough into six equal pieces and form each one into a ball. Roll the balls into flat rounds about 6 inches (15 cm) in diameter. Brush them with the ghee or vegetable oil. Bring the sides to the centre and twist them together to form a purse-shape. Turn the dough over, twisted side down and roll it out into a 7 inch (18 cm) round.

Heat a griddle on a medium heat and brush it with the ghee or oil. Cook the first Paratha for about 2 minutes on the first side, or until the top begins to look as though it is drying. Brush it with a little of the ghee and cook for a further minute, or until the underside becomes slightly speckled brown. Turn the Paratha over and cook it until the second side is speckled and the whole is cooked through. Wrap up the Paratha in a warmed cloth as soon as it is done and cook the rest in the same way.

Rich Flaky Parathas

Make the dough in the same way. Divide it into six pieces, roll out each piece into a circle and brush it with melted ghee. Fold it into quarters and roll it out again. Repeat the process four times. Cook as for the plain Parathas above. You may need a little extra ghee for cooking.

Spiced Parathas

The method for these is taken from Madhur Jaffrey's book, *Eastern Vegetarian Cooking*. The addition of spices is my own. Make Paratha dough in the usual way, omitting the lovage seeds.

When you melt the ghee or clarified butter, add 1 teaspoon each of ground turmeric, ground coriander and cumin seeds. If you are using oil, warm it gently with the spices.

Divide the dough into six pieces and roll them out until they are very thin rounds, about 10 inches (25.5 cm) in diameter. Brush them with the spiced ghee and then roll each one up tightly into a long rope. Brush the rope with more and then coil it up into a small cone. Flatten the cone slightly to make sure it is going to stay together, put it on to a plate and cover it with clingfilm. Shape the remaining pieces of dough in the same way. Cover and refrigerate them for 1 hour 30 minutes or up to 8 hours.

Roll the cones into rounds about 6 inches (1.5 cm) in diameter. Heat a griddle on a medium heat and brush it with melted ghee or oil. Lay a Paratha on the griddle and cook it for about 3 minutes, or until the top begins to look dry. Brush the surface with melted ghee and continue cooking, without turning it over, until the underside is speckled brown. Turn the Paratha over and cook it until the second side is also speckled brown. Wrap the Paratha in a warmed cloth and cook the rest in the same way.

● *Spiced Parathas*

Stuffed Parathas

To make them even more interesting and substantial, Parathas are stuffed with a variety of spiced ingredients before being rolled out. In India, grated white radishes, raw and highly spiced, are one of the most popular filling ingredients. Other stuffings are made from cooked ingredients, and include spiced potatoes, spiced minced lamb, lentils or another cooked vegetable such as cauliflower.

Roll out the Parathas as in the basic recipe. In the centre of each one place about 2 teaspoons of the filling. Bring the sides of the dough together and twist them to form a packet. Turn the packet over and roll it out as in the basic recipe.

To make radish-stuffed parathas you need to buy the long, white radish which is sometimes called mooli. Grate about 3 oz (75 g) and mix it with 1 tablespoon chopped fresh coriander, 1 finely-chopped fresh green chilli, ½ teaspoon each of ground ginger and coriander and ½ teaspoon cumin seeds. Let the mixture stand for 1 hour, so that the flavours can combine, before using.

For potato Parathas, use 4 oz (110 g) mashed potatoes mixed with 1 tablespoon chopped fresh coriander, ½ teaspoon salt, ¼ teaspoon each ground ginger, paprika and chilli powder, plus the juice of ½ lime.

Indian bread can also be deep fried to make Puris. These are puffed and risen, crispy on the outside and soft in the middle, and are eaten with almost all Indian meat dishes. They can be made completely from Chapati flour or with a mixture combining Chapati and plain white flours. In India, Puris are cooked in deep oil in a *karhai*, which is similar to a Chinese wok. Although they are easy to make, it is said that it takes many years of practice to perfect them so that they are delicious and light. A saying in Benares (Varanasi), in the region of Uttar Pradesh, is that if twenty-five puris were stacked on a plate and a coin was dropped on them from above, it should still be possible to hear the chink as the coin hits the plate. A variation on the plain Puri are Banana Puris, made by mixing mashed banana and just ordinary plain white flour. They are slightly sweet and go superbly with curries. They can also be served, sprinkled with icing sugar, as a dessert.

There are also Potato Puris, made by mixing mashed potatoes, curry spices and white flour.

Puris

To make twelve Puris:

8 oz (225 g) Chapati flour
½ teaspoon salt
2 tablespoons melted ghee or vegetable oil
4 fl oz (125 ml) water, or milk and water mixed, slightly warm
oil for deep frying

Place the flour and salt in a bowl and rub in the ghee or oil. Make a well in the centre and pour half the liquid into it and begin to mix in the flour. Gradually add the rest of the liquid to make a stiff dough. Turn the dough on to a floured board and knead it for about 5 minutes, until it becomes smooth and elastic. Return the dough to the bowl, cover it with a damp cloth and leave it in a cool place for 1 hour.

Divide the dough into twelve small balls and roll each one into a 5 inch (12.5 cm) diameter round.

Heat a pan of deep oil on a medium heat. Carefully drop in one Puri. It will sink to the bottom and then gradually rise to the surface. Using a perforated spoon, keep pushing it gently under the surface of the oil so it puffs up. Turn it over and, still pushing with the spoon, cook it for about one minute more or until it is evenly puffed and golden brown all over. Lift it out on to a double layer of paper towels to drain, and cook the rest in the same way.

Kachoris

When a Puri is stuffed with a spiced mixture it becomes a Kachori. Use any of the cooked fillings that are given for stuffed Parathas. Roll the dough into twelve, 5 inch (12.5 cm) rounds and then spread about 2 teaspoons of the filling on one side. Fold the rounds in half. Roll them out again into 5 inch (12.5 cm) rounds, sealing the filling inside. Deep fry the rounds as for Parathas.

Kachoris are often served with Hindu vegetarian meals. All the constituents of the meal – different curries, pickles and rice, are arranged on large, individual plates called thalis. In the centre of the arrangement are Kachoris and Roti.

Benares (Varanasi) is the city to which Hindu pilgrims from all over India come to celebrate the Festival of Divali, or Festival of Lights, their equivalent of the New Year. Whilst they are there they visit Kachori Gulley, a street where the traders specialize in Puris and Kachoris.

One of the few traditional leavened breads you will find in India is Naan, which is also eaten in Pakistan, Bangladesh and Afghanistan.

There are many different versions of Naan. Some contain yeast, some baking powder, some bicarbonate of soda and others a mixture. Some contain eggs and some milk. The similarities are that all use white flour and the main liquid ingredient is yoghurt. Naan is found only in the north of India where it is baked in the dome-shaped clay tandoors that are found behind every Punjabi home. It is also baked commercially.

The dough for Naan is mixed and left to rise for a long time, often overnight. Once risen it is kneaded and pulled apart into small pieces. The baker takes a piece of dough and slaps it between the palms of his hands so that it becomes an oval shape, thicker at the edges than in the middle. He scatters it with sesame or poppy seeds and a little chopped onion, and throws it against the sides of the tandoor. Here, because of the dome shape of the oven, it sticks at one point only, becoming tear-drop shaped as it hangs over the fire. After a few minutes cooking, the Naan will become slightly risen and light brown. The outer parts will be soft and the centre parts crisp. The Naan is taken from the tandoor and eaten while hot and fresh.

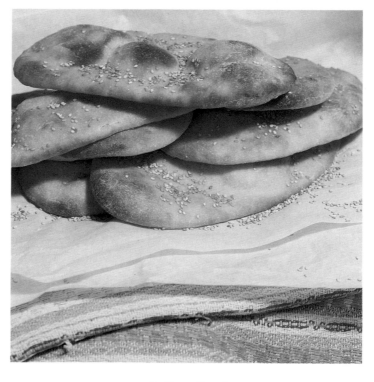

● *Naan Bread*

Naan Bread

To make eight flat breads:

1 lb (450 g) strong plain flour
½ teaspoon salt
½ teaspoon bicarbonate of soda
8 fl oz (225 ml) plain yoghurt
½ oz (15 g) fresh yeast or ½ tablespoon dried
1 oz (25 g) ghee or clarified butter; plus extra, melted
2 eggs, beaten
sesame seeds and finely chopped onion, optional

Place the flour, salt and bicarbonate of soda in a bowl. Gently warm the yoghurt and stir in the yeast. Leave this to stand – five minutes for fresh yeast and 15 for dried. Make a well in the flour and stir in the yoghurt mixture, the ghee and the eggs. Mix everything to a dough. Turn it on to a floured board and knead it until it is soft and springy (about 10 minutes). Return it to the bowl, cover it and leave it in a warm place for about 2 hours to double in size.

Preheat the oven to 400°F/200°C/gas 6. Knead the dough again and divide it into eight equal pieces. Roll each piece into an oval shape about 10 inches (25 cms) long. Leave them in a warm place for 10 minutes to prove. Spread foil over baking sheets and lightly oil it. Heat the baking sheets and foil in the oven. Lay the Naan on the foil and brush them quickly with melted ghee or butter. Scatter them with sesame seeds and/or chopped onion, if you are using them. Bake the Naan for 7 minutes, or until they are only just browned.

Serve them warm.

In Gujarat, in the north-west of India, millet is the staple grain. It is very often ground at home to make a flour that is said to be more nutritious than wheat flour and one which is much prized by the vegetarian population. To celebrate the new harvest, fresh millet kernels are eaten with sugar balls. Later, when the grains are ground, the flour is made into Batloo, a flat, dull-brown coloured griddle bread which is patterned with indentations made by the ball of the cook's finger. Dhebras are flat millet breads, made with a dough that is mixed with chopped spinach and green chillies. Again they are griddle-baked and they are served with plain yoghurt and a sweet green mango chutney.

Kashmir, in the far north, is renowned for its wonderful variety of different breads which are very much influenced by the cooking of Afghanistan and Central Asia. Most of the breads are small, like large buns. They are plain, or slightly sweet or salty, and some are scattered with poppy or sesame seeds. Girda are chewy and can be served with a type of clotted cream or with a Moslem porridge of meat and grains called *harissa*. Kulcha are made in flat, square shapes and decorated with pricked patterns, and Bakirkhani are soft with a hole in the centre.

The Shirmal is a tandoor-cooked bread which is a speciality of Lucknow, the Moslem capital of the region of Uttar Pradesh. It is baked in the street bazaars and makes a lunchtime snack or an accompaniment to a main meal. Yesterday's Shirmal may well turn up for breakfast to be eaten with butter and preserves. Its characteristic is that, when traditionally made, a Shirmal is gently coloured yellow, through the use of saffron. However, according to Madhur Jaffrey in her book *A Taste of India*, saffron is now so expensive that artificial colours are used, producing an orange-red bread the colour of tandoori chicken. Much further south, in Andhra Pradesh, Shirmal are eaten at breakfast with a spiced lamb stew called *nahari*. Here you will also find *Feni*, saucer-sized bread which is soaked in milk and eaten with sugar as a dessert.

Shirmal

To make eight Shirmal:

1 lb (450 g) ordinary plain flour
1 teaspoon salt
2 teaspoons sugar
5 oz (150 g) ghee or clarified butter
10 fl oz (275 ml) milk
a few saffron strands soaked in 5 fl oz (150 ml) milk for 2 hours

Place the flour, salt and sugar in a mixing bowl and rub in 3½ oz (100 g) of the ghee. Gradually mix in the milk to make a soft dough. Turn the dough on to a floured work surface and knead it until it is soft and smooth. Return it to the bowl, cover it and leave it in a cool place for 2 hours. Knead it again and leave it for 1 hour more.

Preheat the oven to 500°F/240°C/gas 9. In the oven, heat a large, cast-iron frying pan. Turn the grill to high.

Divide the dough into eight small balls and roll them flat, into 6 inch (15 cm) diameter rounds. Prick them all over with a fork. Place one round on a heated frying pan and bake it for 2 minutes. Sprinkle it with a little saffron milk and cook it for a further 3 minutes. Place it under the grill for 10 seconds. Sprinkle a little more saffron milk over it and brush it with a little of the remaining ghee.

Wrap the Shirmal in aluminium foil to keep it warm and cook the others in the same way.

CHINA AND SOUTH-EAST ASIA

In China and the other South-East Asian countries, rice has been the staple food for many centuries and wheat products, especially bread, have always taken second place. However, the Chinese do regularly eat Steamed Breads – the recipe for which is only slightly different from that for a basic Western bread dough.
Large loaves are a rarity in China. It is more typical for dough to be formed into small buns. Plainer ones are served as accompaniments to other dishes, and sweet ones are eaten as snacks.

● *Springtime bun festival, Cheung Chau Island, China*

CHINA

For culinary purposes, China can be divided into four distinct regions: the north, which includes the provinces of Shantung, Honan, Hopei and the city of Beijing; the coastal area centred on Fukien but including Shanghai; the inland areas of Szechuan and Yunnan; and the southern region of Canton.

Rice is grown in the coastal, inland and southern areas, but in the north, where the climate is colder, conditions are better for wheat-growing than for paddy fields. Although the northern Chinese depend mainly upon wheat for their energy supply, the bulk of it is not made into bread, but into noodles. However, in the far north, where there has been a Mongol influence, you may find bread being served with strips of barbecued lamb.

In most Chinese recipe books you will find no salt used in Steamed Breads, but a little extra sugar instead; and in some the warm water is replaced with warm milk. The dough is usually formed into small buns which are served as an accompaniment to other dishes. These buns come in many different shapes, two of which are given below.

Chinese Steamed Breads are usually cooked in a bamboo steamer or over simmering water in a wok. An ordinary steamer can be used. The bread itself is bland. It should be eaten hot, with rich meats and sauces.

Man To

To make thirty-two single, or sixteen double, steamed rolls:

1 oz (25 g) fresh yeast or 1 tablespoon dried
1 tablespoon sugar
12 fl oz (300 ml) warm water
1 lb (450 g) strong plain flour

In a small bowl, sprinkle the yeast and sugar into 4 tablespoons of the water and leave – five minutes for fresh yeast and 15 for dried. Place the flour in a bowl and make a well in the centre. Pour in the yeast mixture and the remaining water. Mix everything to a dough. Turn it on to a floured work surface and knead it until it is smooth. Return it to the bowl, cover it and leave it in a warm place for 1 hour or until it has doubled in size.

Punch down the dough with the back of your fist, cover it again and leave it for a further 20 minutes.

Knead the dough again and shape it into rolls (see below). Bring the water in the bottom of a steamer to the boil. Place the rolls in the steamer, leaving a 1 inch (2.5 cm) gap between them. Cook them for 10 minutes, or until they are firm and cooked through. Serve them hot.

If the rolls have to be cooked in two batches, cook the first batch and lift them out. When the second batch have been in the steamer for 8 minutes, put the first ones back on top to heat through. Serve them all hot.

Single Flower Rolls:

Divide the dough in half. Roll out and cut each piece into a rectangle, about 8 × 12 inches (20 × 30 cms) and brush it with sesame oil (sunflower oil can also be used). Roll the pieces up along one long side to make a rolled cylinder about 1½ inches (4 cm) in diameter. With a very sharp knife (the Chinese would use a sharp cleaver), cut the cylinder into pieces about ¾ inch (2 cm) long. Using a chopstick or rounded skewer parallel with the cut, press down in the centre of each separate piece. The layers will push out to the sides, making a pattern of two oval spirals joined in the centre.

177

● *Man To (see page 177)*

Double Flower Rolls:

Divide the dough in half and roll and cut pieces as above. Place one piece of dough on top of another (because these are on end to end, not cut-surface to cut-surface, they will need to be held in position). Press the chopstick down as before, almost to the bottom of the rolls. The shape will be like two joined spirals with two more spirals underneath. These rolls may need an extra couple of minutes cooking time because of their size.

In some restaurants in China, you might find a richer steamed bread, called Shwieh Bai Man To, or Snow-white Steamed Bread, served with 'red cooked' dishes. These are joints of meat that are cooked in a casserole with soy sauce, rice wine, sugar, anise and onions. They are rich and highly flavoured and go well with the plain taste of Steamed Bread.

Shwieh Bai Man To

To make thirty-two single or sixteen double rolls:

1 oz (25 g) fresh yeast or 1 tablespoon dried
2 oz (50 g) sugar
5 fl oz (150 ml) warm water
5 fl oz (150 ml) warm milk
4 tablespoons groundnut oil
½ teaspoon salt
1 lb (450 g) strong plain flour

Place the yeast in a large bowl. Add 1 teaspoon of the sugar and pour in the water. Leave this five minutes for fresh yeast and 15 for dried. Stir in the milk, oil and salt and gradually mix in the flour to make a dough. Turn the dough on to a floured work surface and knead it until it is smooth. Return it to the bowl, cover it and leave it in a warm place for 1 hour to double in size. Punch the dough down with the back of your fist, cover it again and leave it for a further 20 minutes.

Knead the dough for a second time. Shape and steam, as above.

The basic Steamed Bread dough is used in China to make Steamed, Filled Buns which are part of a selection of dishes called Dim Sum, a speciality of Canton. Dim Sum means 'dot on heart' or 'to please the heart'. The special dishes are made and served only in tea houses as they are thought too complicated to be prepared at home. They include Steamed Buns; deep-fried filled dumplings called Wontons, made with an unleavened flour and egg dough; and Spring Rolls, deep fried pancakes. Dim Sum dishes are eaten to accompany Chinese tea, usually in the morning but occasionally in the early afternoon.

Steamed Buns can have either a sweet or a savoury filling.

Steamed Buns with Date and Nut Filling

To make twelve buns:

half quantity of Man To dough (see page 177), risen and kneaded for a second time
2 oz (50 g) stoned Chinese red dates (or ordinary dates if these are not available)
1 oz (25 g) walnuts
1 oz (25 g) almonds
1 tablespoon sesame seeds
2 teaspoons sesame oil

Mince together the dates, walnuts and almonds and mix in the sesame seeds and oil.

Divide the dough into twelve even-sized pieces and roll each piece flat, into a 4 inch (10 cm) round. Place about 2 tablespoons of the filling in the centre of each one. Loosely gather up the sides of the dough so that they meet at the top and twist them round to secure the edges and form a pouch shape. Place the buns on a sheet of greaseproof paper, cover them with a clean cloth and leave them for 20 minutes to prove.

In a steamer, bring the water to the boil. Place the buns in the steamer, leaving a 1 inch (2.5 cm) space between each one. Cover them and steam them for 10 minutes. If you have to cook the buns in two batches, return the first batch to the top of the steamer for the last two minutes, as for the Man To, above.

● *Dining in Yunnan Province, China*

Pork and Water Chestnut Buns

To make twelve buns:

half quantity of Man To dough (see page 177) risen and kneaded for the second time
5 oz (150 g) lean pork
3 tablespoons groundnut oil
2 tablespoons soy sauce
2 spring onions, finely chopped
4 tinned water chestnuts, finely chopped

Very finely chop the pork. Heat the oil in a wok or frying pan on a high heat. Add the pork and stir-fry it until it is cooked through. Add the soy sauce and bring it to the boil. Take the pan from the heat and cool the contents. Mix in the spring onions and water chestnuts.

Shape, fill and cook the buns as above.

The traditional accompaniment to Peking duck is Mandarin Pancakes. The duck and the crispy skin are served separately, along with bowls of cucumber pieces and spring onions. Alongside is a bowl of rich, sweet sauce. The diner takes a Pancake and uses a piece of spring onion to brush a little of the sauce over it. A piece of duck, skin, cucumber and chopped spring onion are placed on the Pancake, which is then rolled and eaten with the fingers.

Mandarin Pancakes

To make twenty-four Pancakes:

1 lb (450 g) ordinary plain flour
10 fl oz (275 ml) boiling water
4 tablespoons sesame oil

Place the flour in a mixing bowl and make a well in the centre. Add the water and 1 tablespoon of the oil and stir the mixture gradually into the flour to make a dough. Turn the dough on to a floured work surface and knead it until it is smooth. Leave it for 10 minutes.

Divide the dough into three equal pieces and roll each piece into a sausage shape about 2 inches (5 cm) in diameter. Cut each one into eight slices. Roll each slice into a thin, flat pancake about 7 inches (18 cm) in diameter. Brush one side of half the pancakes with the remaining oil. Sandwich them together with the remaining pancakes with the oil in the middle.

Heat a griddle or heavy frying pan on a high heat and then reduce the heat to medium. Cook one Pancake sandwich at a time, turning it over when it starts to rise and bubble and when small spots appear on the underside.

When both sides are done, gently peel the Pancakes apart and fold each one in half, oiled side inwards. Place the Pancake on a heatproof plate in a low oven, to keep warm, and cook the rest in the same way.

The duck and other parts of the meal are served inside the folded Pancakes.

● *Family breakfasting on dry bread, Urumchi, China*

SOUTH-EAST ASIA

The cooking of South East Asia is mainly rice-and noodle-based, but in the more Westernized cities, such as Bangkok, there are bakers making Western-type bread. Pan de Sal are small, round white rolls, speckled with crushed crackers. They look extremely attractive and are good served warm with soup. Enseimada is a rich bread, very much like a Brioche in texture. The strange mixture of cheese and sugar actually blends very well if they are sprinkled on while the loaf is still very warm.

Pan de Sal

To make sixteen rolls:
½ oz (15 g) shortening
1 tablespoon salt
1 tablespoon sugar
8 fl oz (225 ml) boiling water
8 fl oz (225 ml) warm water
1 oz (25 g) fresh yeast or 1 tablespoon dried
1 lb (450 g) strong plain flour
4 oz (110 g) plain unsweetened crackers, crumbled

In a large mixing bowl, combine the shortening, salt, sugar and boiling water. Stir, and leave the mixture to cool. Add the warm water and sprinkle in the yeast. Leave it five minutes for fresh yeast and 15 for dried. Gradually mix in the flour to make a dough. Turn it on to a floured work surface and knead it until it is smooth. Return it to the bowl, cover it and leave it in a warm place until it has doubled in size. Knead it again.

Preheat the oven to 425°F/220°C/gas 7. Divide into sixteen round buns. Roll the pieces in the cracker crumbs and lay them on floured baking sheets, spread well apart. Leave them in a warm place for 20 minutes to prove.

Bake the buns for 15 minutes and cool them on wire racks.

● *Pan de Sal*

Enseimada

To make two 8 inch (20 cm) diameter loaves:
1 oz (25 g) fresh yeast or 1 tablespoon dried
6 fl oz (175 ml) warm water
3 oz (75 g) sugar
1 teaspoon salt
4 oz (110 g) butter, softened
6 eggs
1 lb 8 oz (675 g) strong plain flour

Topping:
4 oz (110 g) Edam or Gouda cheese, grated
3 oz (75 g) sugar
2 oz (50 g) butter, softened

In a large mixing bowl, sprinkle the yeast into the water and leave it – five minutes for fresh yeast and 15 for dried. Stir in the sugar, salt, half the butter, the eggs and 12 oz (350 g) of the flour. Beat the mixture with a wooden spoon until it is smooth. Gradually add the remaining flour to make a stiff dough. Turn it out on to a floured work surface and knead it until it is smooth. Return it to the bowl, cover it and leave it in a warm place for 1 hour or until it has doubled in size.

Well grease two 8 inch (20 cm) diameter baking tins. Knead the dough again and divide it in half. Roll each piece into a long rectangle about 6 × 24 inches (15 × 60 cm). Spread them with the remaining butter and roll them up along one long side. Spiral these long rolls into the prepared tins.

Cover the loaves with a clean cloth and leave them in a warm draught-free place for about 1 hour, or until they have approximately doubled in size. Preheat the oven to 375°F/190°C/gas 5. Bake the loaves for 30 minutes, or until they are golden and sound hollow when tapped. Cool them for 15 minutes on wire racks.

To serve, spread the tops of the warm loaves with butter and sprinkle them with the grated cheese and sugar. Cut them into slices.

AUSTRALIA AND NEW ZEALAND

Australia and New Zealand were only discovered by Westerners in the second half of the eighteenth century and consequently were some of the last countries in the world to grow wheat. Their climates were highly suitable and both countries became major producers of the bread-making cereals which had always been the staple food of the European diet.

AUSTRALIA

The first bread cooked by early European settlers in Australia was called Damper. The dough was made with a homemade leaven, was formed into a round, flat loaf, and a cross was cut into the top. This was baked in the coals of an open fire, sometimes literally sitting in the ashes but most often in a round, domed, cast-iron camp-oven which stood on legs over the fire.

Even when permanent towns and settlements sprang up, the Australian way of life continued to be essentially an outdoor one and camping utensils, such as the world-famous billycan, were adapted to the making of bread.

Some of the recipes I have chosen for Australia have been adapted from those I found in a book entitled, simply, *Cookery Book*, produced by the Country Women's Association of Victoria. There are very few recipes for making yeast breads, due, I am told by the Bread Research Institute of Australia, to the fact that bread making at home is not a popular pastime in

Australia. They blame the hot summers and the fact that most people want to be outside as much as possible. Many of the breads are risen with baking powder or bicabonate of soda, and the recipes are quick and easy.

The following Bran Loaf is risen with bicarbonate of soda and steamed in a billycan. If you don't have a suitable can, use a 6 or 7 inch (15 or 18 cm) diameter cake tin.

Bran Loaf

To make one 1 lb (450 g) loaf:

4 oz (110 g) bran
4 oz (110 g) ordinary plain flour
3 oz (75 g) golden syrup
1 tablespoon black treacle
1 teaspoon bicarbonate of soda dissolved in 1 tablespoon milk
8 fl oz (225 ml) milk
6 oz (175 g) mixed sultanas and raisins
2 oz (50 g) walnuts, chopped

Place the bran and flour in a mixing bowl. Stir in the syrup, treacle, bicarbonate of soda and milk, and beat to make a smooth mixture. Fold in the dried fruits and walnuts.

Place the mixture in a buttered billycan or 6 to 7 inch (15 to 18 cm) diameter cake tin. Put on the lid of the billycan, or cover the cake tin tightly with buttered greaseproof paper and aluminium foil.

Bring a saucepan of water to the boil. Lower in the billy or cake tin. Cover the saucepan and steam the bread for 3 hours, topping up the water as and when necessary.

Turn out the bread and cool it on a wire rack. Eat it cut into slices and buttered. When cooked in a billy the bread will be a tall cylinder shape, so you can cut circular slices. When it is cooked in a cake tin you will have to cut it into wedges.

Although Australians may be little interested in baking bread, they very much enjoy eating it and the variety that can be bought is tremendous. Australia has many different communities, particularly in the cities, and besides the ordinary sliced white loaf, which is still the most popular, there are Pitta breads from Greece and the Middle East, Focaccia from Italy, Steamed Chinese Buns, French bread and Croissants, and Bagels for the Jewish community. All these and many more are available from supermarkets and specialist bread shops. The Bread Research Institute is even looking into the best wheats for making Chinese Steamed Breads and noodles, so they can not only supply their own population but also export them.

Many of these different communities have their own festivals and accompanying festive breads, which can be found in their own shops and delicatessens. Easter Breads, for example, are made by the Italians and Greeks, while people of British extraction buy Hot Cross Buns. At harvest-festival time, large wheatsheaf loaves are made, to be displayed in shop windows alongside breads shaped like animals and people.

Over the past twenty years or so, the Australians have become exceptionally health conscious, and this is reflected in their choice of diet – in particular their bread. More people are now enjoying the textures and flavours of whole-wheat and multi-grain breads. These make up 14% of the total bread market; white flour with added grains makes up 18%, but 68% favour plain white. Rye meal, kibbled or cracked (very coarsely milled) grains and extra bran are also added to some loaves.

In my Australian cookery book, I found a recipe for the Grant Loaf. Doris Grant has been extolling the virtues of healthy diets with reduced sugar and plenty of fibre since the early 1960s. It seems dated now, but Doris Grant was the original campaigner. When she was first writing, bread in many countries was predominantly of the white-sliced variety and no one ever thought of making their own. This startlingly easy recipe for whole-wheat bread deserves a place here. There is no better section, for Australians have taken to heart her message. Rather than copy someone else's version, I looked in Doris Grant's later book, *Your Daily Food*, published in 1973, for her own recipe. This is it.

The Grant Loaf

To make three 2 lb (1 kg) loaves:

2 oz (50 g) fresh yeast or 2 tablespoons dried
40 fl oz (1.2 l) warm water
3 teaspoons dark Muscovado sugar
3 lb (1.4 kg) stoneground whole-wheat flour
2 teaspoons salt

In a small bowl, sprinkle the yeast into 5 fl oz (150 ml) of the water and leave it for 5 minutes. Stir in the sugar and leave for a further 10 minutes.

Place the flour and salt in a bowl. Make a well in the centre and pour in the yeast mixture and the remaining water. Knead the mixture in the bowl (see page 13) until it is smooth, elastic and leaves the sides of the bowl clean.

Divide the dough between three greased 2 lb (1 kg) loaf tins. Cover and leave in a warm place for about 30 minutes or until the dough has risen to the top of the tins.

Preheat the oven to 400°F/200°C/gas 6. Bake the loaves for 40 minutes or until a skewer inserted into the centre comes out clean. Turn them on to wire racks to cool.

● *Whole-wheat Apricot and Raisin Loaf*

The following two recipes are real home-baking ones. They contain sugar and fruits and self-raising flour to make them almost like cake, but they are baked in loaf tins and served in buttered slices, so we call them breads. They are both from *Cookery Book*. The first is made from healthy whole-wheat flour and the second, using a tin of pineapple, shows the Australians' originality when it comes to cooking.

The Whole-wheat Apricot and Raisin Loaf has a light texture and spicy, semi-sweet flavour. The Pineapple and Date Loaf is slightly heavier and much sweeter, and probably best eaten without butter.

Whole-wheat Apricot and Raisin Loaf

To make one 1 lb (450 g) loaf:

2 oz (50 g) whole dried apricots
6 fl oz (175 ml) milk
8 oz (225 g) whole-wheat self-raising flour, or plain whole-wheat plus 2 teaspoons baking powder and 1 of bicarbonate of soda
¼ teaspoon salt
½ teaspoon ground mixed spice
2 oz (50 g) butter
2 oz (50 g) caster sugar
2 oz (50 g) raisins
1 egg, beaten

Chop the apricots and soak them in the milk for 4 hours. Preheat the oven to 350°F/180°C/gas 4. Place the flour, salt and mixed spice in a bowl and rub in the butter. Toss in the sugar and raisins. Make a well in the centre and pour in the beaten egg and the milk and apricots. Mix well to make a soft dough.

Place the mixture in a 1 lb (450 g) loaf tin and bake it for 30 minutes, or until a skewer stuck in the centre comes out clean. Turn the loaf on to a wire rack to cool. Serve it sliced and buttered.

Pineapple and Date Loaf

To make one 2 lb (1 kg) loaf:

1 egg, beaten
3 fl oz (90) milk
1½ oz (40 g) butter, melted
1 × 8 oz (225 g) can pineapple and juice, crushed
6 oz (175 g) walnuts, chopped
4 oz (110 g) stoned dates, chopped
12 oz (350 g) self-raising flour
4 oz (110 g) sugar
½ teaspoon salt

Preheat the oven to 350°F/180°C/gas 4. In a large mixing bowl, stir together the egg, milk, butter, pineapple, nuts and dates. Mix together the flour, sugar and salt, and stir them into the pineapple mixture.

Place the mixture in a buttered 2 lb (1 kg) loaf tin and bake it for 50 minutes, or until a skewer inserted into the centre comes out clean.

NEW ZEALAND

Wheat came to New Zealand via Australia. There had never been a variety of grass in the Islands suitable as a good source of grain, and so the Maori people had to wait until the early 1800s before they could grow wheat for themselves. The first wheat in New Zealand was not grown by Europeans, but by Ruatara, chief of the Ngapuhi people. Wheat was, however, grown around mission settlements, and by the 1840s both Europeans and Maoris had well-established wheat fields. Since then, wheat has been one of New Zealand's major arable crops.

The early ovens were the same as in Australia, round and domed and standing on short legs over an open fire. Damper was eaten in New Zealand, too. Sourdough bread was popular and also a bread called Rewena Paraoa, which was raised with a potato starter and was a favourite with the Maoris. Rewena was the Maori word for leaven and paraoa means flour. The bread was first made in the nineteenth century, by Maori farmers who both grew and milled their own wheat. It was baked in the cast-iron camp ovens. Rewena Paraoa is a moist, bouncy, slightly sweet white bread. I cooked mine in an oval casserole and it rose well, developing an attractive cracked top. The bread is very easy to make once the leaven has fermented, as it requires no proving time.

Rewena Paraoa

To make one 2 lb (1 kg) loaf:

Rewena Starter:

4 oz (110 g) raw potato, peeled and sliced
16 fl oz (450 ml) water
1 teaspoon sugar
8 oz (225 g) strong plain flour

Loaf:

10 oz (275 g) strong plain flour
1 teaspoon bicarbonate of soda
1 teaspoon salt
1 tablespoon sugar
1 quantity Rewena starter

To make the starter, first boil the potato in the water until it is soft. Keeping it in the water, break it up with a fork or a potato masher. Cool the potato and water to lukewarm and stir in the sugar and flour. Beat the mixture to make a smooth paste. Place it in a bowl, cover it with clingfilm and leave it in a warm place until it is fermenting. This could take up to four days, depending on the temperature. It may not appear very bubbly, but if you put your ear to it you will hear it working quite loudly.

To make the bread, first preheat the oven to 425°F/220°C/gas 7. Place the flour, bicarbonate of soda, salt and sugar in a mixing bowl and toss them together. Add the Rewena and gradually knead it in to make a soft dough. At first it will seem as though the flour cannot possibly all mix into the starter, but use the kneading in the bowl technique (see page 13) and you will find it goes in easily. The dough will be very sticky, so wash your hands and then coat the dough with flour, after which it should be easy to handle and feel quite springy. Turn it on to a floured work surface and knead it until it is smooth.

Grease a 5 pint (2.25 l) cast-iron casserole or ovenproof bowl, and put in the dough. Cover it with greased foil. Bake the loaf for 40 minutes or until it is risen. Turn it on to a wire rack and return it to the oven for 5 minutes so it becomes golden brown.

When the European settlements became more established, larger camp ovens, were used. These took the form of iron boxes set in brick ovens with a fire top and bottom. Dough mixers came in during the 1890s and the high-speed Chorleywood process, from England, in the 1930s. New Zealand, like every other Western country, went through a stage of favouring white sliced bread from the 1950s to the 1970s and then everyone began to demand bread that was more nutritious.

The New Zealanders, like the Australians, are very health conscious. Even their white flour has a higher extraction from the full grain than that in most of Europe and the United States (78% as opposed to 70%).

There are now many different types of bread available in New Zealand, many of them made with whole-wheat flour or mixed grains. One of the most popular is what they call a Swiss-style Mixed Grain bread. The recipes in this section are adapted from *The Cook's Bread Book* by Mary Browne, Helen Leach and Nancy Tichborne. Their mixed-grain bread contains added gluten and is made with easy-bake yeast. I have missed out the gluten and have used fresh or normal dried yeast. If you have difficulty obtaining cracked rye, use all cracked wheat. The bread is moist, with whole pieces of the grain included in the mixture, and with a delicious nutty flavour.

Mixed Grain Bread

To make one 2 lb (1 kg) loaf:

2 oz (50 g) cracked wheat
2 oz (50 g) cracked rye
cold water
1 oz (25 g) fresh yeast or 1 tablespoon dried
16 fl oz (450 ml) warm water
4 tablespoons skimmed milk powder
1 teaspoon salt
1 lb 2 oz (500 g) whole-wheat flour

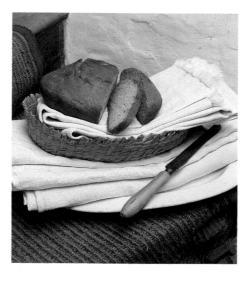

● *Rewena Paraoa (see page 185)*

Place the cracked grains in a saucepan and cover them with cold water. Bring them to the boil, simmer them for 1 minute, drain them and cool them to lukewarm.

In a large mixing bowl, sprinkle the yeast into about one third of the warm water and leave it – five minutes for fresh yeast and 15 for dried. Stir in the remaining water, the skimmed milk powder, the salt and the cracked grains. Gradually mix in the flour to make a very moist dough. Knead it in the bowl until it begins to change texture (see page 13). Transfer the dough to a greased 2 lb (1 kg) bread tin, cover it with a clean cloth and leave it in a warm place for 30 minutes or until it rises to about ½ inch (1 cm) above the top of the tin. Preheat the oven to 400°F/200°C/gas 6.

Bake the loaf for 45 minutes or until it sounds hollow when tapped. Turn it on to a wire rack to cool.

However much bread was baked in commercial bakeries, New Zealanders still enjoyed making bread at home, and there were always bread sections in the local country shows. The more recent interest in ecology and natural living has revived the skill.

This billycan-baked loaf, below, is slightly similar to the Australian Bran Loaf, and can be found in several old New Zealand cookery books. It is soft and moist, and typical of the loaves made on New Zealand farms in the early part of the twentieth century. It is very slightly sweet and is best cut into slices or wedges (depending on whether you have used a billy or a baking tin) and buttered. It goes equally well with cheese or preserves.

Brown Billy Loaf

To make one 1 lb (450 g) loaf:
4 oz (110 g) ordinary plain flour
4 oz (110 g) whole-wheat flour
1 teaspoon bicarbonate of soda
2 teaspoons cream of tartar
½ teaspoon salt
2 oz (50 g) bran
1½ tablespoons sugar
1 oz (25 g) butter, in small pieces
1 tablespoon golden syrup
4 tablespoons boiling water
5 fl oz (150 ml) milk

Preheat the oven to 350°F/180°C/gas 4. Place the flours, bicarbonate of soda, cream of tartar, salt, bran and sugar in a large mixing bowl and toss together. Place the butter and golden syrup in a jug and stir in the boiling water. Stir until the butter has melted. Stir the mixture into the dry ingredients in the bowl. Stir in the milk to make a thick batter.

Spoon the batter into a greased billy, or into a greased 7 inch (18 cm) diameter cake tin. Cover it with a greased lid or foil.

Bake the loaf for 1 to 1¼ hours, or until a skewer inserted in the centre comes out clean. Turn the loaf on to a wire rack to cool.

● *Mixed Grain Bread*

Index

Index

ACKNOWLEDGEMENTS

The publishers wish to thank all individuals, photographers' institutions, and photographic agencies who have kindly supplied photographs for publication in this book.

© **Andes Press Agency**, page 134. © **Bildhuset**, page 119/© Ole Christiansen, page 107. © **Cephas**, page 160, 180/© Stuart Boreham, page 28 (centre)/© Nigel Blythe, page 27/© Mick Rock, page 28 (right), 90 (top and bottom)/© Peter Stowell, page 70. © **Robert Estall Photographs**, page 123. © **Chris Fairclough Colour Library**, page 43. © **Robert Harding Picture Library**, pages 37, 45, 62, 65, 67, 69, 111, 115/© Nigel Blythe, page 38/© Nick Servian, page 64. © **The Hutchison Library**, pages 129, 135, 141, 158, 162, 170, 176, 177, 179/© Dave Brinicombe, pages 103, 148/© Sarah Errington, pages 98, 142/© Robert Francis, page 151 (far right)/© Bernard Gerard, page 116/© Jeremy Horner, page 149/© Chris Johnson, page 161/© Bernard Régent, pages 118, 156/© Liba Taylor, pages 95, 100/© John Wright, page 144/© **Images of India Picture Agency**, page 168. **Photobank** © Adrian Baker, page 36/© Peter Baker, page 140. © **Pictures Colour Library Ltd**, pages 15, 25, 88, 151 (far left and centre)/© G. Haubois, page 28 (far left). © **John Sims**, pages 49, 55. © **Tony Stone Worldwide**, pages 48, 86, 94, 106, 172/© M. Brylewski, page 26/© Julian Calder, page 22/© Mike Caldwell, page 80/© Joe Cornish, page 59/© Lorentz Gullachsen, page 82/© Gary Irving, page 122/© Zigy Kaluzny, page 9/© Mike McCabe, page 182/© Andy Sacks, pages 6, 8, 13, 132 /© Philip Temple, page 81. © **David Williams Picture Library**, page 121. © **Zefa**, pages 72, 73. © **Zul**, page 50.

We would also like to thank the proprietors of **Ye Olde Tuck Shoppe**, Rye, East Sussex, England, for kindly allowing us to take photographs in their bakery. Thanks also to **Didier Degaille**, from Clarke's Bread, for his invaluable assistance.

The author wishes to thank the many national embassies, agricultural federations and baking institutions who answered questions and provided information. Special thanks too, to **Piers** and **Amanda Garnham** of Bartley Mill, Frant, East Sussex, England, for their help and inspiration.